Internet Collapses and Other InfoWorld Punditry

Bob Metcalfe

IDG Books Worldwide, Inc.
An International Data Group Company

Foster City, CA ✦ Chicago, IL ✦ Indianapolis, IN ✦ New York, NY

Internet Collapses and Other InfoWorld Punditry

Published by

IDG Books Worldwide, Inc.

An International Data Group Company

919 E. Hillsdale Blvd., Suite 400

Foster City, CA 94404

www.idgbooks.com (IDG Books Worldwide Web site)

Library of Congress Catalog Card No.: 00-103671

ISBN: 0-7645-3503-X

Printed in the United States of America

10 9 8 7 6 5 4 3 2

1O/QV/QU/QQ/IN

Distributed in the United States by IDG Books Worldwide, Inc.

Distributed by CDG Books Canada Inc. for Canada; by Transworld Publishers Limited in the United Kingdom; by IDG Norge Books for Norway; by IDG Sweden Books for Sweden; by IDG Books Australia Publishing Corporation Pty. Ltd. for Australia and New Zealand; by TransQuest Publishers Pte Ltd. for Singapore, Malaysia, Thailand, Indonesia, and Hong Kong; by Gotop Information Inc. for Taiwan; by ICG Muse, Inc. for Japan; by Intersoft for South Africa; by Eyrolles for France; by International Thomson Publishing for Germany, Austria, and Switzerland; by Distribuidora Cuspide for Argentina; by LR International for Brazil; by Galileo Libros for Chile; by Ediciones ZETA S.C.R. Ltda. for Peru; by WS Computer Publishing Corporation, Inc., for the Philippines; by Contemporanea de Ediciones for Venezuela; by Express Computer Distributors for the Caribbean and West Indies; by Micronesia Media Distributor, Inc. for Micronesia; by Chips Computadoras S.A. de C.V. for Mexico; by Editorial Norma de Panama S.A. for Panama; by American Bookshops for Finland.

For general information on IDG Books Worldwide's books in the U.S., please call our Consumer Customer Service department at 800-762-2974. For reseller information, including discounts and premium sales, please call our Reseller Customer Service department at 800-434-3422.

For information on where to purchase IDG Books Worldwide's books outside the U.S., please contact our International Sales department at 317-596-5530 or fax 317-572-4002.

For consumer information on foreign language translations, please contact our Customer Service department at 800-434-3422, fax 317-572-4002, or e-mail rights@idgbooks.com.

For information on licensing foreign or domestic rights, please phone +1-650-653-7098.

For sales inquiries and special prices for bulk quantities, please contact our Order Services department at 800-434-3422 or write to the address above.

For information on using IDG Books Worldwide's books in the classroom or for ordering examination copies, please contact our Educational Sales department at 800-434-2086 or fax 317-572-4005.

For press review copies, author interviews, or other publicity information, please contact our Public Relations department at 650-653-7000 or fax 650-653-7500.

For authorization to photocopy items for corporate, personal, or educational use, please contact Copyright Clearance Center, 222 Rosewood Drive, Danvers, MA 01923, or fax 978-750-4470.

ABOUT IDG BOOKS WORLDWIDE

Welcome to the world of IDG Books Worldwide.

IDG Books Worldwide, Inc., is a subsidiary of International Data Group, the world's largest publisher of computer-related information and the leading global provider of information services on information technology. IDG was founded more than 30 years ago by Patrick J. McGovern and now employs more than 9,000 people worldwide. IDG publishes more than 290 computer publications in over 75 countries. More than 90 million people read one or more IDG publications each month.

Launched in 1990, IDG Books Worldwide is today the #1 publisher of best-selling computer books in the United States. We are proud to have received eight awards from the Computer Press Association in recognition of editorial excellence and three from Computer Currents' First Annual Readers' Choice Awards. Our best-selling ...*For Dummies®* series has more than 50 million copies in print with translations in 31 languages. IDG Books Worldwide, through a joint venture with IDG's Hi-Tech Beijing, became the first U.S. publisher to publish a computer book in the People's Republic of China. In record time, IDG Books Worldwide has become the first choice for millions of readers around the world who want to learn how to better manage their businesses.

Our mission is simple: Every one of our books is designed to bring extra value and skill-building instructions to the reader. Our books are written by experts who understand and care about our readers. The knowledge base of our editorial staff comes from years of experience in publishing, education, and journalism — experience we use to produce books to carry us into the new millennium. In short, we care about books, so we attract the best people. We devote special attention to details such as audience, interior design, use of icons, and illustrations. And because we use an efficient process of authoring, editing, and desktop publishing our books electronically, we can spend more time ensuring superior content and less time on the technicalities of making books.

You can count on our commitment to deliver high-quality books at competitive prices on topics you want to read about. At IDG Books Worldwide, we continue in the IDG tradition of delivering quality for more than 30 years. You'll find no better book on a subject than one from IDG Books Worldwide.

John Kilcullen
Chairman and CEO
IDG Books Worldwide, Inc.

Eighth Annual Computer Press Awards ⪈1992

Ninth Annual Computer Press Awards ⪈1993

Tenth Annual Computer Press Awards ⪈1994

Eleventh Annual Computer Press Awards ⪈1995

IDG is the world's leading IT media, research and exposition company. Founded in 1964, IDG had 1997 revenues of $2.05 billion and has more than 9,000 employees worldwide. IDG offers the widest range of media options that reach IT buyers in 75 countries representing 95% of worldwide IT spending. IDG's diverse product and services portfolio spans six key areas including print publishing, online publishing, expositions and conferences, market research, education and training, and global marketing services. More than 90 million people read one or more of IDG's 290 magazines and newspapers, including IDG's leading global brands — Computerworld, PC World, Network World, Macworld and the Channel World family of publications. IDG Books Worldwide is one of the fastest-growing computer book publishers in the world, with more than 700 titles in 36 languages. The "...For Dummies®" series alone has more than 50 million copies in print. IDG offers online users the largest network of technology-specific Web sites around the world through IDG.net (http://www.idg.net), which comprises more than 225 targeted Web sites in 55 countries worldwide. International Data Corporation (IDC) is the world's largest provider of information technology data, analysis and consulting, with research centers in over 41 countries and more than 400 research analysts worldwide. IDG World Expo is a leading producer of more than 168 globally branded conferences and expositions in 35 countries including E3 (Electronic Entertainment Expo), Macworld Expo, ComNet, Windows World Expo, ICE (Internet Commerce Expo), Agenda, DEMO, and Spotlight. IDG's training subsidiary, ExecuTrain, is the world's largest computer training company, with more than 230 locations worldwide and 785 training courses. IDG Marketing Services helps industry-leading IT companies build international brand recognition by developing global integrated marketing programs via IDG's print, online and exposition products worldwide. Further information about the company can be found at www.idg.com.   1/26/00

Credits

Editorial Director
Mary C. Corder

**Publishing Director,
General User Group**
Andy Cummings

Acquisitions Editor
Steve Hayes

Senior Editor, Freelance
Constance Carlisle

Development Editor
Nancy Stevenson

Project Coordinator
Melissa Stauffer

Graphics and Production Specialists
Tracy K. Oliver, Kathie S. Schutte

Proofreaders
Brian Massey, Carl Pierce, Toni Settle

Indexer
Sharon Hilgenberg

Special Help
Teresa Artman, Dwight Ramsey

About the Author

Bob Metcalfe

Technology pundit Bob Metcalfe was born in Brooklyn, New York in 1946. He graduated from the Massachusetts Institute of Technology in 1969 with Bachelors Degrees in Electrical Engineering and Management. In 1970, he received a Masters Degree in Applied Mathematics from Harvard University and in 1973, his Ph.D. in Computer Science. His Ph.D. dissertation, Packet Communication, was about the early Internet.

For the next eight years, Metcalfe worked at the Xerox Palo Alto Research Center, where he invented Ethernet, the local computer networking standard that now connects 100 million computers to the Internet. In 1979, Metcalfe founded 3Com Corporation, the $6 billion computer networking company, where he was at various times chairman, president, CEO, vice president of sales and marketing, and general manager of several divisions. He retired from 3Com in 1990. While at Xerox and 3Com, Metcalfe was for eight years a consulting professor of electrical engineering at Stanford University.

After leaving 3Com, he spent a year as visiting fellow in the Computer Laboratory at the University of Cambridge, England. Metcalfe now serves on the board of trustees of MIT, where he was 1997-98 President of the Alumni Association. He is on the visiting committee to the MIT Department of Electrical Engineering and Computer Science and on the board of MIT's Technolgy Review Magazine.

In 1980, Metcalfe received the Grace Murray Hopper Award from the Association for Computing Machinery (ACM). In 1988, he received the Alexander Graham Bell Medal from the Institute of Electrical and Electronics Engineers (IEEE). In 1993, Metcalfe received the Exploratorium Award for Public Understanding of Science. In 1996, Metcalfe received the IEEE's highest award, the IEEE Medal of Honor. Metcalfe was elected to the American Academy of Arts and Sciences and to the National Academy of Engineering in 1997.

Metcalfe joined International Data Group in 1992, first as Publisher/CEO of *InfoWorld*. He is now a director, vice president, and technology pundit, writing columns, giving speeches, and organizing conferences, mostly about the Internet. He has written his internationally syndicated column in *InfoWorld* weekly since 1992, and it is now read by over half a million information technology professionals in the United States alone. Metcalfe's office is in Boston, and he lives with his family on a farm in midcoast Maine. His e-mail address is metcalfe@infoworld.com.

Dedication

To Ruth, Bob, Robyn, Julia, and Max Metcalfe.

Foreword

By George Gilder

Producing Bob Metcalfe, they threw away the seven-layer model, the network adapter, the interface modulator, and the plug and play protocols. They discarded the politically correct spec sheet, DNA compiler, and the Winsock connectors. They delivered the goods — a unique American inventor and entrepreneur who also turns out to be a supreme wit, and the gifted author of this hot potato tome you hold in your palpitating palms.

Don't throw it down. If you have what it takes — asbestos neurons and an itch to know the truth of tomorrow's technologies — your mind will adjust. Soon you will join the legions of Bob Metcalfe connoisseurs, fanning the flames of his runaway careers in business, journalism, oratory, and politics.

You didn't know about the politics? Well, read on. Combining the looks and hair of young Ted Kennedy with the brains of Richard Feynman and the sense and style of Steve Forbes, he would be a superb President. But such a fate would be redundant. In business, he has already pioneered the most fertile technologies of his age and thus, as much as any other man, he has shaped and defined his era.

Famous as the inventor of Ethernet, the dominant form of business computer networking, perhaps soon to enter your home in a cable modem, Metcalfe launched the essential communications model for a varied world of smart PCs. He thus provided a crucial enabler for the rise of the personal computer as it increasingly displaced centralized systems linked to dumb terminals such as TVs, phones, and switchboards. He crucially foresaw that in order to allow change on the edges, the Ethernet would have to be media neutral. "Who knows," he asked in his original Ethernet memo, "what other media will prove better than cable — maybe radio or telephone circuits, or power wiring, or frequency-multiplexed cable TV or microwave."

That meant, in an indispensable insight, locating all the functions of the network in the computers attached to it, rather than in switches and specialized equipment at the center. This basic principle is crucial to the Internet. An effervescent force at Xerox PARC, the institutional source of computer mice and icons, among other inventions, Metcalfe helped weave the interfaces among the original personal computers and workstations.

Outmaneuvered by IBM in the committee politics of networking standards, he and his company, 3Com, overwhelmed the industry giant in the networking marketplace.

The prophet of Metcalfe's Law, ordaining, in essence, that network value rises by the square of the number of the terminals linked to it, he outlined the dynamics of the World Wide Web. The scourge of what he terms the "telopolies," he is also author of the canonical modem joke:

"Translating digital bits into voice frequencies in order to be transmitted across a digital network, modems are performing a grossly unnatural act. And the modems know it. You can tell by the way they whine and hiss and squeal every time we force them to do it."

Possibly reflecting in part the ardor of demand for his roisterously insightful speeches, otherwise hard to pry into his schedule, professional societies galore have barraged him with a stream of extravagant honors (most recently the IEEE's Medal of Honor and the Communications Industry Association's "Industry Legend Award"). Indeed, his career in business has been such a swashbuckling success, that I have always been baffled at why on earth he should wish to join us humble scriveners in the world of journalism.

Here, in this incandescent collection of his columns and other writings, is his triumphant answer. He is simply the world's best writer on technology. Others try hard. From the telecommunications side, Bob Lucky, for example, offers more Olympian prose and more delicate humor. Nicholas Negroponte weaves more elegant and sustained analogies. Esther Dyson gives a more acute account of the unending ramifications of computer software and networks in communities and societies. We all ache to please our readers. We labor to master the technologies. But Metcalfe is already there, the master of the networks that engage us all, and he blows sulphurous gas into the wounds we incurred in efforts to learn his technology by also writing more crisply, authoritatively, knowledgeably, and explosively than any of us.

A guide to all the seven levels of network architecture, from the wires and switches of the physical layer to the network applications in a computer, Metcalfe is also unabashed by levels eight and nine (regulation and politics). His career has precisely prepared him to appraise the most important developments in the world of the Internet and the personal computer, from the physical layer to the embattled interfaces between the operating system, the browser, the network, Bill Gates, Janet Reno, and you, the users of all this gallimaufry of devices and programs.

In this book, for example, you will find the column in which he was the first to predict that the browser would become the new operating system for network computers. You will find the best analysis of the virtues of money, and the implications of digital commerce, and the need for an information meter. You will find the heart rending story of Metcalfe's romance and disillusion with ISDN. You will read a hilarious account of his encounter with the US Patent Office over his "favorite bogus patent," including his fear that the patent commissioner is catching "Potomac fever, for which they tell me the only known cure is embalming fluid." You will find out how the Internet resembles the system of roads and bridges around San Francisco, except that nobody tries to solve the problem of Bay Area congestion by throwing random cars off the Bay Bridge. You will learn about the constant crashes of the Internet and you will find a less than fully contrite and humble account of why he ate his Internet crash column anyway. Best of all, Metcalfe's gifts as writer and raconteur leaven his awesome fund of knowledge and experience and make it all seethe and sing.

So plunge in. Join the growing legions of Metcalfe fans. Read this volume. Soon you will be hissing and squealing and guffawing like teenage modems in love.

George Gilder is President of Gilder Technology Group, Incorporated, located in Housatonic, Massachusetts, and is the author of ten books, including the worldwide bestseller Wealth and Poverty Microcosm, Life After Television, and Telecosm.

Preface

This book contains original columns written by Bob Metcalfe between 1991 and 2000. Because we have reproduced them essentially as they first appeared, a few Web site addresses you encounter may now be invalid. It was our feeling that the references give you context for some of Bob's comments, and so they have been left intact.

Acknowledgments

Life is more than a little luck, and my biggest stroke of it was being born to Ruth and Bob Metcalfe.

I'm also lucky to have a column in *InfoWorld*, to have an archive of my columns at www.infoworld.com/metcalfe, and to have *InfoWorld's* permission to print some of my best here for your convenience.

I don't think I need much editing, of course, but I get a lot, and I'm grateful for it. Thanks to my many *InfoWorld* editors, most of whom I've outlasted, including Stewart Alsop, Rachel Parker, and Sandy Reed. Michael Vizard, Kate McLucas and Jessica Davis were, at last report, the stuckees.

And thanks to Pat McGovern, founder and chairman of International Data Group, InfoWorld's parent at idg.com. Pat thought way back in 1992 that I should be a pundit. And he let me start at the top, at *InfoWorld*.

This is my third attempt to publish a book of columns. I am grateful to Janice Maloney for working on the first, which I had to abandon in a time crunch. I am grateful to Harvey Ardman for working on the second, which I had to abandon in a time crunch. And since three strikes you're out, I'm grateful to Halley Suitt who, conspiring with my assistant Sally Sinclair, finally forced me to finish.

It's punditry's give and take that I enjoy most, and so I'm grateful to those who took time to write rebuttals. Of course the people who disagree with me most refused to answer our inquiries, and they can roast in hell for all I care.

I entered journalism thinking the profession needed more old engineer-entrepreneur pundits. Now that I see much better what journalists are up against, I am grateful to my many colleagues, despite their being frequently wrong, for their collegiality.

IDG Books has always wanted to publish this book — Punditry for Dummies? — and I'm grateful for that, but more so for their sticking with me through two previous unfinished manuscripts, and most recently for accepting that this is just a columns book that needs to be published, not through their usual processes, but in Internet time.

Last but not least, I'm grateful to my readers, the people who buy information technology, frequently from engineer-entrepreneurs like I used to be. I'm grateful to the
half million or so of you who have never bothered to contact me. I'm grateful to the
many who write often that you are canceling your *InfoWorld* subscriptions because
I'm such a jerk. And I'm grateful to the relatively few who take time now and then to
offer me words of encouragement.

If you bought this book, thank you on behalf of Julia and Max Metcalfe, who my wife
Robyn and I hope someday will write how lucky they were to have us as parents.

Contents at a Glance

Contents

Let's Not Call it Cyberspace

Just imagine if you could take a step back several years and name one of the biggest phenomena of our time. What would you come up with? Might our online environs have ended up named after your cat or your mother? See what I came up with in 1994 by reading this chapter, which eases you into the world of punditry. Here's where you, dear reader, learn how sci-fi writer William Gibson, the Greeks, and a theoretical study at MIT all somehow relate to that popular name for the online world, cyberspace.

Maybe We Shouldn't Be Calling It Cyberspace

April 25, 1994

The discovery, exploration, and settlement of cyberspace, now in full swing, is the biggest thing since North America.

What exactly is cyberspace? It's hard to explain — you had to be there — but here's my best shot. By the way, I'd like to suggest we change its name.

Cyberspace is a place created by electronic networks — telephone, television, computer — and we go there in our minds, as disembodied intellect. It's a big place, or many places, growing in another dimension. We go there perpendicularly out of the flatland of space and time. Far out, it may curve back on itself.

Cyberspace is exactly where you are when you're on the phone with your mom — you're not at her house, and she's not at yours, but both of you are together in cyberspace. You're in cyberspace when channel surfing with your TV remote control, when flaming on the Internet with E-mail, or when in a chat room with beautiful strangers. And, dear InfoWorld reader, you enter cyberspace when you get behind the keyboard of your personal computer and venture out onto a LAN for business purposes. You're deep into industrialized cyberspace when launching mission-critical transactions using client/server software over an intercorporate WAN.

Cyberspace is in many ways an uncharted wilderness, a frontier, just like North America in 1492 (if you're Italian), 1100 years ago (if you're Norwegian), or back 10 millennia (if you're Cherokee). Many users of America Online recently wandered out onto the Internet to find that there are aborigines in some far reaches of cyberspace and that conquistadors are not welcome.

Cyberspace is a much better word for this electronic wilderness than digital convergence, data superhighway, or national information infrastructure. But a new frontier called cyberspace is as foreboding as a new ship called Titanic, a new restaurant called The Donner Party, or a new enterprise operating system called Windows NT.

The popular press now often refers brightly to cyberspace. I doubt they've ever read the cyberzine Mondo 2000, home to the dark side of cyberthis and cyberthat, where they know the CIA didn't kill JFK because they've seen him recently with Hitler. Paranoid anti-technology outlaw cyberpunks dressed in black, or in any other color, for that matter, are not good role models for the future citizens of, er, well, cyberspace — where did we get that word?

The first mention of cyberspace was in William Gibson's twisted 1984 sci-fi novel *Neuromancer* — a classic to some, but definitely not a cure for chronic depression. What I'm saying is that when setting off on a day of one-upping the industrial revolution, start at dawn with a cold shower and a hot breakfast, not with *Neuromancer*, which leaves you feeling hung over, alone, and missing a lung.

The word cyberspace, like cyborg, I suppose, comes from cybernetics, which is what in the 1940s MIT's Norbert Wiener called his theoretical study of control systems. Cybernetics in turn comes from the Greek for steering or control. Therefore, cyberspace means "control places." No wonder civil libertarians are so worked up over cyberspace's brave new Orwellian clockwork bladerunners.

So, as I proposed when soliciting suggestions two weeks ago, maybe we shouldn't call it cyberspace, but something else, more hopeful, and with less of an attitude. The obvious alternative is, of course, infoworld. I'll let you guess why Gibson didn't choose infoworld over cyberspace in 1984.

How about infospace, datasphere, or computerland (also already taken)? Or, working with information superhighway, how about infobahn or, my favorite, Iway? Another tack would be to name cyberspace, like North America, after one of its early explorers — Marconia, Cerfdom, or Disneyland (again, taken). My nomination of this kind would be Liderland, honoring the late J.C.R. Licklider, who set in motion the wheels that brought us the Internet.

Or we could rename cyberspace and at the same time gather funds for its further development. We could make this into a naming opportunity for some private donor. I'd gladly give $10,000 to have it called MetcalfeWorld.

Do I hear a billion to call it Ellisonia or Gatespace?

Look, we black-clad, depressive anarchists could have done a lot worse, pal

Rebuttal by Bruce Sterling

Bruce Sterling, *"cyberpunk,"* is the author of The Difference Engine (with William Gibson). *Purportedly a novelist by trade, he actually spends most of his time aimlessly messing with computers, modems, and fax machines. His nonfiction work includes the book The Hacker Crackdown: Law and Disorder on the Electronic Frontier, and articles for The New York Times, Newsday, Whole Earth Review, Wired and The Magazine of Fantasy & Science Fiction.*

Okay, I admit it — if you're Bob Metcalfe, then reading William Gibson's classic novel *Neuromancer* probably does leave you feeling hung over, alone, and missing a lung. I feel exactly the same way when I read Windows documentation.

You really wanna know why the word "cyberspace" caught on; why it's now used by people like Supreme Court justices, guys who couldn't squint through their bifocals long enough to read *Neuromancer*? It's because William Gibson is a literary genius, that's why. Gibson saw society's deep need for a neologism and he coined one that stuck, whereas poor Bob Metcalfe is a writer merely by avocation. In real life, he's a guy who does weird, inexplicable, boring stuff with colored wires.

Despite his mean-spirited attempt to deprive the world of a bit of poetry, I give Metcalfe some credit for this article. The poor guy vaguely understands the menace to his interests here — his horrifying realization that electronic engineers can't name their own damn products. But then when he rolls up his sleeves, licks his mechanical pencil, and starts in on the job himself, look at that lame stuff he comes up with. "Liderland?" "Infoworld?" "Gatespace?" Oh yeah! Those trip right off the old tongue, Bob.

I'll tell you the great, untold story of the term "cyberspace." Back in the glamour days of so-called virtual reality, colleagues in Bob's industry were so desperate to have a name for their vaporware that they actually tried to trademark the word "cyberspace." Gibson had to hire a lawyer and threaten court action to get these little weasels to back off. Thanks to Gibson's noble effort at his own expense, he allowed the word that he developed to remain in the public domain, so that cats like Metcalfe can use it without having to pay for a site license. And where's his payback? Here's Bob Metcalfe — an engineer — making fun of the way cyberpunks dress.

Look — if it weren't for the fact that hairy-eyed visionaries grabbed this technology and made it their own, we'd have a very different name for it. It would be called "Prodigy," and it would be wholly-owned by IBM and Sears. It would be about as exciting as Boy Scout semaphore classes. Instead, we've got a term and a technology that are going to define the zeitgeist of the 1990s for decades to come. Live with it. Get over it. It's too late now.

Microsoft versus the Computer Industry

This chapter offers a rollicking ride on the Microsoft monopoly roller coaster. Along the way I made some pretty on-target predictions about things like a Microsoft online service that Bill Gates would have the gall to bundle with Windows, the emergence of robust web browsers and their tie-in to operating systems, and the bloody Web Wars between Microsoft and Netscape.

See if you can spot my shifting point of view as you read these articles. Learn that Bill Gates is not (quite) evil incarnate, is not a skunk, married well, and takes joy in mooning ogres. Read on...

Is Microsoft Abusing Its Power? Smaller Vendors Find that the Software Giant Casts a Long Shadow

ComputerWorld 2/25/91

"Do you think Microsoft is doing anything illegal?" my venture capitalist friend asked as we stood outside the San Francisco hotel ballroom in which Go Corp. had just announced its pen-based operating system for notebook personal computers.

The subject of Microsoft had come up that day because Microsoft was seen preempting Go, as it has done to other small companies in recent years, by projecting vaguely similar future capabilities in its own products. Anticipating Go's announcements, Microsoft had been talking about plans for pen-based extensions to its DOS-based Windows graphical user interface.

With tens of millions of DOS installations giving it an operating system monopoly, Microsoft's product futures formed a chilling cloud over the Go party. The same chill is felt by the whole PC industry, including several companies with which I'm involved. So, despite my love for lawyer jokes, I decided to take my friend's legal question seriously. "Well, I'm not a lawyer," I answered, "but let's see, there's the Sherman Act. As I recall, that discourages monopolistic collusion on price and anticompetitive territory allocations. There's the Clayton Act. I think that proscribes unfair trade practices, such as tying the sale of one product to another. And, oh yeah, there's the Robinson-Patman Act, which I think requires companies to offer like prices to customers."

My friend was not happy with the amateur legal checklist. "No, Bob," he said, "I was thinking more along the lines of RICO (Racketeer-Influenced and Corrupt Organization Act), which aims to break up organized crime."

Concerns about Microsoft's dominance of the PC software industry are now common and no joking matter, but still, I had to laugh. I thought about all those intelligent young people now streaming by the hundreds to join Microsoft in Redmond, Wash. Is it the Mann Act that outlaws the transport of minors across state lines for immoral purposes? Had we just created a new joke genre?

I was laughing, but my friend wasn't. He was deadly serious. Joking aside, is Microsoft abusing its monopoly?

The word monopoly reminds me of IBM, especially in the 1960's. As I recall my mother telling me, it was often alleged back then that IBM abused its mainframe monopoly by making preemptive announcements to thwart competition. A case in point was its announcement of a subsequently aborted mainframe (the 360/191, I think it was) to rain on Control Data's 6600 parade. IBM was sued, eventually submitted to a consent decree and has since limited such preemptive behavior.

Is Microsoft in a similar situation? Do its hints of future pen-based extensions to Windows constitute unfair competition with Go? I think so. When you begin to dominate an industry, you take on new responsibilities and certain new standards of behavior.

Other Microsoft tactics, also reminiscent of alleged IBM misbehavior in the 1960's, surround its vertical integration into application software. We've all heard how Microsoft got the PC software industry ramping up on OS/2 and Presentation Manager and then suddenly switched to Windows. And what about the abrupt introduction of a new, extended-memory programming interface with the latest version of Windows?

Does this kind of behavior constitute unfair competition against other applications developers who do not have the advantage of early access to Microsoft's operating system plans? I think so. I think that if the DOS world is to remain a level playing field for the development of exciting new applications, DOS' suppliers must divest its applications business.

Evidence of abuse of monopoly power may also be found in what many consider Microsoft's extortionate (catch the RICO connection?) software licensing terms. Do you have a choice not to license DOS on Microsoft's terms? Yes, you can opt for Unix or Digital Research's DR-DOS. But considering their market shares are these real alternatives?

Bill Gates was once my friend. I haven't visited with him since long before Microsoft and my former company, 3Com, entered into their ill-fated partnership on OS/2 LAN Manager. That was way back, when Bill, the programming language and operating system maven, was also still friends with application software developers and PC manufacturers. At that time, Bill was high-mindedly advocating open PC industry standards as liberation from the coercively proprietary mainframe world.

Now, with Microsoft on top, most of Bill's remaining friends are his shareholders. Bill's speeches, long a source of vision for the open PC industry, have become self-serving outlines of Microsoft's rapacious product plans. Bill's industry partnerships have turned one-sided and sour. And Bill's company, known in the past for drawing new customers to a burgeoning industry, is spending too much of its considerable energy on damaging dependent competitors in a stagnant market.

If Microsoft's abuse of its monopoly isn't illegal, it ought to be.

Financial Analyst Sees a Bleak Future for the PC Industry

September 14, 1992

When we met for breakfast in Woodside, just north of Silicon Valley, in a power booth at Buck's, Ruthann Quindlen was gloomy about PC software. Ruthann has specialized in PC software for 10 years at Alex. Brown & Sons, the oldest U.S. investment bank. She used to write for InfoWorld, and we are friends so maybe I'm biased saying Ruthann is the leading banker to PC software companies — selling their stock, taking them public, merging them, and recently advising all but one that their futures are bleak.

"When second quarter financials were reported in July," she grumbled over her omelet, "it confirmed for me that the PC software industry is doomed. Windows is killing the goose that lays the golden eggs."

Having in the past accused Microsoft of abusing its monopoly, I nodded agreement.

"No, Bob," Ruthann corrected, "I'm not joining those who vilify Microsoft. I'm not blaming Microsoft — even they will be hurt by the coming stagnation."

Next, Ruthann admitted she had been wrong. Not wrong about Microsoft — she was Alex. Brown's analyst on Microsoft's IPO, way back in 1986 when sales were a mere $140 million. No, she regrets saying (in a Microsoft videotape even) that Windows was going to create opportunities for small PC software companies. Now it is clear that Windows is killing small PC software companies, and — her eyes grew dark — the big ones, too.

Ruthann ran through some recent reports of slowing growth, earnings shortfalls, and/or falling stock prices — Adobe, Aldus, Borland, Lotus, Micrografx, Quarterdeck, Software Publishing, Stac, Symantec, WordPerfect.

Surrounded by this devastation, Microsoft reported 50 percent growth to $2.8 billion in sales for the year ending June — and all that growth has obviously come at someone's expense.

Playing devil's advocate, I noted that market consolidations are normal. Why should InfoWorld readers care if Microsoft ends up the only PC software company? There would be fewer compatibility problems, and Microsoft could spend less time battling competitors and more on serving their loyal customers, right? Ruthann summarized the history of monopolies — complacency, gouging, slow if any growth, lack of innovation and, an Ice Age later, with or without the FTC's help, overthrow of the monopoly.

Ruthann had hoped Windows would grow the market and restart the PC apps game anew on a level playing field. But no. The companies that Ruthann is gloomy about — most of them — sell through the two-tier retail channel.

Forget that Microsoft might be using undocumented Windows calls — no vilification here. It's just that she underestimated how hard it is to develop Windows apps. And she underestimated Microsoft's head start on Windows. And she underestimated the shelf-space bottleneck.

"Yes, Microsoft shipped a million copies of Windows last quarter, but as Egghead just reported, too many did not sell through. Were they returned to Microsoft? Fat chance. Windows absorbed all the credit lines of the thinly financed retail channel. We have a two-tier python swallowing a huge Windows mouse."

Well, aren't Windows apps doing well? "Yes, but it's hard to tell whose, which is my major point — Windows apps all look alike. And when differentiation is hard, distribution controls. And who controls distribution? Microsoft. Who else has the product breadth to, say, give PowerPoint away in a Word/Excel bundle? Whose brand is reassuringly on both the Windows operating system and on its Windows apps? The only Windows apps doing well are Microsoft's."

I repeated my two-year-old suggestion that Microsoft divide into two companies — operating systems and apps. Ruthann countered by asking whether OSes should come with their own GUIs, utilities, networking, databases, and native apps for usability, performance, and price. Well, maybe.

Ruthann sees no exit from a downward spiral of the industry. She shrugs off the small numbers of Macintosh, Unix, and OS/2. Taligent? No wonder Apple is going into consumer electronics.

The FTC Lets the Microsoft Monopoly Walk

May 3, 1993

After two years investigating anticompetitive behaviors by Microsoft, our Federal Trade Commission met in February and took no action — not even a slap on the wrist.

Now, some of us are just plain sore that Bill Gates is richer than we are.

But maybe the FTC found that Bill Gates doesn't take home all that much — less than the $1 million that President Bill Clinton says is fair.

Or maybe Microsoft is actually not abusing its considerable monopoly powers.

Maybe the FTC found nothing more than wimpish whining from losing competitors and inept former partners like IBM and me.

Or maybe you PC systems managers think that Microsoft's products are so great that Microsoft deserves its monopoly powers. Maybe the FTC found that what's good for Microsoft is good for America.

Or maybe, looking at various market segments in just the right light, the FTC found that Microsoft has no monopoly power at all, just a small share of, say, the market for things that are flat and go round.

Or maybe the FTC will be back soon. Maybe Bill — the one with the Air Force — will soon decide how many election promises he can afford to keep. Maybe the FTC will soon realize that Democrats are running the show now.

According to investment banking firm Goldman Sachs, Microsoft's share of IBM-compatible PC operating systems revenues went from 83 percent in 1991 to 87 percent in 1992.

Some say Microsoft's applications market share is enabled by leveraging monopoly power in operating systems. In word processing, Microsoft had 22 percent revenue share in 1990 vs. WordPerfect's 55 percent. Just two years later, Microsoft and WordPerfect were tied at 44 percent each.

In spreadsheets, Microsoft had 19 percent revenue share in 1990 vs. Lotus' 68 percent. Just two years later, Microsoft had 42 percent share and Lotus 48 percent. Adding in Macintosh, Microsoft is the spreadsheet leader.

Over the 12 months ending this June, Microsoft's system software revenues will, again according to Goldman Sachs, grow a healthy 17 percent to $1.3 billion, while application software revenues will jump 54 percent to $2.1 billion. Yes, I think the FTC will be back.

There is a silly story going around about how free market forces alone will keep Microsoft from 100 percent market share, just as with IBM, which collapsed under its own weight without government interference.

Nonsense.

Facts are that IBM endured decades of antitrust scrutiny, which forced it to curtail anticompetitive practices such as including undocumented interfaces, making premature product announcements, and bundling software with its hardware — the term bundling was invented only after IBM was forced to unbundle. Only this scrutiny made it possible for companies such as DEC, Intel, Apple, Sun, Microsoft, and others to grow, preparing for the day, decades later, when, perhaps inevitably, complacency brought IBM down.

I talked to Jon Lazarus, Microsoft vice president of systems strategy. Jon's charter is to be sure that other companies can build their success on Microsoft's systems software. I met with Jon as he was preparing to celebrate the shipment of the 25 millionth copy of Windows.

Jon said he regrets the recent flap over undocumented interfaces in Windows. He says these were unintentional, the normal result of programmer sloppiness, and that they gave Microsoft's own application developers no material advantage.

Jon laments the pressures put on companies like Microsoft to disclose product plans prematurely. Buyers say they need to know the future so they can plan better and influence product evolution. So can you really blame Microsoft for preannouncing Windows NT in April 1991? Jon defends Microsoft's software bundles. For example, it makes good sense to bundle operating systems with user interfaces, networking, electronic mail, and utilities, he says. It's also good sense to bundle applications such as word processing, spreadsheets, and presentation graphics at really low prices.

Isn't bundling what buyers want?

So maybe we shouldn't want government to rein in Microsoft. Maybe we should trust good faith and free market forces.

But, note that Microsoft prospers only because of the copyright monopolies granted by the government. Because copyrights were created out of thin air for entirely different purposes than PC software, perhaps they should be dropped, or at least cut back, so PC software companies can compete unencumbered by government. How's that for free market macho?

What If Microsoft Ties On-line into a Windows Bundle?

August 15, 1994

This week's what-if question involves: Microsoft's two most unannounced products; entrepreneur Steve Case; CompuServe's acquisition price; billionaire Paul Allen; a pool party thrown by antitrust watchdog Anne Bingaman; O.J. Simpson's plea bargain; and (gag) the information superhighway.

You may not like some possible answers to this week's what-if question if the results of *InfoWorld's* readers' poll on the information superhighway are any indication. The results, which appeared in the September 26, 1994, issue of *InfoWorld*, will show how much you want government to stay out of the Iway business.

In preparing for our poll on the Iway, I dropped in on Steve Case, CEO of America Online (AOL), in Vienna, Va. Case did not surprise me when he said what AOL needs from the Iway is faster and cheaper networking to homes. AOL will connect its millionth home this month. Case, ever the scrappy entrepreneur, also did not surprise me by hand-delivering the diskette I needed to become an AOL subscriber.

But Case did surprise me when he admitted that the on-line services competitor he worries about most is neither Prodigy nor CompuServe, with their millions of subscribers. No, Case worries most about Microsoft, which last I heard has on-line subscribers numbering zero.

After learning of Steve's surprising concern about Microsoft, reports of two recent fascinating events resonated in my inquiring mind. The first event was a pool party thrown by Anne Bingaman, antitrust chief of the U.S. Department of Justice, celebrating her settlement with Microsoft over anticompetitive practices in the PC software market.

Anybody who has negotiated a software license with Microsoft understands why a pool party was appropriate.

While they debate in Washington just how wet Bingaman is, the PC industry is acting as if O.J. Simpson's prosecutor went on TV announcing that in return for dropping all charges, Simpson has agreed not to drive after dark on certain specified interstates.

In defending her settlement, Bingaman admitted, "I wish it were five years ago. I know it's late." I wonder if Bingaman understands just how long five years is in the PC industry. Hey, if Democrats are good for anything, it's supposed to be antitrust enforcement. Does the word "settlement" mean justice is done with Microsoft? If so, Bingaman's successor will likely be at poolside in five years, again lamenting antitrust oversight that Microsoft should be getting right now, say in answer to this week's what-if question.

Meanwhile, back at AOL, our second fascinating event regards Paul Allen.

Allen cofounded Microsoft, owns billions in Microsoft stock, serves on Microsoft's board of directors, is the nicest guy in the world, and recently made a $20 million profit by selling most of his stock in ... AOL. Allen must know something we don't about Microsoft's plans for competing with AOL.

So, now on to this week's what-if question. What if Microsoft ties its own new on-line service into a Windows bundle? Or, paraphrasing, after Microsoft announces that it is entering the on-line services business, either with "Marvel" or by buying CompuServe for something like $2 billion, would it be OK with you if software needed to use Microsoft's own on-line service came bundled in the same box with Windows, say starting with Chicago next year?

Buyers of PC products and on-line services might forget about the long term and answer, "Great, one more capability tied in with Windows at that same low price — goodie, goodie, goodie." Or, bless your hearts, you might say, "Hey, I want Windows cheaper, without Microsoft's on-line software, and then I'll choose whatever the best on-line services are out there."

AOL's Case might have scrappily answered this week's what-if question by saying, "OK, go ahead Bill and Paul, bundle, and may the best on-line service provider (AOL) win." But when I asked Case, he said, "No."

Microsoft is shipping millions of Windows diskettes each week and could kill AOL, not by offering a better on-line service mind you, but simply by tying in the sale of its fledgling on-line service with its market-dominating OS. Even most Republicans accept that this would be an antitrust no-no.

Justice's Bingaman could say, "No, Microsoft, you really can't use your monopoly in PC software to power on to Al Gore's Iway."

Ms. Bingaman, how about closing this barn door right now, and not five years after the horses have escaped?

At Demo 95: Web Is Our Next-Generation OS

February 27, 1995
Demo 95 drew 700 personal computer industry insiders to Palm Springs this month. We celebrated premieres of eight hot new PC products there and sat down to demos of 70 others. All were carefully selected by *InfoWorld* Publishing Co.'s David Coursey for readers of his P.C. Letter.

Now, here's what I say happened at Demo 95.

First, because I'm now too often accused of Microsoft-bashing, I must say that Melinda French's demonstration of Microsoft's Bob was a great relief to the Demo crowd. We were reassured that Bob is a promising experiment in user interface design and that Bill Gates has indeed married well.

Second, Windows 95 (on Coursey's VaporList since December 1993) showed up at Demo for an on-stage product showdown against OS/2 Warp 3.0 (available since October 1994). OS/2 was demonstrated doing many more things at once than I'll ever want to do. Windows 95 survived one of the most adventurous demos I've ever seen, with the actual plugging in of various adapter cards during the playing of angry rock videos.

Iway-wise, Windows 95 reappeared in Demo's on-line services session along with America Online, Apple's eWorld, CompuServe, Lotus' InterNotes, Microsoft Network (when it's ready, maybe in August), Netscape, and Prodigy. There was the usual agonizing over "content" vs. "community." But now the term "context" is clearing up how all this content and community fits into some grand scheme of things.

And there was, of course, the mad scramble to get on-line services onto the Internet's World Wide Web.

Which brings us to Demo 95's parade of Web browsers. On stage for 5-minute demos were Frontier Technology with Super TCP Pro, Spry with Mosaic In A Box, Netscape Communications with Netscape Navigator and Netsite, California Software with InterAp, and Quarterdeck with Windows Personal Web Server. They were all showing everything new under the sun within their Web browsers, especially multithreading, which gives you something to do while large image files hyperlink down at less than ISDN speeds.

America Online's InternetWorks comes as a DLL with its Windows client software.The DLL adds multithreading, OLE 2 support, persistent caching, progressive rendering, and APIs for custom development. Suddenly I saw Web browsers as, yes, client/server middleware for Internet screen scraping.

Multithreading and APIs are features of operating systems, and they bring us to this week's conceptual breakthrough: Web browsers are now viewed as a hot new application category. Soon, like Microsoft Windows before and Microsoft's Bob after, these former Web browsers will be euphemized as "operating environments" or some such, and every OS will have one. Right after that, as their APIs mature, they will graduate — like Windows may — to becoming full-fledged OSes all by themselves.

Consider files. The earliest OSes had only sequential access to unnamed files. Next came random access and the invention of file names and directories. Then structured data, with self-describing files, as in SQL databases.

The Web now advances files again, with hyperlinking — moving directory information into files, with pointers not only to other files but to pieces of other files, and not only to files on the local computer, but to files anywhere in the Web. It's suddenly clear that hyperlinking must be driven down into OS file systems. Why should hyperlinking be something you do only with files outside your computer? Consider user interfaces. In the beginning there were batch job control languages. Then there were interactive command-line interfaces. And lately GUIs. Over the Internet, it was Telnet starting in the 1970s, then the X Window System, and now the Web browser — which is, yes, a client/server GUI hyperlinking OS.

Web browsers and servers are surely our next-generation OS. What I can't figure is whether the new Web OS standard will come from IBM, Apple, Microsoft, Oracle, Novell, or some new OS company we've heard little of.

Resist Microsoft's Invitation to Win95's Maiden Voyage

July 10, 1995

After PC Expo, the lobster yacht *Enthusiasm* motored out of New York harbor's Hell's Gate headed for Southampton, Newport, Woods Hole, Provincetown, Boston, and points Down East into Maine. My crew was swashbuckling software entrepreneur Fred Gibbons, who launched Software Publishing Corp. in 1980 and floated it to $150 million with PFS and Harvard Graphics.

Fred and I spent our dockside evenings arguing about Aug. 24, 1995, the day Microsoft insists that it will ship and you will buy Windows 95 and the new Microsoft Network (MSN).

There's not a lot about Aug. 24 that Fred and I are sure about. We are both absolutely positive that it will be a Thursday. But I'm the only one who thinks that Aug. 24 will be long remembered as the day Microsoft's wave broke.

Windows 95 and the MSN may not ship on Aug. 24. There are the bugs, of course.

In late June, for example, I witnessed a demo of MSN that promptly sank when MSN's client failed to plug and play a modem driver. Until then, I had not confused the new Microsoft network with the old ones — remember MS Net and LAN Manager? But Microsoft officers have decided to ship Windows 95, despite warnings from their programmers below decks. So bugs will not delay the ship date. The real schedule threats are from the Department of Justice and other antitrust watchdogs around the world.

Bundling MSN with Windows is such a blatant exercise of monopoly power that the Department of Justice will almost surely fire across Microsoft's bow. I suspect Microsoft is by now hoping for Justice to wade in. If forced to pull MSN, Microsoft can blame Justice for a further delay of Windows 95, a delay that its programmers can use to plug their leaks.

Now, even if Windows 95 ships on Aug. 24, I'm not so sure you'll be aboard. You might not end up thinking of Windows 95 as an irresistible upgrade of Windows 3.11.

You might think of Windows 95 as an entirely new operating system on its maiden voyage. You might wait six months for Windows 95 1.1 — Windows 96. Or, you might RISC skipping Windows 95 to hold out for Windows NT 96, or something even better that escapes the 14-year-old Intel-DOS platform.

OK, so maybe you will shove off with Windows 95, MSN, and the new hardware needed to float them — the pressure on you must be enormous. Then, all your users will be, Microsoft says, one button away from MSN. Think of all those modem drivers to be plugged and maybe played. Think of all that traffic suddenly converging on MSN. I'm not sure you'll enjoy surfing the tsunami of MSN newbies.

I believe not bundling MSN with Windows 95 will foster competition in on-line services. But maybe you IS managers, after finding your users all suddenly at sea with MSN, can think of better reasons for not bundling the product.

Now, assume that millions of Windows users do suddenly find themselves surfing MSN. You can bet many will then want the real thing, to be on the open Internet, which MSN is not.

Sure, Windows 95 bundles a TCP/IP stack and a Web browser. But deep down in its dark little heart, Microsoft really wants your users on MSN and really wants content providers to lock themselves into MSN's development tool — Blackbird.

Microsoft wants everybody to adopt its proprietary on-line service in August 1995 in exactly the same way everybody adopted its proprietary operating system in August 1981.

Well, Windows 95 and MSN may ship on Aug. 24, and you may be able to get them for way less than Microsoft's mandated minimum advertised price of $89. But, even so, I do hereby give you permission not to run out to buy large quantities of the Windows 95 1.0 bundle.

In any event, Microsoft will have again failed to ship on time. They will have again shipped too many bugs and not enough promised features. They will have again abused their growing monopoly powers. And they will have again not embraced openness — this time the Internet's. So if there's any Justice, on Aug. 24, 1995, Microsoft's wave will break.

Microsoft and Netscape Open New Fronts in Web Wars

August 21, 1995

After its phenomenal stock offering two weeks ago, Netscape Communications Corp. is well on its way to becoming the Microsoft of the Internet. But then, of course, after Thursday's shipment of Windows 95 and the Microsoft Network (MSN), Microsoft Corp. is too. Microsoft and Netscape are now the principal antagonists in a war for control of the software that runs the World Wide Web.

At this point, I should say that *InfoWorld's* owner, International Data Group (IDG), of which I am a vice president, is a big Netscape customer and was invited some months ago to invest $2 million. I should also say that Microsoft is one of IDG's largest advertising customers. There, I feel much better now.

At *InfoWorld's* Spotlight conference a few weeks ago, John Shewchuk, MSN's group general manager for tools and applications, demonstrated Blackbird, the multimedia development tool for MSN content. Blackbird is cool.

On the phone with Shewchuk, I learned something that most of Netscape's new shareholders probably don't know yet, which is that Blackbird has now been announced, not just as the development tool for MSN, but separately from MSN as a complete set of tools, viewers, and servers. Blackbird will be offered to you as "MSN in a box" in direct competition with Netscape.

Blackbird viewers will be a lot like Web browsers, except they will be on the client end of an advanced distributed object system for browsing Blackbird-generated multimedia content including Hypertext Markup Language (HTML). Blackbird servers will be a lot like Web servers, except they will also handle Blackbird's multimedia objects. Blackbird will be backward-compatible, Microsoft-controlled fourth-generation Web software.

In the Web's first generation, Tim Berners-Lee launched the Uniform Resource Locator (URL), Hypertext Transfer Protocol (HTTP), and HTML standards with prototype Unix-based servers and browsers. A few people noticed that the Web might be better than Gopher. In the second generation, Marc Andreessen and Eric Bina developed NCSA Mosaic at the University of Illinois. Several million then suddenly noticed that the Web might be better than sex. In the third generation, Andreessen and Bina left NCSA to found Netscape.

The Web Wars began as Netscape wondered if it could stand to remain compatible with standards that were out of its control under Berners-Lee in the World Wide Web Consortium (W3C) at MIT. Now, in this fourth generation, the Web Wars escalate as Blackbird advances Web technology using Microsoft-controlled standards. According to Shewchuk, Blackbird, not MSN or Netscape, is the future of the Web.

MSN ships this week with a component manager that can download Blackbird viewers. Blackbird viewers don't need MSN to operate, and Blackbird servers running on Windows NT will enable you to set up Blackbird webs with MSN nowhere in sight.

Blackbird is multimedia object technology based on Microsoft OLE. It has its own URLs, namely OLE monikers. It has its own multimedia markup language, not just HTML. And it improves considerably on HTTP by optimizing for high latency on the sprawling and now increasingly clogged Internet.

Imagine using Netscape, or any of the other NCSA Mosaic clones, including Microsoft's. Eventually you click a hyperlink and find yourself looking at a Blackbird page that, because you are not using a Blackbird viewer, you can't see in its full glory, if at all. So, you download a Blackbird viewer, which lets you continue browsing the old Web while giving you access to the dazzling multimedia objects on the new Microsoft Blackbird Web. And you're hooked.

Expect fierce competition between Microsoft and Netscape. The important question is not whether Microsoft or Netscape wins, but whether we'll end up choosing our Web standards from those developed in an open computing consortium or those controlled by Microsoft.

Will Blackbird do to Netscape during the Web Wars what DOS/Windows did to Unix during the OS Wars? It's a good bet, especially if W3C follows in the footsteps of any of the various defunct Unix consortia. The most likely cause of Blackbird's undoing would be if distributed multimedia OLE turns out a dog.

Netscape's Tools Will Give Blackbird Reason to Squawk

September 18, 1995

This week, Netscape Communications Corp., in Mountain View, Calif., will attempt to deserve its astronomical $2 billion stock market valuation. The valuation is astronomical because, calling a spade a shovel, Netscape remains unprofitable 18 months after its founding by a recent college graduate reported to have 9,000 lines of code which he mostly has been giving away.

Marc Andreessen's Navigator is a rewrite of Mosaic, the fabulously successful Internet browsing software that Andreessen and friends developed. And, Andreessen has been able to attract world-class adult supervision and a crack programming team to his company. But $2 billion?

Well, by distributing its Navigator free to Mosaic's installed base over the Internet, Netscape has accumulated millions of users and what, at the busy intersection of Information Superhighway and Wall Street, they call "mystique."

Many investors bought into Netscape, including my employer — *InfoWorld*'s owner — which, I hasten to disclose, invested $2 million prior to Netscape's historic public offering.

This week Netscape is announcing products that promise to transform it into an even more rapidly growing and soon-to-be obscenely profitable provider, not just of Web browsers, but of the indispensable next-generation Internet operating system.

Yes, Netscape this week announces products aimed not only at winning the Web Wars against other Mosaic clones and Microsoft's Blackbird, but also at winning the much bigger OS Wars. (See "Microsoft and Netscape open some new fronts in escalating Web Wars," August 21, 1995.) These products would turn Windows 95, for example, into just a mundane collection of not entirely debugged device drivers, says Andreessen.

Of course, to reopen the OS Wars, win against Microsoft, and grow into its $2 billion valuation, Netscape can no longer just give Navigators away free for 90 days in hopes that you will eventually pay for them. Netscape now has to sell you large numbers of its Internet OS and interactive multimedia application development tools. Recently Andreessen told me more about that.

First, Netscape is not just a browser company. It mostly sells Web server software — $11.9 million last quarter. Second, Netscape servers are sold mainly to meet internal information needs. Up to 90 percent of Web servers are behind fire walls, on what might be called "intranets."

Third, Netscape's Internet OS will operate on top of Windows 3.1, Windows 95, NT, Macintosh, and Unix. Netscape is not abandoning those sticking with Windows 3.1 while waiting for something better.

Fourth, Netscape's new Navigators are not just browsers, but suites of Internet applications, for browsing, forms, mail, news, FTP, chat, and beyond to live on-line applications and interactive multimedia. So, Netscape will be competing not only with other Mosaic clones and Blackbird, but also with Lotus Notes.

Fifth, the Netscape OS is not just for Netscape applications, but will come, like any good OS, with programming interfaces and tools for application developers. These additions include tools for Web publishing; viewers for diverse document types including Adobe Acrobat, Macromind Director, and Apple QuickTime; Sun Microsystem's Java "applets" to run cross-platform on both clients and servers; and a scripting language.

Sixth, Netscape's "client/server/server" Internet OS will provide facilities for backend transaction processing, elaborating the client/server model with navigating clients and application servers and database servers.

Andreessen kindly offered to demonstrate just how limited and flaky Blackbird is, which would have confirmed what I've heard elsewhere, including from reliable sources inside Microsoft. I declined the demo, but the offer started me wondering. Netscape's transformation this week is going to require the shipment of quite a lot of software — too much it occurs to me for less than two years of development.

Will Netscape's transformation be vaporware?

Will Netscape Eat Hat, Being Too Busy for Web Conference?

January 8, 1996

In the shadows a young man waited for the microphone. He stood at the back of the audience of 2,000 attendees of the Fourth International World Wide Web Conference last month in Boston. I had just summarized the conference for the crowd and was itching for questions.

"Dr. Metcalfe," the young man asked respectfully, "exactly what article of clothing will you eat, if not your hat, when the Internet fails to collapse in 1996?" The young man was, of course, referring to my Dec. 4, 1995, column in which I listed 10 factors that would lead in 1996 to a catastrophic collapse of the Internet.

That column has me buried in mail, thank you. I'm getting so much response I can't answer it all, for which I apologize.

To deny a repeated accusation, no, I am not shorting Netscape stock. Because I am a pundit, my stocks are in a blind trust that does not go short. My employer, International Data Group, is way long (a minority investor).

And no, I don't think it contradictory to predict the Internet's collapse and then argue that it's the next big thing. This seeming contradiction is resolved by clarifying that the collapse will be temporary and will lead us into the Next Generation Internet.

Anyway, will I eat my hat if the Internet fails to collapse in 1996? Well, I can't just willy-nilly rise to this challenge. How will we actually know when the Internet has collapsed? Will the collapse last a minute, which certainly has happened already, or a year? Can I still, at my age, digest a hat? So, in front of 2,000 witnesses, I swore that if, in my judgment, the Internet fails to collapse in 1996, I will eat my "collapse column" at the Web Conference in 1997.

As for the Web Conference in 1995 (WWW4), I complained in my terminal keynote about all the attention Hypertext Markup Language programming got. I complained about the unprojectability of the Third WWW User Survey. And I complained about the only subject hyped even more than the Web, namely Java, about which the audience agreed that expectations have been set too high.

Three sessions interested me most. One was about Millicent, a micropayments system in development at Digital Equipment Corp.'s Systems Research Center, Palo Alto, CA.

Another was Tim Berners-Lee's projection for the Web over the next five years. Berners-Lee, creator of the Web and now director of the World Wide Web

Consortium at MIT, said that Web browsers would soon disappear. The third most interesting session featured Microsoft and Sun Microsystems negotiating their big Java deal on stage. I commend both companies for pursuing Java and hope, along with most *InfoWorld* readers, that their deal gets done.

Now, it was very odd that there were no Netscape speakers at WWW4 and no Netscape booth. In session after session the audience all around me kept whispering, where's Netscape? Conference attendees speculated about a falling out between Netscape's Marc Andreessen, who is now worth $100 million, and Tim Berners-Lee, who is not.

Another theory was that Netscape is pulling out of the World Wide Web Consortium to go its own proprietary way on Web standards.

As for me, I worried, because Microsoft has said it will bundle with Windows everything that Netscape planned to sell, that Netscape's Andreessen, Jim Barksdale, and Jim Clark had thrown in the towel, sold their stock to America Online, and gone home.

Before giving my conference wrap-up, I called Netscape and asked point blank why they were not at WWW4.

Their spokeswoman said the simple truth was that Netscape has only 400 people and one trade show booth, and they were too busy with the many Web conferences surrounding WWW4. Nothing more than that. In fact, she said, there were five technical people from Netscape headquarters at WWW4 and certainly some Netscape representatives from the Boston area.

To set minds at ease, I reported this simple truth to the 2,000 attendees at WWW4 and asked the Netscapees in the audience to raise their hands. None did. Uh oh.

Tying IE4 with Windows May Be Incentive for Netscape

October 14, 1996

Microsoft Corp. was pooh-poohing the Internet only a year ago. It gilded its Wintel clunkers with the Microsoft Network in hopes of killing, not the Internet, but America Online.

When I moved into *InfoWorld*'s new Internet section, I hoped to get out of Microsoft's way. True, Nicholas Petreley was left alone to stand up to Microsoft's rapacious PC software monopoly, but, on the other hand, I looked forward to taking on the Internet's bioanarchic intelligentsia, pushovers compared with Microsoft.

Since last year, however, Microsoft officials have decided to "embrace and extend" the Internet and thereby to wander again into my beat. So, hey, Microsoft execs, just when you thought it was safe to misbehave monopolistically again, I'm back. And this week I've got a great idea for you: Netscape and our Department of Justice.

Many people say that Microsoft's next Web browser, Internet Explorer 4.0 (IE4), will be the death of Netscape Communications Corp. Netscape's only hope, they say, is if the antitrust watchdogs at Justice enjoin Microsoft from various anticompetitive practices.

Recall how Justice forced Microsoft to stop using its monopoly powers to coerce PC vendors into buying only Windows — five years after the damage was done.

Next, recall how Justice prevented Microsoft from buying rather than competing with Intuit Inc. — we all helped with that one. Now Justice should punish Microsoft for attempted abuse of its monopoly powers in Internet markets — this time before the damage is done.

Microsoft Executive Vice President Bob Herbold, a great guy who used to head information systems and advertising at Proctor & Gamble, demonstrated IE4 last month near Disneyland in Anaheim, Calif. Herbold's IE4 demonstration was cool, until it crashed in front of 1,000 people attending the first Internet Commerce Expo. I felt the pain of the IE4 product manager on stage with Herbold when his projected demonstration screen went plaid.

Microsoft Chairman Bill Gates, another great guy who also is not evil incarnate, demonstrated IE4 a week later near EuroDisney in Paris. Again, IE4 crashed in front of 1,000 people who were attending the International Data Corp. European Information Technology Forum.

Gates had a different IE4 product manager on stage with him in Paris, which made me wonder whether Herbold's had already been shot.

You might ask, and so should Justice, why Herbold and Gates would twice risk the embarrassment of those IE4 crashes, especially because IE3 is, in addition to being free, so very new? The answer is that Microsoft is rushing to freeze the market for Internet clients, to pre-empt that market's leader, Netscape, and to keep people from buying Navigator until IE4 can be delivered.

IBM long ago got sued because of such abuses of monopoly power — pre-emptive pre-announcements — which damage competitors much more than they help customers.

Now it's Microsoft's turn to be enjoined from perpetuating its monopoly by commenting on future products, especially products that later fail to ship on schedule, if at all.

Netscape is now asking Justice to prevent Microsoft from tying IE4 with Windows, but surprise, I can't agree. The idea of unifying Windows desktops and Internet browsers is one I've advocated for more than a year. Even if I didn't give Microsoft the idea, it is a good one.

So how does Justice keep Microsoft from unfairly locking out its Internet competitors while not preventing the integration of desktops and browsers? In Paris, Gates told us that IE4 would become part of the new Windows "active desktop." He said that Microsoft was simply replacing the current desktop module of Windows with new software including IE4.

And so here is this week's great idea: If Microsoft can replace the desktop module of Windows to produce a unified desktop and browser, then so can Netscape. Justice should insist that Microsoft further enhance, document, support — and not abruptly change — its desktop programming interfaces in Windows (among others) so that other software companies can use those interfaces to compete by offering integrated desktops, browsers, and who knows what exciting else.

Microsoft is Mooning the Ogre of Public Desire to Have Competing Choices

November 3, 1997

Since 1991, I've been warning Bill Gates that Microsoft should act its size. Microsoft is no longer a spunky start-up. It is a multinational monopoly. Borrowing a phrase from Fortune Magazine's Stewart Alsop (former *InfoWorld* editor), I'll try putting it another way: Bill, stop mooning the ogre. Stop mooning public opinion and the various government agencies sworn to uphold antitrust law.

Gates simply does not understand that we the people demand what I call "freedom of choice among competing alternatives," or FOCACA for short.

At Agenda 98 in Scottsdale, Ariz., the conference Alsop and I co-produced in mid-October, Alsop asked Gates if he understands that his company's anti-competitive practices are angering the Ogre of FOCACA. Gates was defiant. If customers choose Microsoft products, isn't it as simple as that?

Maybe Gates should study what happened to the tobacco industry while making that argument.

Gates says Microsoft should not be punished for its success, that Microsoft is a better judge of what to integrate in software than are the bureaucrats in Washington, and that in suing Microsoft, Joe Klein, who heads the Antitrust Division of the U.S. Department of Justice, is just responding to political pressure from Microsoft's whining competitors. I would say it's equally likely that Klein's move on Gates followed a misunderstood memo urging Attorney General Janet Reno to prosecute "Bill."

At times Gates sounds wounded. It's as if he went and built this fine company under the free enterprise system and now the government is ungratefully "reigning" on his parade. Gates apparently forgets that, while growing Microsoft, he was supported by various governments with corporate, contract, and copyright law, to name just three. And governments were there protecting him from IBM and others with antitrust law. Hey, Bill, it's simply Microsoft's turn to obey antitrust law.

Well, rather than just complain, let me explain how Microsoft should have introduced Internet Explorer leading up to Windows 98. In short, Microsoft should have served customers while bending over backward not to exclude competitors — offering excellent products while preserving FOCACA.

First, Microsoft should not have introduced Explorer for "free." That is mooning the ogre. Sure, Netscape did it at first, but Netscape was a spunky start-up. Microsoft should have introduced Explorer under terms and conditions similar to Netscape's at the time, say for $39. Selling products below cost, or "dumping," especially for free by a multinational monopoly, is frowned upon by the ogre of FOCACA. It is against long-standing law.

Second, Microsoft should have been careful not to tie or bundle the sale of Explorer to the sale of its monopoly product Windows. That is mooning the ogre. Even the world's largest PC manufacturer, Compaq, had to bow to Microsoft's tying of Explorer to Windows. Such tying is anti-FOCACA and illegal. Microsoft monopoly power is so intimidating that a Compaq vice president is now saying he preferred Explorer even without the threatening letters from Microsoft. If so, why the letters?

Third, Microsoft should not have tried to pretend that Explorer is "integrated" into Windows 95. That is mooning the ogre. Microsoft is right to integrate Web browsing into the Window's desktop. I wrote that here not long ago. (See "Tying IE4 with Windows may be an incentive for Netscape, other vendors," Oct. 14, 1996)

However, to preserve FOCACA, Microsoft should have enunciated the programming interfaces between the integrated desktop and the rest of Windows. It should have made sure that other browser suppliers had effective access to those interfaces before moving to bundle Explorer into Windows 98. Explorer is clearly not "integrated" into Windows 3.x, Windows 95, or Windows NT, and Bill, I'm technical enough to know this. Windows can run without Explorer. Windows can browse the Web with Netscape instead. Explorer can run on non-Windows platforms. Integrated? How stupid does Microsoft's head lawyer Bill Neukom think the ogre is?

Another negative aspect of Microsoft's mooning the ogre is that it is distracting the ogre from more important work. While Joe Klein is fighting with Microsoft, the United States Telephone Association (USTA) is conspicuously conspiring to delay the information age. We have 1,200 local telephone companies with $100 billion in revenues and not one iota of competition among them. If Gates would just listen to me, the ogre would be free to turn on the USTA, which offers much less FOCACA than Microsoft.

Survival Lessons: Skunks, Microsoft, and Bill Gates' 1998 Antitrust Epiphany

February 16, 1998

The skunk is, like Microsoft, nocturnal and omnivorous. And after a millennia of natural selection, the skunk is, like Microsoft, an exquisite survival machine. So, catching moonlight in a pair of scanning eyes, the skunk instinctively knows, like Microsoft, exactly what to do.

The skunk watches in the dark. Prey or predator? If it thinks the flashing eyes are those of an approaching predator, the skunk arches its back and flares its fur. Next, the skunk hisses, stamps its feet, and, like Microsoft, puckers its rectal musk nipples.

With the eyes still coming, the skunk enters its final escalation. It swings up onto its front feet, raises its tail, and squirts its musk between the eyes. The skunk's smelly blinding musk usually ends such nighttime encounters. But not this time.

This time, it turns out, the predator's eyes are the approaching headlights of an 18-wheel truck. Bearing down at 65 miles per hour, the truck doesn't hear the skunk's hissing, nor smell its musk. All that evolution notwithstanding, never noticing the skunk, the truck runs it over.

Like a skunk, Microsoft is now hissing defiantly into what it mistakes for the approaching eyes of another Digital Research, VisiCorp, Software Publishing, WordPerfect, Lotus, or Novell. This time, however, Microsoft is squirting musk into the headlights of the onrushing 18-wheeler that we call the Antitrust Division of the U.S. Department of Justice.

Microsoft is squirting insults at the Department of Justice prosecutors, Federal judges, expert witnesses, and the computer industry's vast right-wing conspiracy. Gates cannot defy the Justice Department the way Bill Clinton does. Gates cannot beat Ralph Nader at the Beltway game. Gates has not yet understood the politics of his predicament nor the public opinions that power them.

When Gates says the Department of Justice is not qualified to direct software innovation, or that Microsoft is being punished for its success, he's simply not getting it. He's transfixed by the lights of the Department of Justice's onrushing 18-wheeler.

Microsoft illegally dumped, tied, and exclusively distributed Internet Explorer in violation of a specific consent degree and long-standing antitrust law. No amount of Microsoft musk is going to blind the Justice Department to this.

Mind you, if Microsoft stops squirting soon, the Justice Department will allow the true integration of Internet Explorer into the desktop of what's now called Windows

98 — that's not really the issue. The integrated browser is a good idea, even if I said so myself (see "Tying IE4 with Windows may be an incentive for Netscape, other vendors").

And then the Justice Department will not go away; it will be around forever reminding Microsoft of the real issue, which is that Microsoft must serve customers while bending over backward not to stifle competition. Microsoft must give competitors a chance to compete and customers a chance to choose.

Microsoft should change its stripes. It should not dump or tie. It should open all of its important programming interfaces. It should not force resellers to exclude competing products. It should build "Chinese walls" between its various divisions — better yet, spin them off. And it should pay dividends from its mountain of monopoly profits.

Microsoft should stop using fear, uncertainty, and doubt against competitors. It should stop preemptively announcing nonexistent products, for example Pen Windows in 1991, and Windows 98 in 1995. It should stop raining on parades, as it does by naming its Palm PC after the 3Com PalmPilot.

Microsoft is obsessed with defeating the Department of Justice. Similar to the way 3Com, when I was there, was obsessed with defeating Novell. Or like IBM, before Lou Gerstner, was obsessed with defeating Microsoft. Or like Microsoft itself, in 1995, when it was obsessed with defeating the Internet.

It took changes of leadership to save 3Com and IBM. In the case of Microsoft defeating the Internet, it took Gates having his famous 1996 Internet Epiphany.

Well, I know Bill Gates, and he's no skunk. He's too smart to take Microsoft under the Department of Justice's 18-wheeler. I predict Gates will have a 1998 Antitrust Epiphany. I hope he'll call me first with the scoop. And I don't mean just kinder and gentler public relations. Gates will soon look into the Justice Department's eyes and see, as he finally saw in the Internet's, something to scamper off into the woods about without making a big stink.

Refusal to rebut

A letter from Nathan Myhrvold, Microsoft

I asked both Bill Gates and Nathan Myhrvold of Microsoft to rebut this chapter. Bill declined politely. Nathan also declined, in the following letter, which I happen to think fills the bill splendidly. I thank him for allowing me to quote it. Since writing this letter Nathan has taken a leave from Microsoft and seems to be having fun.

Dear Bob,

Thanks for offering me an opportunity to rebut your columns about Microsoft, but I'm going to have to pass. Bill's going to pass on this one, too. His reason for not doing this, like mine, is not having enough time to go around. I don't think that I can write a 700-word rebuttal, and I certainly don't have time for 200-words. Mark Twain once wrote that he was writing a long letter because he didn't have time to write a short one. Even for lesser writers such as myself, the principle holds.

In any event, even with tons of time, I don't think that this particular material is suitable for a rebuttal. The point of a real "rebuttal" is to highlight flaws in somebody's arguments, or to provide an alternative argument. A thinking person reading a column and its rebuttal should, between the two, see the development of competing ideas and be able to make a judgment about the merits of each.

But your Microsoft columns, especially the last one, are not about making an argument or developing ideas. They are a set of assertions without argument or proof being offered. And, like a lot of things in the press, they are written with the volume turned up – full of rude analogies, sweeping statements, and replete with strong words like "illegally", and puerile ones like "rectal musk nipples." I suppose it takes that to get noticed in the din of hype surrounding these topics.

It's your book and your opinions, so you are certainly entitled to write it however you would like. However, given what your articles are, I don't see how can I do a rebuttal in the true sense. I could say you are wrong with the same flat assertion, but that is just a descent into name-calling. So, where you compare our company to a skunk, what should I say? Claim we are really more like some other mammal? Or reply in kind with a pungent, derogative comparison for you? Neither is the sort of thing I want to do.

Sorry, but I don't see much scope for me to do anything with this. Good luck with your book.

Nathan

Wire Up Your Home and Stay There, but Not with ISDN/ADSL!

This series of columns is like a map leading you on a journey through the evolution of a large and complicated infrastructure. The route taken to provide us all with hi-tech phone service has been a rather tortuous one, as you'll see. It required a walk in the forest of the organizational miasma that defines telcos; a stroll down the lane of tariffs, overpriced services, and market competition for our dollars by giant telopolies; and a ride through a long, dark tunnel of protocols, switches and packet splitting.

The bottom line: don't ask how we got here: today's telephone technology (no matter when the Year of ISDN really happened) is a wonder and it's getting better all the time. It's so wonderful that I've (almost) forgotten the bad old days of POTS (plain old telephone service) and make daily reaffirmations of my devotion to the telecommuting lifestyle all this technology has made possible.

ISDN Is the Information Age Infrastructure

December 7, 1992

The unfortunate gap that exists between the computer and telephone industries was never more evident than on November 16, 1992 — the day the Information Age began in America.

Many of our readers, most of the InfoWorld Publishing Company, and the entire computer industry spent November 16 on the road to Comdex in Las Vegas. I took the road less traveled — I was with the entire telephone industry in Reston, Virginia, at a big event they called the Golden Splice, to celebrate the first transcontinental all-digital telephone call.

The symbolic Golden Spike was driven in 1869 at Promontory, Utah, to complete the first transcontinental railroad, providing infrastructure for the Westward Expansion and the Industrial Age. The telephone companies liken their new nationwide digital network to the Golden Spike — the Golden Splice symbolizes the infrastructure for the Information Age.

Let history record that I was master of ceremonies at the Golden Splice event and the one who proclaimed the birth of the Information Age. You weren't there to yell "Outrageous!" on behalf of the computer industry, so I reminded the 200 telephone executives that more than 100,000 of you were, at that very minute, in a similar but somewhat larger room in Las Vegas, celebrating the 50 millionth personal computer in America.

Most computer folks would place the beginning of the Information Age well before this year — maybe 10, 25, or even 50 years ago. But, I said, from some vantage point in the remote future, squinting back across the broad sweep of history upon the Agrarian, Industrial, and Information Ages, today's 50 million PCs might look like horse-drawn wagons on the dusty trails that crisscrossed America before the Golden Spike.

The dusty trails I described are today's tired telephone modems. I know that millions of America's horse-drawn PCs are blessed today with Ethernet, and some of these are internetworked remotely with T1 lines (for big bucks). But the rest, the vast majority, are moseying along at 1,200 or maybe 14,400 bits per second. Imagine how much more wonderful our personal computers could be with ISDN's 10 to 100 times more bandwidth at a cost not much higher than today's 100-year-old analog voice telephones. Maybe ISDN is networking for the rest of us.

The first transcontinental all-digital telephone call on November 16 was actually a four-way ISDN videoconference among Reston, Chicago, Los Angeles, and Huntsville, Alabama, at 384 kilobits per second. Four groups of kids spoke to us, and to one another, about the pictures they had drawn depicting the uses of ISDN in education, health care, telecommuting, and entertainment.

They then sent their pictures via ISDN to Reston, where they were combined into a poster and sent back.

Of course, ISDN has been a long time coming, and there are quite a few more ISDN railroads to build. But it's my assessment that an important crossover point has been reached. Not only is there now a demonstrable national standard for ISDN, National ISDN-1, but an impressive number of National ISDN-1 telephone switches (22) have already been installed, including the two needed to connect my house with InfoWorld.

And the accelerating ISDN deployment program reviewed at the Golden Splice event shows substantial penetration of the major markets during 1993 — more than half of the customers served by the seven regional telephone companies will have National ISDN service by the end of 1994.

The ISDN exhibits that accompanied the Golden Splice event revealed the opportunities in ISDN's Information Age. The room was, of course, filled with PCs and workstations. And, speaking of modems, Hayes was there. I saw NetWare over ISDN, Windows groupware over ISDN, TCP/IP and OSI over ISDN, teleconferencing galore, and exciting new ISDN applications, many not previously posssible.

I urge you to look into ISDN. If you would like more information, contact Bell Communications Research or the Corporation for Open Systems International.

One-Stop Shops Could Put ISDN Over the Top

March 8, 1993

Many of you have written, as if I've just fallen off the turnip truck, to say that the Integrated Services Digital Network really is not here yet or will never be. So, I'm back to say again that, like LANs 10 years ago, ISDN is taking off. And here's what needs fixing.

For more than a decade, telephone companies have been working on ISDN to replace everybody's plain old analog telephones with new switched digital transmission services. Operating at a basic rate of 144K per second, ISDN promises to make it economical to carry "remote" computer data 10 to 100 times faster than is typical today.

Bob Puissant agrees with me and thinks that ISDN is a winner. Of course, he'd better — he's director of business development of data services for Ameritech, one of the phone companies most deeply committed to ISDN deployment.

Bob is working on the problem I have been talking with telcos about: They talk ISDN, I talk PCs. This needs fixing because when ISDN carries much data, virtually all of it will be among PCs. By that time we PC people will have to talk about ISDN in our own PC language.

Of course Bob and I have very little to talk about until ISDN gets widely deployed. Bellcore is about to release Report SR-2102, Issue 3, which shows percentages of the millions of telephone lines in 1992 through which each of the telcos could have provided ISDN service and the plans for 1994.

However, you cannot just make an ISDN data call to any of the millions of ISDN subscribers around the country. In fact, in most cases initially, you can only call other subscribers served by the same central office. But, in the meantime, as telcos work to interconnect the increasing numbers of ISDN-capable switches in their central offices, some important applications can take off.

One obstacle to deployment is the difficulty telcos have getting consistent ISDN tariffs approved out of the 50 public utilities commissions. If the trend continues toward usage fees rather than monthly fees, ISDN can be as affordable as today's business phone service. With Al Gore wanting us to invest in national information infrastructure, he should consider national tariffs that would accelerate ISDN deployment by the telcos.

Federal regulations also prevent your telco from selling you what you need to connect your PCs to the ISDN digital subscriber line they provide. Various third parties have to provide you with (ahem) "Customer Premises Equipment" or CPE. That includes network termination equipment, maybe a home network controller, customer premises RJ-45 wiring, some mixture of analog and digital phones, and terminal (like LAN) adapters that plug into your PCs.

ISDN needs simple one-stop shopping in a market driven by many small and energetic third parties — you know, like the PC industry. Bob reports that Ameritech is working to provide "whole products" through a growing channel of distributors, which may soon include PC channels. Ameritech is also forming alliances with PC product companies — Intel is a recent and important example.

One of Ameritech's lead ISDN applications is corporate work-at-home, sometimes called telecommuting. It seems to me that ISDN's speed advantage over dial-up modems is enough to make work-at-home fly. And enabling people to work more at home attacks some of society's biggest problems — pollution, productivity, parking, fossil-fuel depletion, road repair, climactic changes, child care, and, oh yes, keeping vague appointments with telephone installers.

Pacific Bell has promised that in April I will have ISDN service between my office and home. We'll give this ISDN-WAH thing a try.

How Fast Is ISDN, Really? A Very Early Look

August 2, 1993

Many readers respond excitedly to my ISDN columns, half wanting to share bad experiences from the 1980s and half wanting to know more. I reply that ISDN has come a long way in the last couple of years and deserves another look, such as my Very Early Look on the subject of speed.

I've had my ISDN service for several weeks now. When my Apple PowerBook Duo 230 slides into its dock at my home, a 144Kb-per-second (Kbps) ISDN line silently connects my tiny home Ethernet to InfoWorld's big one. And then my NetWare servers, LaserWriters, electronic mail, Lotus Notes, and Internet services are all right there, yes, almost as if I were in my office a half-hour's drive away.

For my ISDN service I chose book-sized Ethernet-ISDN remote bridges from Combinet Inc. I use a changing mix of operating systems and networking protocols, and a bridge handles them all, whereas an ISDN card would not.

Combinet's bridges — one at my home, one at InfoWorld — give me "bandwidth on demand" through the ISDN Basic Rate Interface (2B+D) that connects them. When my Duo sends a packet to an address not on my home Ethernet, my home bridge dials an ISDN "B" channel to its counterpart at InfoWorld, which passes the packet at 64Kbps on to the InfoWorld network.

Dialing takes less than 4 seconds. The 64Kbps channel is kept open until there are no packets bridged for a while. When packet traffic increases, the second ISDN B channel is dialed, boosting bandwidth to 128Kbps. And all this goes on silently, automatically, without dial tones, with little (if any) perceptible delay.

So, is ISDN fast enough to extend LANs remotely so you could use them for, say, telecommuting? Yes. For example, I no longer user Remote cc:Mail from home, but cc:Mail itself, and it's only a little more sluggish than usual. On file transfers I'm getting 90Kbps uncompressed, which is brisk for most of what I do. In the longer term, multiplying 128Kbps by a compression factor of four, I expect to get upward of 500Kbps through my ISDN line, but I'm not there yet.

For my Very Early Look at ISDN speeds, I used my wristwatch to time the launching of MacWrite, a program file of 3.7MB.

As I sat at InfoWorld, it took 7 seconds to launch MacWrite directly from my Duo's hard disk — which gives a reference disk-to-memory speed of just over 500Kbps. I copied MacWrite to InfoWorld's NetWare server and then launched it: 9 seconds at just over 400Kbps.

At home, I launched MacWrite (only for test purposes) from the same InfoWorld NetWare server, but through ISDN this time: 40 seconds at 90Kbps.

Why don't I see 500Kbps from home? There are several reasons, and the good news is they are all being fixed.

First, I really don't have two 64Kbps lines between my home and InfoWorld. My Pacific Bell ISDN service is still provided through the 56Kbps lines, so for now my ISDN line (two channels) passes a maximum of 112Kbps.

Second, my Duo uses AppleTalk, which, like IPX, requires an acknowledgment for each data packet. Therefore, even when two 56Kbps channels are dialed, AppleTalk uses them alternately, one at a time, not getting the benefit of both. The best I can expect for now through my ISDN line is 56Kbps.

Looking ahead, Pacific Bell will be upgrading its ISDN service to use 64Kbps circuits. Some protocols, such as TCP/IP, already can exploit parallel channels, and AppleTalk and IPX (with "burst mode") can be fixed. Also, Combinet plans to upgrade its bridges to use a standard packet-slicing technique so current LAN protocols can get the benefit of multiple ISDN channels. In the meantime, I'm getting only 56Kbps through my ISDN line.

But how can I get 90Kbps through a 56Kbps channel? It turns out Combinet bridges compress packets, so I launch MacWrite compressed by half, getting me 90Kbps.

So, while I'm not yet getting the decompressed 500Kbps, I expect it won't be long in coming. And even the 90Kbps I get now is a big improvement over the remote analog connections, which were bogging me down.

In an upcoming ISDN column, I will get to how much (or how little) all this wonderful ISDN bandwidth costs, so stay tuned.

Telecommuting via ISDN Is Getting Cheaper

August 23, 1993

My advice on what to do about wireless mobile computing: Wire up your home and stay there. Those 50,000 Americans killed in auto accidents every year would probably agree. And ISDN is rapidly making it possible.

But staying home has its downside too. There are 25,000 Americans murdered every year, most near home by people they know. And ISDN unfortunately does cost money, although probably less than you think.

So how much does it cost to telecommute via ISDN? Well, like the cost of driving, it depends on how far from work you live and how fast you want to get there. And it depends on whether you count just the monetary costs of fuel and tolls or also the environmental costs of exhaust and spills, owning a car, highway construction, stress from traffic jams, not seeing your children grow up, parking, and the value (if any) of your time.

To provide the new telecommuting system I've been writing about for a while, InfoWorld pays Pacific Bell for my ISDN line — two 64Kb-per-second (Kbps) digital data channels (2B+D). For installation, which takes six to nine days if within 18,000 feet of an ISDN central office, I paid $70.75. (There is a $150 charge that Pac Bell will waive if I keep the service for two years.) Each month I pay $27.70 to stay connected. I'm InfoWorld's only ISDN user for now, so total installation and monthly charges are double these rates.

In addition, because I live a half-hour's drive from InfoWorld, for each 64Kbps channel I pay 10 cents for the first minute and 4 cents for each additional minute, which is what I pay to make analog voice (or modem) calls to InfoWorld. As with analog service, these usage charges drop by 30 percent after 5 p.m. and by 60 percent after 11 p.m. and on weekends.

Kathie Blankenship, director of switched digital services at Pacific Bell, says ISDN prices are decreasing. Regulators are relating tariffs more to costs and moving away from the subsidization of local residential voice services with higher prices for long-distance business services. Competitive pressures are increasing. In addition, economies of scale are being felt in digital services. In fact, by switching to Pac Bell's newest service, my monthly ISDN charge has already dropped by 40 percent. Blankenship confirms that I now pay one of the lowest ISDN tariffs in the United States. Other telephone companies, please note, the race is on.

Right now I connect via ISDN to InfoWorld continuously while my computer is turned on at home. Staying continuously connected is not necessary, especially given that it takes less than 4 seconds to get connected. Nevertheless, using one 64Kbps channel 2 hours per working day, 21.5 working days per month, via ISDN costs $159.89 per month.

If I were to use two 64Kbps channels continuously for 8 hours per working day, my ISDN charges would hit $883.58 per month. At this level of usage, it would be a lot better to buy a dedicated 1.544Mb-per-second T-1 line.

Considering that I mostly just stare blankly at and occasionally type into MacWrite screens, if my ISDN connections were made, say, in 1-minute bursts every 20 minutes, and if the ISDN lines at InfoWorld were shared, I would pay a lot less, perhaps as little as $40.60 per month.

These costs do not include my home computer, roughly $5,000 with a 20-inch monitor. Nor do they include what's needed to drive the ISDN line — in my case, an Ethernet bridge box that runs $2,500.

ISDN service charges depend heavily on your applications, operating systems, and protocols. So it's key that you PC system managers get involved in specifying any proposed ISDN-based telecommuting systems.

If you are served by Pacific Bell, call for more information on switched data services, including ISDN. Pacific Bell, now in the midst of a billion-dollar program to go 100 percent digital by 1997, reports ISDN inquiries are up strongly — now past 500 calls per week.

What do you think about these ISDN prices? I'm surprised and encouraged. I will soon be on the low end of the above estimates, finding it practical to take my own advice and stay home more.

My wife Robyn, however, may think differently about this. When we were married, she agreed to take me for better or worse, but not for lunch.

Will the Year of the ISDN Be 1994 Or 1995?

December 27, 1993

The Year of the LAN is a longstanding joke, and I freely admit to being the comedian who first declared it in 1982. Despite all the snickering since then, I still think — in my own twisted way — that I was right. I called attention to the necessary conditions being met in 1982 for LANs to begin their rapid proliferation. OK, maybe 1983 would have been a better choice, but some folks today think that LANs may never catch on.

Anyway, I'm now getting ready to risk another decade of ridicule by courageously declaring The Year of the ISDN. If you're one of my regular readers, then you know I'm advocating that personal computer systems managers should all soon wire up with ISDN. We should soon use ISDN for the small office and home office networking that we now do for our companies with analog modems, but with only one-tenth the speed ISDN offers.

Which year? I think The Year of the ISDN is upon us — 1994, or maybe 1995. Up to now, ISDN has been driven by the telephone companies, but now it is the PC industry's turn to steer, and I'm thinking especially of our favorite market legitimizers: Intel and Microsoft. And IBM.

So, I'm delighted to say that the personal computer industry is getting behind ISDN. In keynote speeches, Microsoft chairman Bill Gates now repeatedly highlights the importance of ISDN, and Microsoft reportedly is working hard on ISDN both for its own internal use and for future products.

Intel punctuated 1993 with a series of agreements with major telephone companies — Ameritech, Bell Atlantic, Ericsson, MCI, Pacific Bell, Siemens — on ISDN-based personal computer data and videoconferencing. Intel reportedly is planning major ISDN-related product announcements early in 1994.

My telephone company here in California, Pacific Bell, continues to push ISDN. Last month it initiated a $16 billion program to build fiber and coax communications superhighways. In addition to telephony and broadcast video, ISDN will also be one of the services offered at the 1.5 million home "terminals" PacBell plans to install by the end of 1996.

More good news from my telephone company is that what I pay for my ISDN service at home is headed downward for the second time since I had it installed only a few months ago. I now pay $28 per month for my single line 144Kb-per-second (Kbps) ISDN line. Once connected, I pay 4 cents for the first minute of each 64Kbps local call and 1 cent for every minute thereafter, plus normal telephone toll charges, minus substantial time-of-day discounts.

The California Public Utilities Commission is evaluating a new ISDN tariff proposal. Under the new tariff, beginning in May 1994, my ISDN would cost me about the same as now, except I would get free the first $20 of local charges — about 30 hours per month during prime time. The aim of this new tariff is to offer a flat-rate service in the local area — say, between your home and office, or to an Internet local point of presence — for those who wouldn't use ISDN all that much.

If you want to know more about ISDN, first try calling the data communications office of your local telephone business office. Or look for the October edition of ISDN Tariff Summary, prepared for the North American ISDN Users' Forum (NIUF).

While we're on ISDN, I urge you to consider IBM's new WaveRunner Digital Modem (ISDN) cards. With a WaveRunner your PC can communicate not only with the few other ISDN devices currently out there but also with Switched 56Kbps equipment, Group 3 fax machines, and analog modems. For more information call Linda Davis in the networking group of IBM Direct. While you have her on the phone, ask whether The Year of the ISDN will be 1994 or 1995.

Microsoft's Plans Signal the Year of the ISDN

April 4, 1994

An *InfoWorld* reader called up Ed Foster's Gripe Line recently to complain that in this, The Year of the ISDN (according to me), he's been waiting since December for ISDN service. When I called back to find out which mom-and-pop telephone company in the rural hinterlands needs my encouragement on ISDN, our reader admitted that his office is actually on an island.

To be more specific, our reader is waiting impatiently for ISDN on 57th, between 6th and 7th. Yes, his island is Manhattan. The telco is NYNEX. Ugh.

NYNEX notwithstanding, this really is The Year of the ISDN. This is the year that the PC industry is finally wrenching ISDN out of the hands of the telcos, which since the 1970s have been trying too hard to invent integrated services and not hard enough to deliver digital networks.   Starting this year, the telco ISDN tail will no longer be wagging the PC dog.

One PC company after another is grabbing hold of ISDN now. Intel's launch of ISDN products in January told me that The Year of the ISDN is near. Learning about Microsoft's three major ISDN initiatives tells me The Year is here.

Microsoft ISDN experts Charles Fitzgerald and Ted Osuch explained to me recently Microsoft's three ISDN initiatives, or, to use their exact words, just how far out on the ISDN limb Microsoft has climbed. Way far. First, Microsoft uses ISDN. Ted Osuch is senior telecommunications engineer for Microsoft.

He says they have Primary Rate ISDN at 31 sites worldwide and use ISDN video teleconferencing among Microsoft's U.S., German, Swedish, and Tokyo offices.

But wait, there's more. In July 1992, Microsoft began an ISDN partnership with the two telcos and the public utilities commission that serve the areas around their headquarters. The goal of this partnership, for which Microsoft is to be commended, is not just to hook Microsoft up, but to work toward general availability of ISDN to anyone in the Puget Sound area.

But Microsoft also recognizes that availability isn't enough.

"Microsoft Guidelines for Establishing ISDN Services at Home," now in Revision 1.0.3, tells how to buy residential ISDN service and hardware for home PCs. Order forms are included. And Osuch says he is working to make it easy to buy ISDN from Egghead.

ISDN tariffs paid by Microsoft employees are somewhat higher than here in California, but they are likely to go down.

Microsoft's second ISDN initiative is to support ISDN through its operating systems. Since October 1993, 160 Microsoft executives — yes, including Bill Gates — have been using ISDN to connect their Puget Sound homes to Microsoft. For example, they now use Windows for Workgroups 3.11 over ISDN to connect into the Remote Access Services (RAS) of Windows NT Advanced Server (NTAS) 3.1.

In the future, says Fitzgerald, who is product manager for Microsoft's Telephone Application Programming Interface (TAPI), Microsoft products will support ISDN through TAPI.

The ISDN hardware that Microsoft uses is DigiBoard's PC-IMAC. As many as 20 WFW clients can be connected simultaneously to each NTAS RAS server. Osuch reports that his users get 1.7-to-1 compression and therefore move 200Kb per second (Kbps) through their ISDN lines. He currently provides one ISDN server port for every five clients.

Microsoft's third ISDN initiative is the development of PC telephony applications. Central office switches are like mainframes, PBXs are like minicomputers, and now with ISDN it's time for personal telephony, Fitzgerald and Osuch say.

In sharing this vision, Fitzgerald stops just short of repeating a line from Nolan Bushnell, who once said that we can make telephones as easy to use as PCs (sic).

Say you connect your PC to ISDN and your telephone to your PC. Your PC can dial numbers from your contacts database, letting you set up conference calls with a mouse click. Your PC can also be an answering machine. It can choose to give a busy signal, forward a call, deliver a personal message, or record one. Microsoft says that in the future these integrated services will, thanks to ISDN, be performed more economically by your PC than by your PBX or central office switch.

So, do you give up? Do you at last agree that, except on a few remote islands, 1994 is The Year of the ISDN?

FCC's Doubling of ISDN Rates May Kick Off a User Revolt

April 3, 1995

Our Federal Communications Commission is doubling its surcharges on ISDN. It takes a vivid imagination to see this doubling as good news, but, hey, that's why you keep me around.

The FCC now surcharges you $3 a month for each of your telephone lines. These subscriber line charges (SLCs) are collected by your local telephone monopoly (Nynex, for example), and they pile up in Washington. Your long-distance telco (MCI, for example) also collects surcharges for the FCC, piling them up for each minute of your long-distance calls.

Next, telco lobbyists help FCC analysts assess the costs of local telephone lines. The FCC then redistributes its pile of surcharges as subsidies to the local telcos. The FCC has been redistributing SLCs since the breakup of AT&T, which was using long-distance tolls to subsidize the many miles of copper that fan out to deliver local telephone service.

Today, the FCC continues these subsidies, hoping to keep local telephone service cheap. The FCC does not rely on competition to drive costs down, but rather on the plans of a large bureaucracy, its own protected local monopolies, and their lobbyists. Oh, great. And so who's surprised that the SLC has risen since inception from $1 to $3 per line per month? Then along comes ISDN, which digitizes an existing copper telephone line to get two 64Kbps B channels. Because you've often heard how expensive that last mile of copper line is, you would think ISDN would be met with rejoicing.

Instead, in 1992, when Nynex, on bended knee, brought ISDN before the FCC, MCI (where Internet pioneer Vint Cerf now works) intervened to point out that B channels can each carry a voice call and therefore should really be surcharged as if each were a separate copper line. The FCC agreed with MCI and is now insisting anew that SLCs be collected for each channel of each line, doubling ISDN's surcharges from $3 to $6 per line per month.

This doubling of surcharges is strangely good news to MCI and other long-distance telcos. The more money flowing into the FCC from SLCs, the less money MCI has to kick in to the government per long-distance minute. Local telcos say that this doubling will break the accelerating demand for ISDN.

And so now they're all arguing at the FCC about what "line" means in SLC. You can voice your opinion by writing Chairman Reed E. Hundt, FCC, 1919 M St. N.W., Washington, D.C. 20554.

The FCC's Mark Corbitt offers another explanation for how we ended up with this bizarre ruling: "The FCC opened public debate on the ISDN SLC topic and didn't hear a dissenting word. Where was the computer industry? They're not involved."

So, how can it be good news — other than to MCI — that the FCC is doubling ISDN surcharges? Well, this doubling does serve to confirm that 1994 was The Year of ISDN, like I've been telling you. What better indication of ISDN's growing impact than having the feds swoop down to tax it? It's also good news that this outrageous FCC ISDN SLC ruling is demonstrating at just the right time how dysfunctional our communications regulatory regime and industry structure are, and how the structure is oscillating toward catastrophic collapse. Our outrage will help Congress finally power past the telcos toward a Communications Act of 1995.

Kathie Blankenship recently retired as ISDN queen after many years at Pacific Telesis and now directs marketing at Smart Valley Inc., in Palo Alto, Calif. She says, "A new framework is required. It's time the entire market got opened up. Let there be competition for the local loop, and let the local telcos compete in the long-distance market as well." Got that, Washington?

Argue about SLCs if you want, telcos, but you're rearranging furniture on the deck of the Titanic. Your monopolies have been sheltered from competition long enough, your profits maximized by inflating, not reducing, costs. And now we tens of millions of PC users, knowing that the costs of communication are going down, not up, flatly reject paying more for ISDN. We demand that our networking costs, like our computing costs, be driven down by competition. We want our Iway. Hurry up and sink.

Nortel Combines Best of DSL with Best of Ethernet for 10Mbps Internet Access

March 9, 1998

On March 23, another new Digital Subscriber Line (DSL) technology will be announced by a major telephone equipment manufacturer. And you heard it here first.

EDSL is not what Nortel will call its new technology. Nor will the company call it 10,000Kbps (vs. 56Kbps) modems. Nortel's new DSL will be called EtherLoop, short for Ethernet Local Loop.

Northern Telecom (Nortel) has been in digital telephony since 1976. Its annual sales grew 20 percent in 1997 to $15.5 billion. And its telephone switches now provide 120 million digital lines worldwide.

Jack Terry joined Nortel in 1974. Today, he is assistant vice president of broadband technology and architecture. He is an award-winning fellow of the IEEE. Terry knows everything there is to know about the copper wires running into the telephone central offices of the incumbent local exchange carriers (ILECs). He is the principal inventor of EtherLoop. And I spoke with him last week.

Terry confirms that Asymmetric DSL (ADSL), so popular among Compaq, Intel, Microsoft, and the ILECs, has problems that slowing down won't fix. ADSL wasn't even designed for Internet access. It was designed so ILECs could broadcast video on demand.

To develop EtherLoop for Internet access, Terry started with the basic transmission properties of "binder groups." A binder is a standard telephone cable through which 25 wire pairs snake toward ILEC central offices. And binders are grouped. Any DSL must grapple with the sad fact that signals sent down telephone pairs interfere (crosstalk) within and among binders. A binder group has to be treated as a shared medium.

Terry's primary design criterion for EtherLoop was that it could be deployed by competitive local exchange carriers (CLECs). That and carry Internet packets the way an Ethernet LAN does, rather than broadcast constant bit-rate video streams.

Terry says EtherLoop is "stealth" technology. It can be installed on ILEC binder groups with minimal interference, administration, and cost. No rewiring is required, so EtherLoop requires virtually no service calls. EtherLoop operates through one telephone pair, which can also be carrying plain old telephone service (POTS).

EtherLoop multiplexers near the media distribution frames in ILEC central offices split off POTS for ILEC voice switches and run Ethernet over to CLEC packet switches.

EtherLoop will carry Internet packets from homes and offices at speeds as fast as 10Mbps. Terry estimates that the total transmission capacity of a 50-pair binder group is 250Mbps. Of course, the farther an EtherLoop modem is from its multiplexer in a central office, the slower it operates, approximately 5Mbps as far as 6 kilometers.

EtherLoop's secret is that it does not transmit continuously. Like Ethernet, it transmits packets in bursts.

Between Ethernet (IEEE 802.3) packets, idle EtherLoop multiplexers test their transmission environments and recalculate per-line equalization. ADSL's continuous modem synchronization assures that binder groups are overflowing with transmission energy, much of which becomes the crosstalk ADSL struggles with. EtherLoop reduces power and therefore noise in binder groups.

EtherLoop is agile among transmission rates, frequencies, packet starts, power, and methods of modulation. EtherLoop multiplexers share binder group transmission capacities, avoiding noise at times and frequencies, and like Ethernet, staying out of one another's way.

EtherLoop does not suffer collisions. EtherLoop modems only speak when spoken to by EtherLoop multiplexers.

EtherLoop is coming to market with a multiplexer chip that handles as many as eight telephone pairs. This chip contributes to EtherLoop's 10-to-1 power-space advantage over ADSL. Rotation among pairs is maintained, Terry says, to minimize delay for IP telephony.

Terry wants EtherLoop to be a standard so Nortel will submit it to the International Telecommunication Union or to the IEEE.

Nortel is also submitting EtherLoop to a "publishable technical audit" by Bellcore. Terry expects to receive a clean bill of spectral compatibility from Bellcore.

It's easy to predict that ILECs will try to prevent CLECs from deploying EtherLoop, claiming interference in binder groups with POTS and ADSL services. The Bellcore audit will help Nortel's CLECs overcome ILEC foot-dragging at public utility commissions.

Let's wish EtherLoop well in the fierce competition ahead among DSLs, ILECs, and CLECs.

Early Good News from Rural MVL DSL Trial: Big Boost to Internet Speed

July 6, 1998

A digital subscriber line (DSL) now shares the 22,000-foot copper pair that brings plain old telephone service (POTS) to our farm in Maine.

Thanks to our very own little DSL trial, we now enjoy continuous Internet at hundreds of kilobits per second.

Your farm, however, especially if you live on a remote island such as Manhattan, is probably stuck with a dial-up analog telephone modem that busies your POTS line and runs at a tenth the speed. I'd like to help solve this problem by reporting that, unless you're a bumbling and/or conniving telephone monopoly, DSL isn't all that hard.

Paradyne is a major DSL supplier spun off from AT&T and is providing Multiple Virtual Line (MVL) equipment for our DSL trial.

The Lincolnville Telephone Company (LTC) operates the telephone central office 22,000 feet from our farm. Feisty little LTC also operates our cable TV service and is an ISP.

Midcoast Internet Solutions is our farm's equally feisty little ISP.

The hard part of our trial was connecting Paradyne's DSL equipment in LTC's central office to Midcoast's Internet point of presence (POP). LTC ran a 1.5Mbps T1 line to Midcoast's POP, which is 45 minutes southwest by car. Today's price for such a T1 line is $1,000 per month.

LTC installed Paradyne's MVL splitter, controller, and DSL access multiplexer (DSLAM) in one refrigerator-size rack in LTC's central office. This took about four hours (at a cost of $200).

The other end of my 22,000-foot telephone pair runs through an inch-thick "binder group" into a car-size main distribution frame (MDF) in LTC's central office. From there it goes into Paradyne's breadbox-size splitter, which runs POTS back to the MDF and then on to LTC's truck-size voice switch.

Paradyne's splitter takes the DSL from my telephone pair and runs it down its rack to Paradyne's breadbox-size DSLAM. Internet packets flow up and down the rack between the DSLAM and Paradyne's breadbox-size controller. The controller exchanges my packets with a specified ISP, in this case with Midcoast, via T1.

On my desk up at the farm, I have Paradyne's book-size 768Kbps MVL modem. My 22,000-foot POTS line snaps into one RJ-11 port. My telephone snaps into another. And into the modem's RJ-45 port snaps any Ethernet device — for now my Macintosh, later our Ethernet hub.

The MVL modem senses its DSLAM, and together they monitor at what rate they can reliably exchange packets. In my case, 22,000 feet from a central office in rural Maine, this turns out to be 320Kbps. When I pick up my phone to make a voice call, MVL drops to 192Kbps.

How much does MVL cost? Paradyne has a starter kit for feisty little telephone companies and ISPs. For the first 20 subscribers, it's $20,000, or after discounts, $1,000 per subscriber, including all MVL central office equipment and subscriber-installed DSL modems.

After another engineering iteration and rollout to 100,000 subscribers, Paradyne says MVL will drop below $400.

Well, $1,000 could be written off in 24 months at $42 per month. At $400, your farm's MVL could be written off over five years at $7 per month.

Good news, yes, but there are some complications.

None of these monthly costs includes the Internet service behind the DSL. For example, I now pay Midcoast $350 per month for the Internet services behind the 56Kbps line I now lease from LTC for $250 per month.

The Internet response I'm actually getting through MVL is not yet nearly 10 times that of POTS. There are many Internet bottlenecks.

We don't know if we would get 320Kbps were other MVL subscribers to share our binder groups. What if we lived closer to LTC and got MVL's full 768Kbps?

Paradyne's MVL is not based on standards being pursued by the Universal ADSL Working Group and the Home Phoneline Networking Alliance.

DSL should start small and evolve competitively with improving technologies and growing markets, like Ethernet did. But this is not how regulated telephone monopolies work. I'm worried that, even if our little DSL trial is successful, it will be discontinued by our public utilities commission, or overpriced out of the barnyard based on today's 56Kbps and T1 lines. Stay tuned.

More from Maine's Rural MVL DSL Front: Pick Your Speed and Pay Your Toll

July 13, 1998

My athletic trainer, Jodie, wants to try her new goniometer on me, but I'm not up for it. She has even offered to let me use it in evaluating my new Digital Subscriber Line (DSL).

Last week, I reported here about a group of us in rural Maine trying a new DSL technology, Multiple Virtual Line (MVL), developed by Paradyne. We are joined in this trial by our feisty little Lincolnville telephone company and our feistier little Internet service provider, Midcoast Internet Solutions.

Thanks to Paradyne's MVL, I'm now enjoying 320Kbps Internet access through the same 22,000-foot copper pair that carries plain old telephone service (POTS) along meandering Route 52 and up Gould Hill to our rare-livestock farm.

Last week's good news was that MVL now costs $1,000 per subscriber for the first 20 subscribers, including all central-office equipment and subscriber-installed modems. Furthermore, because of volume, Paradyne sees MVL dropping soon to $400 per subscriber. I depreciate $400 over five years at, not $1,000 per month, or even $100 per month, as telephone monopolies and public utilities commissions might, but less than $10 per month.

This week, there's more good news, and some other news, from our MVL trial.

It's good news that when downloading software I net between 200Kbps and 300Kbps, depending on which servers are being used and who is using them, and that's before compression. So now I'm updating all my software because I don't have to batch my downloads overnight at one tenth the speed.

The *other* MVL news is that Web access through MVL is only slightly faster than my $600-per-month 56Kbps Internet service. As I've been telling you, the Internet has many bottlenecks, not just local access.

Not used to having customers as fast as 56Kbps, Midcoast does not cache Web pages after downloading them though the Internet's bogging backbones.

Some other news is that MVL operates as fast as 768Kbps, but I'm getting only 320Kbps. So I could double my speed again by moving closer to my central office or by getting Paradyne to install a DSL access multiplexer (DSLAM) in the digital telco box at the bottom of Gould Hill.

Our trial does not demonstrate what happens if all of my neighbors were to get MVL, too. With their POTS lines sharing long 25-pair binder groups with mine, my peak MVL rate might drop to less than 320Kbps, as it does (to 192Kbps) when I take my phone off the hook.

Paradyne developed MVL because larger Asymmetrical DSL (ADSL) trials have been plagued by cross talk. For example, Bell Atlantic now says you can't install ADSL beyond 15,000 feet. But MVL uses lower frequencies and less power than ADSL, so it will probably have lower cross talk and go farther. But we'll have to wait until somebody tries 100,000 MVL subscribers out of one central office.

Now, it used to make sense to charge a fixed monthly fee for DSL, plus whatever ISPs charge to carry packets through the Internet. It's highly debatable whether ISP charges should be fixed for a given access speed or vary based on traffic. I'm now wondering the same about DSL.

Say your telephone company adds MVL to your POTS by installing $400 of equipment. Does this mean you should pay for installation plus $10 per month to cover maintenance, depreciation, and profit?

What if you're getting 320Kbps and your neighbor closer to the central office is getting 768Kbps? Shouldn't your price be less? Or should you pay more because your bits are being carried further? Or would distance premiums exactly balance speed discounts in a flat monthly fee? Don't think so.

And what if, as neighbors sign on, your MVL service starts to rate-adapt down to 100Kbps? Shouldn't your price go down proportionately? Or does the increased value of connecting to more of your neighbors exactly balance with speed discounts in a flat monthly fee? Don't think so.

If DSLs are to be rate-adaptive, then pricing should vary with distance from the central office, the speed your service adapts down to, and the traffic carried.

Mind you, I'm doing this without Jodie's goniometer, but seems to me that you should pay traffic charges for rate-adaptive DSLs, for Internet access, and for Internet backbone use.

Now a lot of you are opposed to metered Internet usage. I chalk this up to how expensive metering has been under the telephone monopolies. But competition can get us to the low metered rates we deserve in an Internet guided by sound economics.

Puzzling Over a Light Bulb, a Liar, and When G.Lite Will Be under the Xmas Tree

August 31, 1998

This week, I won't be saying much more about the impeachment of Bill Clinton. Instead, during what's left of the summer, let's work on three little puzzles and a big one involving digital subscriber lines (DSL).

✦ *The Coffee-Tea Puzzle.* (See "If unwanted e-mail is in the eye of the beholder then I want a spam button," Aug, 3.) If you start with two identical glasses, one half full of coffee and the other half full of tea, and you pour some of the coffee into the tea, and then you pour the same amount of the mixture back into the coffee, is the coffee more diluted than the tea, or vice versa?

All but one of an astounding number of responding readers — you know who you are — found that the coffee and tea are equally diluted. Bravo!

Some of you noted that equal dilution results in the cases where none, all, and certain fixed amounts of the coffee are poured into the tea. Others of you, like me, recalled enough algebra to prove equal dilution for all pourings between none and all, assuming that the coffee and tea are thoroughly mixed.

Now, I am proud of us, but I am also totally in awe of those who concluded without algebra that the dilutions are exactly equal, and in fact the mixing does not even have to be thorough. However much tea makes it back to dilute the coffee, exactly the same amount of coffee is left behind to dilute the tea, so what's the big deal? I hope this puzzle was fun for you too.

This equal dilution result comes in handy when discussing what happens when the computer and telephone industries mix.

✦ *The Light Switches Puzzle.* Like Monty Hall's three doors (see "Microsoft, government got you down? Try these mind puzzles for a lift," June 8), you are presented now with three identical light switches. One of the switches is connected to a light bulb in a room downstairs that you cannot see. The other two switches are connected to nothing. The puzzle is, after flipping the switches all you want, and assuming you can go downstairs to look at the bulb once and only once, how can you find out which switch is connected to the bulb?

No, you cannot see the wiring. May I have your answers, please?

✦ *The Liar Puzzle.* This puzzle is not about Bill Clinton, upon whose impeachment I cannot dwell here. There are two people standing at a fork in the road. One of them, Ken, always tells the truth. The other, Bill, always lies.

You don't know who's who. What one question do you ask one of them to find out which road to go down?

✦ *The UAWG Puzzle.* Last January, Compaq, Intel, and Microsoft — otherwise known as CIM — announced their formation of the Universal ADSL Working Group. They were joined in UAWG by the few remaining Baby Bells and many other companies who ought to have known better.

UAWG's aim was to produce a splitterless (no new in-home wiring) version of the ANSI T1.413 Asymmetrical DSL (ADSL) standard in time for Christmas. G.Lite, as the International Telecommunications Union (ITU) will call UAWG's consumer ADSL standard, was to plug and play at 1.5Mbps downstream, 512Kbps upstream. And thanks to CIM's UAWG, G.Lite products were to be on store shelves by Christmas.

The big puzzle now is: Which Christmas?

CIM agrees with me that dial-up telephone modems are not nearly what their customers need for Internet access. So they rushed off looking for a quick way to break the bandwidth bottleneck.

CIM was told by telephone monopolies — the very same people who promised ISDN — that ADSL is the way to go, the standard, 8Mbps downstream and 1.5Mbps upstream. And inexplicably, as I wrote here in February (see "Compaq, Intel, Microsoft back the wrong standard for fast Internet access," Feb. 9), CIM believed the Baby Bells who had decided, after an elaborate political process, that ADSL could be slowed down to make it usable by consumers.

Trouble is, ADSL, having been designed for video on demand, does not really work well for Internet access. And now UAWG is discovering, confidential sources report, that slowing ADSL down does not solve its problems.

It's now clear that Universal ADSL will not appear on PC store shelves in time for Christmas 1998. And from UAWG leaks that I am now pursuing, it's beginning to look like Christmas 1999 is a reach. So at which, if any, Christmas will G.Lite appear?

Hungry for DSL, I'm rooting for UAWG, but its politics are trying to sweep ADSL's problems — which I, among others, warned them about — under the rug. You work on this week's puzzles, and I'll keep digging into UAWG to see if it can be saved.

Universal ADSL Working Group Is Speeding G.Lite Down a Road to Nowhere

September 7, 1998
Compaq, Intel, and Microsoft are leading an industry consortium in the development of a consumer standard for high-speed Internet access through telephone lines. And although it may not seem that way from what I have to say below, I'm rooting for them.

Trouble is, the consortium is doomed, or at least it's showing all the signs. The consortium is mired in standards bodies and their acronyms, none of which I've used yet in this week's column. It has decided to rely on technology decisions made by telephone monopolies, back when said monopolies thought video on demand, not Internet access, was the next big thing. Worse, the consortium is now trying to sweep its various problems under various rugs.

Compaq, Intel, and Microsoft, otherwise known as CIM, have attracted more than 70 members to their Universal ADSL Working Group (UAWG). UAWG is rushing to specify a plug-and-play version of Asymmetric Digital Subscriber Line (ADSL), which it hopes will receive an initial blessing as G.Lite from the International Telecommunications Union (ITU) at its October meeting in Geneva.

UAWG is determined that G.Lite will be based on American National Standards Institute (ANSI) T1.413 ADSL using Discrete Multitone Technology (DMT) modulation. And as if ANSI and ITU weren't enough, UAWG is being rooted on by yet another consortium, the more than 300 members of the ADSL Forum.

UAWG is right that today's analog dial-up telephone modems are not adequate for Internet access from homes. UAWG is right that packetizing phone lines is the leading alternative to dial-up modems. UAWG is right that an international standard would greatly accelerate the proliferation of Digital Subscriber Line (DSL) technology.

UAWG is wrong, however, in assuming that ADSL can simply be slowed down to reach far into many distant homes without rewiring them. I warned about this right after UAWG was formed. (See "Compaq, Intel, Microsoft back the wrong standard for fast Internet access," Feb. 9.)

Back then I argued that because Nortel and Paradyne have both recently introduced non-ADSL DSLs, there must be something wrong with DMT. And now sources within UAWG are telling me that I'm starting to look right.

But UAWG is not admitting the problems it's having with ADSL. Go to its Web pages and look for any bad news at all. Nothing but glad tidings and the claim that G.Lite will be the preferred modem standard, not by Christmas 1998 or 1999, but by 2000. Slip.

Efforts to hurry G.Lite through ITU are running into reality. Conscientious engineers are now trying to insist that the modeling and testing of actual home wiring be made part of the ITU specs. The leadership, however, is working hard to hold to schedule and maintain appearances.

For example, you will not read on UAWG's Web pages that DMT's developer, Stanford Professor John Cioffi, is admitting DMT cannot smoothly handle telephones going on and off hook on shared G.Lite lines.

Others complain that it is not realistic to model home wiring as a simple star of Category 3 copper wiring. It's just that because of DMT's high frequencies and power, G.Lite will require in-line phone filters; or new $50 telephones; or the full-rate ADSL splitters that UAWG was aiming to eliminate with G.Lite; or ugly deployment restrictions to keep G.Lite from interfering with plain old telephone service, T1, ISDN, and itself.

I may yet be proven wrong about ADSL being broken beyond UAWG's repair, but I'm positive that UAWG's current telephone company politics and propaganda will, if not fixed, prove fatal. UAWG proceedings should be opened up so that we all can track its problems and progress. Now, out in front of all this, the few remaining Baby Bells are talking quite a bit about their upcoming launches of DSL service — they are feeling the competition of cable modem companies. And it sounds like ISDN all over again.

If I were cynical, I'd suggest that telopolies want UAWG to fail. The longer they can delay DSL deployment, the more time they have to prepare for their retirements by gouging us for T1 services.

Before we see a universal DSL standard, I think we're going to see chips that automatically sense and support various combinations of V.90 56Kbps modems, DMT and Carrierless Amplitute and Phase Modulation ADSL, G.Lite, Paradyne's Multiple Virtual Line, Nortel's EtherLoop, and others. These chips will be valuable in absorbing differences among emerging standards and in adapting to wiring differences.

The hard part will be getting the various DSLs deployed in, under, around, and through the telephone monopolies and their public utilities commissions.

The Direct Access Internet Race Gives You Two Choices: DOCSIS and UADSL

October 5, 1998

Here's more good news for frustrated dial-up users of today's bogged Internet. There's a new standard called the Data Over Cable Service Interface Specification. DOCSIS is the cable television industry's answer to the telephone industry's Universal Asymmetric Digital Subscriber Line, UADSL.

See my critique of UADSL ("Universal ADSL Working Group is speeding G.Lite down a road to nowhere," Sept. 7) and a response from the UADSL Working Group (To the Editor, Sept. 28).

The good news is that both DOCSIS and UADSL are poised for major deployment in 1999, maybe into millions of U.S. households. They will compete fiercely in building the next-generation Direct Access Internet™.

Note that we have several "nextgen Internets" including Gigabit Ethernet, IPv6, quality of service, secure, Java, voice-over-IP, and multicast Internets. And of course there's my Pay-As-We-Go Internet™, which was coldly received here the week before last.

We are also moving to a nextgen Direct Access Internet. DOCSIS, UADSL, and their many dark-horse competitors will replace indirect (dial-up, kilobit, circuit-switched) access to the Internet with direct (continuous, megabit, packet-switched) access.

So here's what I heard about DOCSIS from some folks at Motorola. They have installed 300,000 cable modems and estimate that to eventually be 70 percent of the market, with virtually zero churn. If you are a subscriber of RoadRunner, MediaOne, or @Home, you likely have a Motorola modem. The second-largest supplier, with less than 30 percent share, is LANCity, which was acquired by Bay Networks, which was acquired by Nortel. Other suppliers are in the noise, such as General Instrument with maybe 5 percent, but then there's lots of noise.

The immediate goal of DOCSIS is to get you T1-like direct access to the Internet for $40 per month. If you've ever tried to get T1, you understand how telcos might be threatened by this — cable companies have to watch their backs.

In the short term, after checking with your cable operator, you're to go out to Circuit City, buy a cable modem for less than $200, plug it into your cable television set-top box, and connect your PC. Chances are your operator will roll his or her truck out to your house to prepare the cabling, but after that, heaven.

In the longer term, you will buy set-top boxes containing cable modems, digital video disc drives, Ethernet, and telephone jacks (which has telcos worried even more). Next, you will have cable-ready PCs with factory-installed DOCSIS cards. Eventually, we're talking cable-ready network computers.

Applying the liar puzzle solution

Remember the puzzle with a fork in the road and there are two men, one who always lies (Bill) and the other who always tells the truth (Ken), but you don't know who, and you get only a single question? The solution is to ask one which road the other would say was wrong, and take it. So, I asked Motorola what UADSL proponents say about DOCSIS.

First, UADSL proponents say DOCSIS bandwidth is shared among many subscribers. But DOCSIS systems can operate to 100 kilometers with a 37Mbps downstream channel and multiple upstream channels. As new subscribers sign up, old ones are reassigned to additional upstream channels or to added services on the same hybrid-fiber-cable (HFC) plant.

Second, UADSL proponents say DOCSIS is insecure. But, not counting software security at higher layers, DOCSIS uses the 56-bit Data Encryption Standard with new keys daily.

And third, UADSL proponents say DOCSIS requires two-way HFC infrastructure that cable television companies don't have and cannot afford. And this is the heart of the matter.

DOCSIS is a standard based on the 700,000 cable modems that will be installed on two-way HFC by the end of 1998. Of 100 million U.S. households, 95 million are passed by cable television, 65 million subscribe, and 13 million are already two-way HFC. By 2000, more than 70 percent will have two-way HFC, Motorola says.

Hundreds of thousands of us already enjoy direct Internet access at home. Get it ASAP, using UADSL, DOCSIS, or something better. If you can't, attack the monopolies standing in your way. If you can't get direct access in your neighborhood soon, move somewhere that is serious about the Information Age.

How About Skipping G.lite and Getting On with the All-Optical Internet?

June 28, 1999

Telephone-company executives are still reeling from their hasty introduction of the Princess telephone in 1959.

So it's understandable that to date, telcos have installed 100,000 Digital Subscriber Lines (DSLs) on their copper — far less than the one million cable television modems (CTMs).

It goes back to 1957, when AT&T unveiled a "bedroom phone" with a light for nightstands. But after Sputnik, in two years flat, AT&T repositioned the Princess telephone as a "woman's phone" in four entirely new colors, despite scant evidence that housewives wanted to use telephones.

Such bold, Bell-ringing dynamism.

How could they have known Princess colors would open the public's eyes to telephone choice? And there followed the FCC's Carterfone decision in 1968, AT&T divestiture in 1984, the Telecommunications Act of 1996, and the DSL Interoperability Showcase at SuperComm99 in Atlanta.

Older but wiser, members of the United States Telephone Association (USTA) are not rushing into always-on, high-speed Internet access to homes, many of which still don't have Princess telephones.

USTA makes a big show of technology developments, standards making, market trials, deployment plans, and interoperability showcases. Meanwhile, it lobbies and litigates to deter competition.

To treat my hard-earned bias against telco monopolies, I attended the Universal Asymmetric DSL Working Group (UAWG) Interoperability Showcase at SuperComm99. More than 30 telephone equipment vendors demonstrated compatible combinations of customer premises and central office equipment using a new ADSL variant called G.lite. Lite is intended to accelerate deployment of always-on, high-speed Internet access to homes.

At a press conference, UAWG declared victory with G.lite and disbanded. UAWG was founded by Compaq, Intel, and Microsoft in Jan. 1998. G.lite will henceforth be taken up by the ADSL Forum.

Despite their denials, I think Compaq, Intel, and Microsoft are bailing out of G.lite. They have no reason to care whether DSLs beat CTMs. Perhaps they're starting to agree with me that G.lite doesn't work all that well, or that telcos are not great partners.

The most convincing part of the UAWG press conference was Compaq's disclosure that it has shipped 100,000 Presarios with G.lite ADSL modems. These were combo cards including V.90 dial-up modems (56Kbps), full-rate ADSL (8Mbps down and 768Kbps up), and G.lite ADSL (1.5Mbps down and 384Kbps up).

I wonder how many people will keep on using V.90, or jump to full-rate ADSL, rather than compromise on G.lite ADSL. I kept hearing that the Internet can operate at up to about 400Kbps, so V.90 and ISDN are too slow, full-rate ADSL is too fast, and G.lite is just right.

Well, I don't buy this, nor am I enthusiastic about ADSL — full-rate or lite.

Even the ADSL Forum says it's diversifying and should probably be called the DSL Forum. Sounds like the (A)DSL Forum is bailing out of G.lite, and maybe even ADSL too. It denies this vehemently. Today's alphabet soup of DSLs includes HDSL, ADSL, SDSL, VDSL, MVL, SuperLine, and EtherLoop. There will be many more flavors of DSL before we're through.

Too many G.lite proponents think homes will each have one Compaq-Intel-Microsoft PC. They offer DSL cards with Windows support. How will a home's several non-Windows computers be connected?

ADSL fans are about to discover that even more important than high-speed Internet access is always-on Internet access. They will be surprised by new applications that are only practical with always-on access.

Soon, we'll realize that CTMs and DSLs are copper retrofits promoted by monopolies that own a lot of copper. We're going to start encouraging competition to bypass old Bell copper by deploying the all-optical Internet.

Liar, Liar, Pants On Fire, Your Nose Is Longer than a Copper Telephone Wire

September 20, 1999

Too bad that what should be the leading always-on, high-speed, residential Internet access technology isn't.

Last year, 10 times more cable television modems (CTMs) were deployed than Digital Subscriber Lines (DSLs). This year, DSL is spreading, but it is tangled in "Digital Subscriber Lies."

I'm not against DSLs, but because its copper lines are in the hands of telephone monopolies (telepolies), I've been pessimistic, and rightly so.

True, I declared Asymmetrical Digital Subscriber Line (ADSL) Lite dead after the Universal ADSL Working Group (UAWG) turned it over to the ADSL Forum. In the very act of thanking UAWG, the ADSL Forum declared it was really the DSL Forum and scheduled its next two boondoggles for Hawaii and Switzerland. Rest in peace.

True, I've warned you about telepolies prematurely choosing ADSL as a standard. There will be many more DSL technologies before we're through.

But, I'm enthusiastic about non-ADSL DSLs. They should be prominent among dial-up telephone modems, ISDN, CTMs, DSLs, mobile wireless, fixed wireless, satellites, power lines, and fiber to the home.

Now, if it's optimism you want, let me introduce you to Dave Burstein's DSL Prime. I read it and suggest you do too.

But be careful about Digital Subscriber Lies. Go read, for example, how DSL Prime's estimates of DSL deployment, around 160,000 at the end of June, "are based on company numbers, not arbitrary guesswork." That's reassuring.

ADSL has been a lie all along. The telepolies needed a ploy to get public utilities commissions to grant them higher profits. After ISDN, they promised ADSL for video on demand. After that fizzled, they came up with ADSL Lite.

Anti-Bell activist Bruce Kushnick is about to sue the telepolies over their broken promises to deploy the information superhighway. He is alleging $37 billion of ISDN, DSL, and fiber fraud by the telepolies.

Another lie: CTM "party lines" have security problems, but DSLs don't. Have you followed where telephone lines go outside your house? For how long do we depend on physical disconnection for security?

Another lie: CTMs share transmission media, while DSLs don't; so CTMs are slow, and DSLs are fast. This is three lies in one.

First, DSLs do share a medium, namely the "binder groups," through which twisted copper lines wind their way back to central offices. More DSLs per group, more cross talk, slower speeds.

Second, the upstream trunks are the likely bottleneck for high-speed access. DSL providers are just as capable of scrimping on those as CTM providers. And third, both CTM and DSL providers can substantially boost bandwidth by pushing optical fibers outward to subscribers.

Another lie: CTM providers, especially AT&T, will "bundle" content with their CTM services, undermining our First Amendment rights. Fact is, AT&T's services give access to all Internet content, not just AT&T's. I'm with the Federal Communications Commission Chairman Kennard and AT&T on this.

Rich Shapero, a venture capitalist deep into DSL, reports that deployers such as Covad, Northpoint, and Rhythms are hampered by the inability of telopolies to provision copper for other than their own DSL services.

Shapero says this is not the telopolies lying. It's the residual incompetence of long-term monopolies. He wants the telopolies fully divested. He wants them broken up into switching companies and local-loop companies — "loopcos" — providing copper to all comers.

But, the telopolies have already proven to be competent DSL providers. Not ADSL, but HDSL, or High-bit-rate Digital Subscriber Line, providers. They call it T1 and charge 10 times more than they should for it. This would indicate that the telopolies are lying more than they are incompetent.

Well, OK, it's probably too close to call.

Dragging their feet on broadband access?

Rebuttal by Arno Penzias

Arno Penzias, Nobel Prize winner for research that enabled a better understanding of the origins of the universe, is the former head of research at Bell Labs. He began his career in 1961 when he joined Bell Laboratories, taking part in the Echo and Telstar communications satellite experiments. He is best known for his work in radio astronomy. Currently he is a Venture Partner at New Enterprise Associates in Silicon Valley.

Dear Bob,

ISDN? It's all about sending digits over nominally analog wires, no? Been happening since at least the mid-fifties. In that case, the wires stretched from a 'client' at Dartmouth College's campus, to a Bell Labs 'server' in New Jersey. Not a lot of bits per second in those days, but data rates have been climbing steadily ever since.

For tens-of-millions of Internet users, those bits still travel disguised (by modems) as plain old analog telephone signals. It may not be as fast as we'd like, but you can't beat the price. Modem users get all-you-can-surf service for a fixed monthly rate, kept low by government regulators so as to make residential telephone service as widely available as possible. (That's the system that got the phone lines to your corner of Maine in the first place, I hope you realize.) Under this model, Telcos are supposed to make up any revenue shortfalls from business customers and fees on long distance phone calls.

Why am I telling you all of this? You seem bemused by Local Exchange Company reluctance to promote a new $30/month service (DSL) that makes an existing $3000/month service (T1) largely unnecessary. But not to worry. The fact that 80 percent of new T-1 lines are provisioned with DSL hardware has attracted interest from IXCs and CLECs. They would like nothing better than to grab business customers from the ILECs under those economics.

With competition for business customers heating up and prices dropping, the ILECs are now trying to get FCC permission to enter the long-distance business directly, in return for opening up their local access business to competition. In practice, that means offering to rent their copper wires to the CLECs. (Yes Bob, fiber will come to your house some day. But remember that less than one US office building in ten has a fiber connection today, letalone residential customers). But from a CLEC perspective, rented copper wires only make economic sense with DSL-based service packages. So, a land-grab race looks likely.

As amply reflected in your columns, Telcos rarely (if ever) move as fast as expected. Nonetheless, status quo seems impossible. For example, consider AT&T's 'bet the company' venture into cable-based communications services. This rapid penetration of cable modems has drawn growing attention from Internet heavyweights, forcing the CLECs to pace themselves accordingly. That's what we call competition.

And, finally, don't count out the ILECs just yet. Technology just might save (at least some of) their bacon. On the operations side, I'm seeing lots of promising new technology advances, such as rapid provisioning of multiple DSL circuits, and neat ways of exploiting some of the

(continued)

(continued)

potential bandwidth that now sits unused in metropolitan fiber rings. Deployment of such tools could unlock much of the value that lies in the ILECs' core assets and keep them in the ball game.

Loathe as I am to compete with you in punditry, I won't try to predict which service providers will be left standing at the end of this coming shake-out; but whichever providers survive, I'm pretty sure that they won't be dragging their feet on broadband access as some are today.

Keep smiling,

Arno

Wireless Computing Will Flop...Or Will It?

Back in 1993, there was a big to-do about wireless PCs. In my wisdom I attacked the concept of wireless on several levels. I started by dealing with the brain-frying potential of low-level electromagnetic radiation and the danger of holding a cellular phone to your ear for hours on end. Then I segued to my famous portapotty analogy, stressing the inconvenient side of the lack of plumbing inherent in wireless computing. Not to mention the inefficiency of broadcasting information all over the place to reach a single person's wireless device.

Well, years rolled by and the millennium approached, and I finally realized I had been wrong about wireless (among other things). And the very lady who helped me see the wireless light, Dawn Lepore, has graciously joined me in this chapter to point out the error of my ways.

Wireless Nets Give Me a Warm Feeling Inside

July 26, 1993

At a recent wireless LAN demo, I got a funny warm feeling inside about cellular radio technologies in the frequency bands around 2.4 gigahertz.

Having worked at Raytheon back in the 1960s, when the Radarange was new, I guessed that 2.4 gigs is about where microwave ovens operate. The LAN guy explained frequency hopping to avoid microwave oven interference. But it wasn't oven interference worrying me just then, it was being inadvertently cooked by my wireless LAN.

Anne Ryder and I returned to InfoWorld and talked about LAN cooking. Anne scrambled off to find what had been written recently on the health hazards of microwave radiation. She came back with a ton. It seems I'm very late to the subject — maybe 25 years late.

You've probably read that microwaves are not the only frequencies in the electromagnetic spectrum in which health hazard alarms are going off.

Radiation (not to be confused with radioactivity) from high-tension power lines are accused of causing leukemia, cellular telephones of causing brain tumors, and computer monitors of causing miscarriages, birth defects, stress, and depression. Then there is the electricity allergy sweeping Sweden, which Forbes wrote about March 8.

I'm writing about these alleged (which is not to say nonexistent) radiation dangers from my normal position — hunched about a foot from a 20-inch color monitor. I guess I really shouldn't worry about wireless LAN radiation while pushing my face into this torrent of gamma rays, X-rays, ultraviolet light, infrared light, heat, microwaves, and the much stronger electromagnetics closer to 60 hertz.

PC companies say there are no scientific data indicating that monitor radiation is a health hazard. And yet Apple, Compaq, and IBM have collectively offered $2.5 million to support further research into the subject at Johns Hopkins University. So you'll forgive me for selecting an 18-point font and rolling my ergonomically correct Herman Miller chair way back.

The most recent radiation scare has been about cellular telephones and the possibility that holding a 600-milliwatt 900-MHz (not quite microwave) radio transmitter up against your head several hours a day might give you brain cancer. This possibility, however remote, is beginning to worry some of the more than 10 million cellular telephone users in the United States, especially us hotshots (no pun intended) with portable models.

I missed it, but a man from Florida appeared on TV with Larry King and accused NEC and GTE of killing his wife with cellular. So far, there is only circumstantial evidence. This woman used a cellular phone a lot and died of a brain tumor. Am I too cynical in thinking that this unfortunate widower has a lawyer working on contingency to sue these deep-pocket companies (one of them Japanese), and that there will eventually be, prior to jury trial, an insurance settlement?

Motorola has taken a strong stand against fearmongering about cellular telephones. I waited in the queue a few seconds for an operator, gave my address, and am awaiting a pamphlet in the mail.

Getting back to wireless LANs, I understand the Federal Communications Commission will only allow them to radiate below a watt, and we won't be pressing them to our heads, so nobody is in danger of getting well done soon.

But who knows what frequencies at what powers over what periods might resonate with various bits of our genetic material, causing what I'd rather not say? Fact is, nobody actually knows.

The scientific community says there is insufficient data to conclude that long-term exposure to low-level electromagnetic radiations is a health hazard.

It also agrees that more government money should be spent on further research, somewhere between the $7 million recently requested and $10 billion.

Just as I drive to work daily knowing that something like 50,000 Americans die in car accidents each year, I am going to continue using my 20-inch monitors and portable cellular telephones. And I'll have a wireless LAN as soon as I can figure out what to do with it. Just to be on the safe side, however, my arms will be extended and my fingers crossed, and I'll be wearing a coconut sunblock, protection factor 15 or greater.

Wireless Computing Will Flop — Permanently

August 16, 1993

Study the photos in computer publications, including this newspaper right now, and you will notice that almost all of the wires are missing. I'll wait while you look.

Hardly any wires, right? So does this mean that the unphotogenic tangle hanging off the back of your desk is a thing of the past? Does this mean that several years of raised hopes about wireless mobile computing have already been realized? Does this mean that, untethered at last, we all can take up the carefree wireless mobile lives of neo-nomads? Answers: No, No, and No.

Furthermore, it is my sad duty to inform you that the coming resounding flop in wireless mobile computing will be, alas, permanent.

There is, I know, an exciting trend toward wirelessness. The relentless progression of smaller, faster, higher capacity, and lower priced computers cries out, "Wires have to go!"

Power cords have to go, replaced by longer-lasting batteries made from sealed lead, nickel cadmium, lithium ion, or maybe plutonium cyclamates (just kidding). And, by the way, let's have a few battery standards so we can share them with our seatmates on planes.

Next, network cables have to go, replaced by higher frequency electromagnetics made from gallium arsenide, spread spectrum, frequency hopping, and packet cellular. And they, too, better work on planes.

Cutting all these cords and cables is exciting, but it isn't inevitable. The truth about wireless computing is that it's not going to pan out.

Simply put, there aren't enough megahertz to go around out there in our increasingly polluted electromagnetic ether. It is an ecologically unsound waste of energy to broadcast bits in all directions when they need to be received in only one. The ether is too scarce to be wasted on non-broadcast communications, and it won't be.

Cellular telephone companies like to brag about carrying up to 19.2Kb per second to and from your delightfully wireless mobile computer. Excuse me, but aren't you finding that 10Mb per second is a little on the slow side; maybe you're going to need ATM at several million multimedia megabits per second?

So after the wireless mobile bubble bursts later this year, we'll get back to stringing fibers. Instead of computing on the road without wires, we will be installing ubiquitous plugs.

This isn't to say there won't be any wireless computing. Wireless mobile computers will eventually be as common as today's pipeless mobile bathrooms.

Portapotties are found on planes and boats, at construction sites, rock concerts, and other places where it is very inconvenient to run pipes. But bathrooms are still predominantly plumbed. For more or less the same reasons, computers will stay wired.

Need more reasons why wireless won't become widespread? There are the privacy challenges of wide-area data broadcasting, which you'll encounter as you demonstrate that you care. What about standards for wireless computer networking, which will settle down right after ISDN, HDTV, PCMCIA, and ATM are resolved. Consider governments around the world reallocating spectrum for use by wireless computer networks, which they will right after whale hunting is stopped. And there are the health risks of prolonged exposure to increasing levels of higher frequency electromagnetic radiations, which I hope are nil.

And finally, what about the vast amounts of money needed for building wireless networking infrastructure, which will be raised right after The Deficit is eliminated?

Of course, many of these issues may be resolved in our lifetimes. So even if I'm wrong about the permanent shortage of real ether, wires will be keeping us civilized for a very long time.

Is it any wonder, then, that the TV industry, which has relied on broadcast radio for most of its history, is in a full-swing switch to cable? Increasingly we will switch data via fiber networks instead of broadcasting it via radio.

And in case you're not upset yet, there's this angle: If half the world's problems are caused by having too many people, the other half are caused by all of us wanting to move around so much — from home to work, from work to our customer's work, from our picturesque hometowns to identical airports, hotels, and tourist traps around the world. So let's just wire up our homes and stay there.

Wirefree RadioMail to Change My Life, in 1994

November 29, 1993

Wireless computers, as I first observed here on August 16, are like pipeless bathrooms, or portapotties: handy on airplanes and boats, and at rock concerts and constructions sites, but not in very many other places. My advice? Forget being a road warrior. Wire up your home and stay there. And if you must go somewhere, plan on plugging in when you arrive.

Now, I'm not yet ready to recant my prediction that the current wireless frenzy will soon flop. But I will admit now that wireless is too big a subject about which to generalize. Wireless networking is like nonelephant biology.

Under wireless come such different species as global positioning, paging, E-mail, cellular telephones, LANs, remote LAN access, remote terminals, personal identification, and personal digital assistant beaming. So, OK, one or two of them might not get selected out.

Much of the E-mail I've received disagreeing with my prediction of a wireless flop was from users of RadioMail, a company here in San Mateo, Calif. Jim Opfer, president of the RadioMail Users Group (RMUG), rejoices in sending me E-mail. He says, basically, "Look Bob, no wires, and this here was sent at 8Kb per second (Kbps) from an outdoor cafe in Los Angeles." RadioMail is anywhere, anytime, and for $89 per month. My wet-blanket replies are generally from home at 50Kbps over ISDN for $28 per month. In one message, which was probably typed while changing lanes on an interstate, Opfer invited me to attend an RMUG meeting. I leaped at the chance.

There was an enthusiastic buzz that evening among the hundred or so RMUG attendees, a good many of whom carried computers smaller than their modems.

Guy Kawasaki, famous for perfecting software evangelism during the launch of the Apple Macintosh, was the evening's volunteer keynote speaker.

Kawasaki said that RadioMail has changed his life. If you don't "get" RadioMail in 30 seconds, he said, you won't ever. And people who don't get RadioMail can safely be ignored. So, not wanting to be ignored, I've decided to delay my RadioMail epiphany until mid-1994, when perhaps it and I will be ready.

RadioMail founder Geoff Goodfellow was the highlight of RMUG, but then I tend to fall for engineer entrepreneurs. Geoff said that RadioMail's two-way cellular packet radio technology is a vast improvement over the one-way pager he wears on his hip. First, paging systems can only afford to carry very short messages — little more than a phone number — because, not knowing where you are, they have to burn bandwidth over very large areas. Second, because paging is not acknowledged, it is unreliable. And, third, paging offers no easy way to respond.

RadioMail is connected to the Internet, so I asked Geoff if I could do wireless file transfers and assume the other privileges of being a TCP/IP network node. No, Geoff said, RadioMail could use TCP/IP, but "that would be wrong." RadioMail cells share only 8Kbps among many users, and the nationwide wired network that connects the cells, provided by Ram Mobile Data, can delay packets for several seconds. So, RadioMail uses the new Mobile Transfer Protocol One (MTP1), avoiding the high overhead of the Internet's aging TCP/IP protocols.

As for radio modems being larger than mobile computers, Geoff says that PCMCIA versions are now coming to market. He expects RadioMail nirvana in mid-1994.

InfoWorld columnist David Strom won the first coveted RMUG award, which recognizes the sending of RadioMail messages from bizarre situations. He was sitting at a New Jersey toll plaza, beaming mail back and forth. I expect to hear soon something about a RadioMail user shaking hands with Elvis Presley while lifting his RadioMail terminal to the sky from a boat on the White House lawn. This year's winner answers his RadioMail while plugged into a kidney dialysis machine. Once PCMCIA radio modems are on the market next year, I plan to win the coveted RMUG award.

Anyway, I think it's time to find a better word for wireless. Knowing the difference between careless and carefree, how about wirefree? And didn't the automobile really start to take off when they stopped calling them horseless carriages? Please, send me your naming ideas for the various species of this nonelephant biology.

Agenda Verdict: Retooling Sites for Wireless Devices Is the Next Big Internet Trend

November 1, 1999

It turns out I was wrong again. Not about the Internet stock crash on Nov. 8 — that would be next week.

No, it turns out I was wrong about wireless.

I've been down on wireless for a long time. When choosing an "ether" for Ethernet back in 1973, I did not choose wireless, even though Ethernet was based on Alohanet, which used radio.

Ethernet was first built on coaxial cable and later on telephone wire, for good reasons. The wireless Alohanet ran expensively at 9.6Kbps, while the first wired Ethernet ran cheaply at 2.94Mbps — more than 300 times faster.

More recently, when wireless Ethernets were trying to be the rage, I again said, "no." Wires (and fibers) are so much better than the real ether. Ubiquitously wired plugs will always be better than slow, expensive, and unreliable wireless. I was right to be down on wireless LANs.

Enthusiasts took offense when I wrote that wireless portable PCs would be as rare as pipeless portable bathrooms.

Wireless PCs would show up as often as portapotties — on boats, in airplanes, at rock concerts, around construction sites.

So, this year, planning for my annual gathering of the computer industry, Agenda 2000, I didn't tee up wireless. (See my Aug. 16 column)

I only realized my mistake in the middle of a panel about electronic commerce. We were talking about moving companies from an old to a new paradigm, from traditional commerce to electronic commerce.

Dawn Lepore is CIO at Charles Schwab, which started as a leader in discount stock brokering and is now a leader online. She sketched how Schwab had organized to get on the Internet and how it is now reorganizing to make the major shift "from the Internet into wireless."

Ever the Internet know-it-all, I interrupted Lepore, pointing out the Internet is independent of media. Surely she need not reorganize Schwab just to handle wireless.

Lepore turned toward me, smiled sweetly, and although in not so many words, firmly made these eye-opening points.

The Internet and wireless are quite different. To treat their differences as a simple matter of media will likely be fatal to your company. Wireless media are slow, unreliable, and intermittently connected, and your system has to deal with this, but that's just the beginning.

Devices to be used in wireless e-commerce, such as cell phones and personal digital assistants, are really not much like PCs. They have only vestigial keyboards, mice, and displays. Information on your Web site cannot just be dumped wirelessly, assuming that there is a PC at the other end.

It's true that HTML anticipates a wide variety of displays, but not wide enough. So there's your Internet (HTML) content, there's your wireless content — don't get them confused — and that's still not all.

Services to be offered wirelessly are not nearly the same as those offered through PCs. Customers will expect different services when riding in a taxi from those they expect when they are sitting at their desks.

So says Dawn Lepore. I was wrong not to make wireless technology a more prominent part of Agenda.

Of course, what I've said about portapotties had to do with wireless PCs. And most people talking about wireless today don't have PCs in mind.

So I could say that I wasn't really wrong about wireless PCs. But then we'd waste a lot of time arguing semantics — like Microsoft spinning this as the PC-Plus, not Post-PC, Era, sure.

I'd rather just admit I was wrong and add wireless to my beat. So, will there be separate Internet and wireless networks? After all this work on converging the Internet, telephone, and television networks, do we now have Internet-wireless divergence?

Bob, get out of the house

Rebuttal by Dawn Lepore

Dawn Lepore is the Vice Chairman and Chief Information Officer of Charles Schwab. Ms. Lepore was one of the leaders in implementing technology at Schwab, making the shift from mainframe to client/server. She also introduced networking applications, and Web-based information systems that have helped contribute to the company's successes in recent years.

Now Bob, your advice to "just stay home" and enjoy a fully-wired, Ethernet-rich house is well intentioned, but is that really practical for the rest of us? Isn't it time to go mobile?

I think you're focusing on the literal meaning of the word "wireless" and not necessarily the possibilities that the wireless network and the plethora of new devices and services can make possible.

Wireless isn't just about transferring data without wires. It's partly about that, but it's also about being mobile. It's about carrying a small device with long battery life that gives you the capability to access information and perform real and secure transactions anywhere.

Getting an email notification at your desktop when you're spending the whole day in meetings or traveling really doesn't help you in making timely decisions. I think people need information everywhere to take action and make decisions when it's most relevant.

And that's what I think is so great about wireless: It's going to be both an evolution and a revolution.

There are some things that you do today on your PC or on the Internet that will move to a wireless platform. In that sense, it's an evolution, letting the tasks we do in our current wired interfaces evolve into a wireless world.

But I also think there's going to be a revolutionary aspect to it; there are going to be new ways of working that we haven't even thought about that will be enabled because of wireless technology.

I think there's an aspect of quick gratification with the use of wireless technology that is very powerful — equally powerful but different from the wired connection that gives us robust graphical information. Each medium has something unique about it, that offers people different, but unique, functionality.

I don't know what the future will look like, but I can imagine people using their phones as wallets. There'll be no need to carry cash or credit cards. Because I never remember to go to the ATM to get cash, it will be a big relief to me to be able to download cash over the Internet to my wireless device of choice.

Phones (or some other device yet to be thought of that is small and convenient) will allow us to do real time financial transactions, transfer money, pay the phone bill, buy groceries, and get a Coke out of a vending machine.

Who knows? Our wireless devices may even replace the keys to our house and our car.

The future of wireless is going to be exciting. Bob, get out of the house and come join the rest of us!

The Oh-So-Slow Internet

The race to speed up Internet access reminds me of one of those movies from the '60s in which a large number of has-been actors jump into odd-looking cars and chase each other across the country. Along the way there's a lot of bumbling, nasty attempts to crash each other, and agonizingly slow progress towards their goal.

The participants in the race for Internet access speed include such notables as AT&T, Time Warner, MIT and Lucent (rather than Dom DeLuise and Red Buttons). The progress (or lack thereof) of their various vehicles has been observed by very frustrated members of World Wide Wait Watchers — in other words, you and me. The articles in this chapter recap the race for you, with pit stops to observe the leaky plumbing that underlies the Internet.

Start Measuring URL Download Times, Then Complain Loudly

August 5, 1996

Internet management is one of those sad oxymorons about which we laugh uncomfortably and do too little. In our daily use of the Internet, we see that managing its reliability and performance isn't going all that well. Because it's hard. It's hard because of our chronic surprise at ramping enrollments. It's hard because of the rapid evolution of demanding Internet applications.

Internet management is also hard because our tools are terrible. A single mistyped ampersand can collapse 100 routers for half a day. Internet service providers (ISPs) don't notice, until we tell them, that our service is out. And when the Internet bogs down, we start getting its notoriously uninformative error messages.

Well, even though it's my job, I'm not one to just sit around complaining. And so, realizing that we cannot manage that which we cannot measure, I offer here today a really good idea about collecting data on the performance and reliability of the Internet. I'm amazed that this idea is not already widely implemented — please let me know if you've heard of it before.

Here's the idea. Every day, all day, millions of Internet users already test the reliability and performance of the Internet, each from his or her unique point of view. For example, they test the reliability and performance of the Internet every time they click on a Web hyperlink. Too bad the results of these tests are not collected.

Too bad that we've been unable to collect these millions of performance and reliability measurements — until now, that is. Here's how: Each time an Internet browser cranks up a URL to download a Web page, have it log the time and results of the download. Then, a new window in our browsers could summarize our test measurements, say for each bookmarked URL or its domain name.

In this new browser window, the user could see at any time how quickly bookmarked URLs have responded recently and the percentage of times they have failed to respond. You could see how much time it takes to look up the names of URLs, how long it takes to get a reply, and how long it takes to complete a download of a given size.

You might also see various trend lines, say on Internet (not Ethernet) retransmission counts and how they vary by time of day or day of the week. With a more organized picture of the Internet service you are getting, you could be more articulate with your company's users, with your IS department, with the ISPs competing for your business, with your favorite services across the Internet, and with the Internet's intelligentsia.

But that's only half the idea. Each time your browser cranks up a URL, it could upload a compact summary of the results of its last download from that URL. Web servers then might log the performance and reliability of access experienced by their clients. This would allow Internet server operators to communicate more forcefully among the ISPs that are vying for their business.

Well, I've run this idea around the Internet a little. Steve Crocker at Cybercash Inc. likes it. And Marc Andreessen at Netscape Communications Corp. likes it. That makes three of us. You? Andreessen wrote to me, "Thanks for the idea! We've kicked the general concept around, and there's been interest in similar things from some of our intranet customers (some want to be able to better measure their 'net; others want their users to be more aware of the impact of their actions on the community's resources). We'll put it on the list for a future release."

Ask your Internet software suppliers to add measurement to their products so that you can better manage the Internet cloud.

This client/server Internet measurement logging idea should eventually be fleshed out in the context of standards. Various clients and servers should be able to aggregate their data to pinpoint the Internet's weak links and bottlenecks.

By the way, how many times did you have to retry downloading this column? How long did it take? Where do you think the bottlenecks are? Are we improving? And what are the chances of your e-mail answers getting through?

The Numbers Show How Slowly the Internet Runs Today

September 30, 1996

My formula for Internet packet delay is $D=H*Q*(R+P/C)$. This formula helps clarify how various forms of Internet "switching," as we discussed last week, will improve Internet reliability and performance.

IP routers forward packets toward their 32-bit destination addresses through circuit after circuit, router to router, hop by hop. At each hop, packets are transmitted, received, queued for routing, routed, queued for transmission, and then forwarded to the next router.

Some Internet engineers quibble that routing and delay are much more complicated than $D=H*Q*(R+P/C)$. True, but we have to start somewhere.

In my formula, D is delay. H is for hop count. Whatever a packet has to go through in a router, it has to go through it H times before it reaches its destination. Hop counts of 10 or more seem typical; the range extends past 30.

H seems to be increasing in the Internet and not only because of growth. Hop counts are higher because of the uncoordinated concatenation of Internet service providers (ISPs).

Q is for queue length. Packets aren't alone at routers but on queues, where they must wait for the packets ahead of them to be routed and transmitted.

Q seems to be increasing in the Internet. Routers only have so much memory, so when queues fill, packets are discarded. More queue memory helps to a point, after which lengthening queues add to delay.

R is for routing time. A router receiving a packet at one port must decide at which other port to queue the packet for forwarding toward its destination.

The packet's address specifies a subnet, which is used to search through a table of subnets, yielding the port for the next hop. Not only are these tables growing — more than 30,000 global routes and 10MB — but routing decisions are now subject to an overlay of highly questionable policies, such as routing packets toward another ISP instead of delivering them along the shortest possible route. R seems to be going up in the Internet. Routers are increasingly incapable of keeping up, in which case packets queued for routing are discarded without notice.

P is for packet length, and C is for circuit speed. At each hop, a packet is delayed by the time needed to transmit it (P/C). Most Internet packets are short, but most of the bytes carried are in long packets. With all that imminent multimedia, the average P increases. The time to transmit a packet (P/C), and therefore the store-and-forward delay it accumulates over a hop, decreases with the speed of the circuit.

Now, I bet that C is decreasing in today's Internet, despite all the big ISPs saying they are upgrading their backbone circuits. Why? C is an average of all the circuits a packet has to hop through.

Increasingly, Internet users are not coming directly onto the Internet through high-speed circuits from LANs but through modems. Also, with the number of ISPs growing, the increasing numbers of hops away from the backbones are through slower circuits. C is probably going down. Does anybody know? Pending data to the contrary, I bet every parameter of Internet delay is going in the wrong direction.

Various forms of Internet switching aim to improve these parameters. Asynchronous Transfer Mode (ATM), for example, by breaking packets into 53-byte cells, aims to reduce P.

Next week, let's look at "tag switching," recently introduced by Cisco Systems Inc., and see how, with and without ATM, tags promise to reduce Internet packet delays and losses due to routing. In the meantime, if you have real data on the parameters of my Internet delay formula, let's hear from you.

Private Iways Will Avoid All Congestion on the 'Net

October 21, 1996

Many of you are asking: "What's the next big thing after intranets?" My answer is extranets. Sadly, like intranets, too many extranets will be private, bypassing the big, bad, bogging Internet.

The buzzword extranet extends a progression begun in the 1970s with ARPAnet, Alohanet, and Ethernet. That progression of nets went to two-syllable Latin prefixes some time around 1983, with the Internet, intranets, and now extranets.

Ever self-promotional, I contend that the buzzword extranet, now in widening use, was coined here on April 8. (See "Summer Olympics to use IBM's 'extranet' 390s, but beware the Ides of July," page 43.) Please send any prior references.

Note also that I hereby reserve for future use our next two major 'Net buzzwords, contranet and circanet.

What we call the Internet (inter meaning between) is a proliferating network of networks that's been running IP since 1983.

What we call intranets (intra meaning inside) are IP networks running inside companies. Intranets run Web applications for internal use by company employees. Intranet is not just another word for LAN. Many intranets are LANs, true, but many LANs don't run IP, and a growing number of intranets are WANs among a company's locations.

What I'm calling extranets (extra meaning outside) are IP networks through which companies run Web applications for external use by customers. Extranets are for electronic commerce.

You might assume that when a company develops a Web site to serve customers, it simply moves that server outside its intranet firewall to allow extranet access over the Internet. Wrong.

The assumption that extranets will go out over the bogging Internet was shattered for me by Bruce Sachs, who is executive vice president of Bay Networks Inc. in Burlington, Mass. Sachs was telling me about virtual private networks (VPNs). Some Internet service providers (ISPs), such as Concentric Network Corp., carry intranet traffic through VPNs. Such traffic need not venture out of its VPN and risk the vagaries of the Internet. Think of such VPNs as outsourced intranets.

Sachs talks about ISPs using VPNs to provide what I call private extranets to connect companies with customers. Again, customer traffic is carried on one ISP's VPN, not touching the Internet.

For example, because the Internet cannot yet provide the performance needed by many multiuser games, you can sign up for a private gaming extranet, which is outsourced through a Bay-equipped Concentric VPN.

Ditto network security for online banking — sign up for an outsourced private financial extranet.

You can tell a company's extranet is "on the Internet" when customers use a URL for access. A company's extranet is "private" when customers use a specified phone number. A private extranet is "outsourced" when the company's phone number dials in to an ISP.

Our InfoWorld extranet is on the Internet. America Online and CompuServe are known for their huge, previously Web-free private extranets. Microsoft Corp. launched Microsoft Network through a private extranet outsourced through Uunet Technologies Inc. You can outsource your private extranet through an ISP such as Concentric.

You can have your extranet on the "commodity" (that is, insecure, unreliable, slow, and cheap) Internet and, for paying customers wanting better service, also on a private extranet.

Thanks to private extranets, the Internet might yet become a low-grade government safety net for schools, libraries, and other tax-supported institutions — not the well-paved Information Superhighway we're hoping to have for electronic commerce. I hope not.

Now, using phone numbers rather than URLs for extranet access is not going to fly in the long-term. Packet access through modems over the circuit-switched analog telephone network is lame. Telephone company central offices, engineered during the past century for voice telephony, are already overloading thanks to, for example, the long holding times of IP calls.

Longer term, customers won't like having a different phone number and all that modem rigmarole for every company with which they do business. We'll all eventually get hooked up with continuously connected packet-oriented transmission facilities.

Remember, you heard it here first: outsourced private extranets. Longer term, extranets will move back onto a better managed, industrial-strength Internet.

Until then, I suggest you join my new club for Internet users, World Wide Wait Watchers.

Hughes Satellite Gives Telcos, TV Needed 'Net Competition

October 28, 1996

Megabit Internet Service will eventually be as universal as hot water, paved roads, alternating electricity, telephone dial tone, and perhaps even color televisions. But eventually is a long time.

So let's ask two questions: First, how long before we get universal megabit Internet service? Second, who will provide it? Too many people are asking now whether we should go with digital subscriber lines (DSL) from telephone monopolies (the same people who promised you ISDN in the 1980s) or cable modems from television monopolies (the same people who promised you interactive television in the 1980s). It seems that we'll decide soon which of the two technologies is better, which is the way to go toward universal Internet service. I worry that we'll fall back on getting this done through government monopolies (the same people who've made "universal service" an oxymoron).

Instead, let's work to be sure that DSL and cable modems have a level playing field on which to compete. For example, telephone company monopolies should not be allowed to buy cable monopolies. And let's be sure that competing Internet on-ramp alternatives include LANs, telephone modems, ISDN, terrestrial wireless links, low-earth-orbiting satellites, and who knows what else.

How about geostationary satellites? Hot on the heels of DirecTV and its announcement this month of DirecPC, Hughes Communications Inc. is now planning Spaceway, another exciting satellite service. Spaceway will offer 92Mbps Internet access directly to homes via geostationary satellites. Spaceway's two-way digital dishes will cost less than $1,000 and could be in service by as early as 1999. So, on your behalf, I visited Hughes, in Long Beach, California.

Why talk about Spaceway now? Why not just wait for *InfoWorld's* Product Reviews when Hughes ships its HS702 satellite and Spaceway's 66-centimeter (26-inch, for you old-timers) ultra-small-aperture terminals? Am I now myself guilty of an anticompetitive pre-emptive preannouncement?

There's too much talk these days about just two alternatives for getting megabit Internet service to homes. Spaceway is another promising Internet on-ramp alternative likely to come of age by the end of the millennium. The HS702 is the geostationary satellite through which Spaceway bits will flow.

Four pairs of HS702s costing $3 billion will redundantly cover the world. Each HS702 is expected to keep 48 of its 64 125-MHz transponder beams in operation for 15 years. Each downlink beam is 92Mbps, for a total of 4.4Gbps per satellite, 35Gbps worldwide.

Spaceway uplinks will come in three flavors. Using a 66-centimeter (26-inch) dish, your Spaceway uplink will send data at 384Kbps, 1.2-meter (47-inch) at 1.5Mbps, and 3.5-meter (11-foot) at 6Mbps.

Hughes is intent on charging by the byte for transmissions using its satellite systems (more than 60 cents per megabyte today using DirecPC). Doesn't the company know it's 'net religion to charge a flat, if not zero, rate? I think Hughes has the right idea, although the rate will have to work its way down.

Hughes is also specifying a service that is 92Mbps into homes but a lot less out. Don't Hughes officials know it's Internet religion to be symmetrical?

Again, I think Hughes and others such as cable-modem manufacturers, trying to reach homes, have the right idea. God and/or Darwin gave us two ears and one mouth — let's take the hint.

And then there's satellite delay. Getting up and down the 40,000 kilometers to Spaceway satellites will take nearly a half second, which is more than twice the transcontinental delay through today's Internet. Hughes says the delay will not be fatal to Internet telephony.

So, at 92Mbps, will Spaceway be the way to connect to the Internet? No. When it comes to stationary point-to-point transmission, optical fibers outshine wireless. The sky would be black with HS702s if Spaceway were used for megabit Internet service for even a small fraction of U.S. households.

Still, Spaceway is something to look to, especially for highly mobile or remote applications. What can we do to encourage Hughes to go ahead with its $3 billion Spaceway investment? The telephone and cable monopolies need this run for their money.

Replace the 'Net's Old Pipes with Shiny HTTP 1.1 for Few Floods, Fast Downloads

March 31, 1997

The World Wide Web is bogging down, and what more proof do you need than the prominent Stop button on your browser and how often you're hitting it lately. Why? Because the Web's plumbing wasn't built for the use it's getting.

Web plumbing includes layer upon layer of protocol software. IP underlies TCP and DNS. These in turn underlie URLs, HTML, and HTTP. All of this plumbing leaks.

Fortunately, the Internet Engineering Task Force (IETF) and the World Wide Web Consortium (W3C) have been working to fix the Internet's plumbing and especially HTTP, the worst of the Web's protocols.

When you're hyperlinking, your browser's HTTP software, now Version 1.0, goes out over the Internet and downloads Web pages. On these pages are many objects, each with its own URL and each to be downloaded in turn before the page can be rendered. It's while waiting for all these objects to be HTTPed that Web users typically hit Stop.

The problem is that HTTP 1.0 sets up and breaks down a separate TCP connection through the entire Internet between browser and server for each and every object on a page. Because most objects are small, the IP packets managing TCP connections often way outnumber those carrying objects. And most of these are wastefully short packets brimming with overhead.

Worse, the control packets that TCP uses to manage its connections are not subject to the congestion controls that TCP provides for data packets. So they flood the Internet.

Worse yet, TCP's congestion algorithms take more time to make estimates and pace transmissions than is allowed by the short connections typical of HTTP 1.0. So they rarely hit their stride on the Web.

Opening and closing TCP connections keeps our clients and servers busy. Sending, receiving, and waiting for packets slows response. Numerous short packets flood routers and are too frequently dropped, which causes TCP to wait before retransmitting — longer each time (such as Ethernet) — soon hanging Web downloads. Stop!

Marc Andreessen noticed this problem way back at the University of Illinois when working on Mosaic. So today's browsers cleverly download Web objects in parallel, opening several TCP connections at once, overlapping download delays. This technique does speed downloads on an empty Internet, sure, but it doesn't reduce the profligate use of packets by HTTP 1.0, which slows downloads on a bogging Internet.

And so here comes HTTP 1.1, a proposed standard (RFC 2068) out of the IETF HTTP working group, which includes Roy Fielding, Jim Gettys, Jeff Mogul, Henrik Frystyk Nielsen, and, of course, Tim Berners-Lee — perpetrator of HTTP 1.0, father of the Web, and spiritual leader of W3C at MIT.

I asked Gettys, a visitor at W3C from Digital, about the IETF's work on HTTP 1.1. In short, HTTP 1.1 offers persistent connections, request pipelining, byte ranges, and other dramatic improvements for which Gettys is very grateful to the IETF team.

Persistence means that object downloads from a Web server are carried more efficiently over one longer TCP connection in fewer, longer packets — all under TCP congestion control.

Pipelining means that many of the object-download requests can be outstanding over one TCP connection.

And ranges mean that downloads of portions of an object can be requested.

The bottom line is that HTTP 1.1 outperforms HTTP 1.0 by reducing packet counts 50 percent to 90 percent and elapsed download times 20 percent to 75 percent.

Before we enjoy substantial improvements, HTTP 1.1 must be implemented and deployed in browsers and servers. If HTTP 1.1 reduced only the number of packets generated per Web-page download, its deployment would be a low priority for most everybody. You see, the Internet does not charge by the packet, and so it's no skin off anybody's nose to flood the Internet with packets that seem to improve their own performance.

Fortunately, even if we aren't the good little Marxists that the Internegentsia expects us to be, HTTP 1.1 will also substantially reduce our response times. So you'll be helping others while helping yourself by demanding HTTP 1.1 from your Web-software suppliers as soon as possible.

Web Performance Measuring May Help You Avoid the Stop Button

April 7, 1997

This is a big week and not just because April 7 is my 51st birthday.

On Monday, Elizabeth Dole and I will be speaking at a Bellcore research meeting. Bellcore was recently spun off by the regional Bell operating companies. In my speech, I will suggest that Bellcore seek an expanded role in managing the operations of our bogging and collapsing Internet. I'll get back to you if that suggestion goes anywhere.

On Tuesday and Wednesday I will be attending and on Thursday I will deliver the keynote speech at the Sixth International World Wide Web Conference, in Santa Clara, Calif. I'll cap that keynote by making the case that I should not have to eat my first Internet collapse column of Dec. 4, 1995. (See "Predicting the Internet's catastrophic collapse and ghost sites galore in 1996.")

In that column I began predicting "collapses" during 1996 of our poorly measured and managed Internet. I'll report back, if need be, on how the column tasted.

Now regardless of whether I eat my words or not, this is the last week that my punditry will appear in the Internet section of *InfoWorld*. I'm moving out in part to make room for a weekly report of the Keynote Business 40 Internet Performance Index.

Next week, Keynote Systems will launch its first Web-site performance measurement products. Keynote, in San Mateo, Calif., joins a flock of new Internet measurement companies offering to help us deal with how often the prominent Stop buttons on our 'net browsers get pushed.

There are various kinds of measurements offered by these new companies. Keynote measures the responsiveness, if any, of Web sites. Such measurements can be conducted on Web servers, in Web clients, among cooperating clients and servers, or by agents — mystery Web-site shoppers. Keynote's first offering, Perspective, a service and software, opens for business next week with more than 20 of 96 planned agent sites around the United States.

Perspective agent sites measure the responsiveness of URLs interesting to Keynote customers. Customers buy measurements from specified agent locations, with specified sampling intervals, for specified URLs.

URL responsiveness measurements are sent to a Perspective server, the one operated by Keynote for its service customers, or a server operated by a Keynote software customer. Concurrently, Perspective Desktop software allows Keynote customers to query the server, charting the responsiveness of interesting URLs or receiving alerts when responsiveness drifts out of specified bounds.

Jim Barrick is founder, CEO, and chief technology officer of Keynote, which, when I visited late last month, had 14 employees in one big room. Barrick is clear about his mission: to shine a bright light on Web performance. Keynote will serve as a "Darwinian accelerator," helping users select Web sites and Internet service providers (ISPs). Keynote will also help Webmasters and ISPs manage their performance.

Data is now accumulating on how Web users behave when URLs are slow to respond — sooner rather than later they hit Stop and wander off in disgust.

One idea Barrick and I discussed was how a Keynote-measured site, upon receiving a poor responsiveness alert from a certain region, might switch from the image-heavy version of its content to the image-light version, thereby speeding response to those users, keeping more of them around.

By pointing its measurement agents at 40 selected Web sites — including InfoWorld's own Web site, *InfoWorld Electric* — Keynote produces an index of Web responsiveness, charts the index week by week, and reports the most (and least) responsive sites. InfoWorld Researcher Jim Battey will report the Keynote 40 in *InfoWorld* and *InfoWorld Electric*. Look for the Index starting next week.

Now in case you're worried, my column is moving to our new penultimate editorial page, End Around, that I'll be sharing with none other than Robert X. Cringely. I'm getting this "bonus" because, thanks to you, my average weekly readership just passed 570,000. From the Ether will continue to accumulate at *InfoWorld Electric*, which I will hope will become more responsive.

So, now at last, I will be sharing a page with Pammy. Look for us in our new location next week.

Cable TV Modems Are Finally Delivering the Net to Homes and Small Offices

February 2, 1998

Internet access through cable TV modems is now finally starting to take off. Be sure to consider this good news when deciding where next to move your home or office.

But first, remember that dial-up telephone modems are an abomination. They cram digital data packets through analog voice circuit switches — the worst of both worlds.

Telephone monopolies don't understand this, but even telephone modems, dumb as they are, know what they are doing is wrong. Just listen to their hissing and screeching every time we force them to do it.

Fortunately, there are alternatives to dial-up modems.

+ *Integrated Services Digital Network (ISDN)* — at 144Kbps, it's too little too late. Also, ISDN continues to cram packet traffic through telco voice circuit switches. ISDN proves the folly of listening to telopoly propaganda.

+ *Digital Subscriber Line (DSL)* — these technologies carry Internet packets over telco copper at megabits per second. When DSL packets arrive at telco central offices, they bypass voice switches. But we don't want DSL promises from telopolies (see ISDN). We want competitive access to telopoly coppertone so various DSLs can fight it out.

+ *Wireless* — This type of access to homes and small businesses bypasses telopolies, so let's root for it, but as for the long-term, only mobile applications are likely to tolerate the low speeds and high costs of wireless modems.

+ *Satellites* — these are an exciting alternative for Internet access, but we'd have to blacken the sky to get the total bandwidth needed. Only mobile and rural needs will be well met.

+ *Power lines* — Power lines are another coppertone infrastructure, especially inside homes and businesses. Why not plug into the Internet with the same prongs that connect you to the power grid?

+ *Cable TV modems* — Last, but not least. What has kept me from rooting for cable modems these last couple of decades has been that, despite many exciting announcements, they simply have not worked. Outside of the lab, it's been repeatedly proven to be difficult to use broadcast (one-way) analog video channels for carrying interactive (two-way) digital data packets.

But now, reports are accumulating that cable modems are working in sufficient numbers to be interesting.

For example, there's the @Home Network, the Time Warner Road Runner High Speed Online Service, and, all around me in Massachusetts, there's MediaOne Express.

Sadly, MediaOne offers high-speed cable modem service in Massachusetts, but not to my townhouse, which is way out on Beacon Street in rural Boston.

So I asked Daniel Dern, fellow Internet pundit, to evaluate MediaOne from where he lives. Dern came back with mostly good news.

MediaOne offers high-speed Internet access to cable TV subscribers for less than $40 per month. The service is 300Kbps upstream and 1.5Mbps downstream. MediaOne provides a modem that plugs into your TV cable, into an AC outlet, and into an Ethernet card in your PC. Thereafter, your Internet access is continuous — no more dialing, no more busy signals, no more logging in, no more hissing and screeching.

Dern reports MediaOne is, in a word, *fast* — it "beats the hell out of a [dial-up telephone] modem." And he has asked that our punditry team keep paying for the service so he can evaluate MediaOne indefinitely.

Now, MediaOne is fast, but only as long as requested Web pages are found locally cached at MediaOne. If not, there's still the World Wide Wait.

Dern worries about MediaOne's security services and complains about the company's privacy policies. Not only might his bits be collected off the shared cable by clever neighbors, but MediaOne itself is monitoring his usage.

MediaOne contracts reserve the right to sell information on Dern to only the worst possible people.

MediaOne's $40 service is for one client computer. It is forbidden to run a server or several clients on a LAN. Early adopters of high-speed Internet access, like you, are quite likely to have LANs and servers, so MediaOne has a four-client service in the works.

So, there's good news about the cable TV alternative to dial-up telephone modems. If you are contemplating a move of home or office, join those now inquiring, not just about the quality of local schools and roads but also about neighborhood availability of cable modem Internet access. If you've already plugged yours in, what is your experience with cable modems?

Beep-Beep! Road Runner's Cable Modem Service Offers Really Fast Internet Access

February 23, 1998

Thanks for your hundreds of e-mails responding to my favorable reporting about MediaOne Express and Internet access using cable TV modems. (See "Cable TV modems are finally delivering the Net to homes and small offices.") Sorry I've had to stop answering them.

And it's virtually unanimous: *InfoWorld* readers with cable modems are confirming in droves that they really like them and are saying good riddance to dial-up telephone modems. I'm hearing not just from happy customers of MediaOne in Massachusetts. Two cable modem users reported in from Camden, Maine, just 11 miles from our farm. And there are many happy users of, among others, @Home and Time Warner's Road Runner from around the country.

Road Runner is named for the speedy Looney Tunes character owned by Time Warner, which now offers cable modem Internet access in eight metro areas.

The company says it has 12.4 million cable subscribers, 1 million of which can get Road Runner, and, since September 1996, more than 16,000 do.

Road Runner is beep-beeping around Portland, Maine.

Mainiacs pay $100 to install the service, which includes a cable modem with an Ethernet port, a choice of Ethernet card for their PCs, and software. Then they pay $40 per month for continuous, unlimited, really fast Internet access. No more busying their telephone lines. No more upgrading their pitiful dial-up telephone modems.

Road Runner's maximum speed downstream is 27Mbps, and its upstream speed is 3Mbps. Speeds seen by users vary depending on how many are assigned to a channel, who's online, and what they're doing. Road Runner says the worst it gets is like ISDN. Current customers report speeds much faster than that.

Yes, Road Runner gets rave reviews. I've heard from many people who have checked on the availability of Road Runner before moving their homes or offices. The service is that compelling.

Road Runner's content editor in Portland is Will Kreth. He walked me around his head end. There is a room full of cable TV equipment. The next room is full of Toshiba cable modems and fibers running toward the cable room. Then there are racks of Internet servers — Web, caching, subscription, security, operations — and routers out to the Internet.

Next door are Kreth's editors. They gather content for Road Runner's Portland Web server. Then there's national content, which comes in via the Net, including Time Warner's *Sports Illustrated* and CNN, and my column.

Kreth said that as soon as Bell Atlantic brings Digital Subscriber Lines (DSL) to Portland, Time Warner will be happy to work a deal to supply Bell Atlantic's content. I observed that when Kreth said this he was not holding his breath.

Speaking of Bell Atlantic, I must remind you that the telopolies will not sit idly by while cable TV companies bring you the Internet. It's possible they might race to deploy DSL for Internet access, which would really be something to see.

But it's more likely that the telopolies will print brochures while lobbying to slow cable companies down. So I'm worried that Time Warner and US West will merge Road Runner and MediaOne.

Telopolies are already conniving with regulators to cap cable prices. Subtle, but this starves cable companies of cash to upgrade for cable modems.

Another telco trick is using "universal service" sentiment to issue regulations saying that cable companies can't serve anyone unless they serve everyone. This aborts start-up competition.

Speaking of monopolies, there is fascinating evidence at Road Runner of anti-competitive behavior by Microsoft.

Consider that Road Runner has found a way to support Motorola or Toshiba modems. They support Hewlett-Packard's HP Unix or Digital Windows NT servers. They support Internet traffic upstream through MCI or Sprint. They support several models of 3Com, Intel, or Standard Microsystems Ethernet cards. And they support Windows or Macintosh PCs. You choose.

However, amid of all this freedom of choice among competing alternatives, there's Internet Explorer. If you use any "proprietary" browser, a browser other than Microsoft's, Road Runner says it cannot support you. The Department of Justice should dig into the negotiations leading to this exclusionary deal.

If you live in an area where cable TV modem access to the Net is available, subscribe now. If not, demand it. Failing that, move.

SuperLine Promises You Broadband Internet Access Over Existing Phone Lines

February 8, 1999

The SuperLine Integrated Access System that was just announced at ComNet in Washington is not so much a technology triumph as it is a business breakthrough.

Starting now, telephone companies can profitably deploy SuperLine to plug big holes in their residential voice offerings and thereby provide broadband Internet access much more widely than ever dreamed for Asymmetric Digital Subscriber Line (ADSL).

The big holes are extra telephone lines for children, offices, modems, and fax machines. Telcos are generally reluctant to market extra lines because they're running out of copper. It costs on average $1,000, and sometimes much more, to run copper for a second line.

Even without marketing, current demand for extra lines from 167 million U.S. subscribers is more than 3 million per year. When marketed, the demand more than doubles. In addition, home Internet access will skyrocket to 33 percent of households during 1999.

Enter SuperLine. Today, for between $500 and $1,000 per household, depending on volume, SuperLine uses copper already carrying plain old telephone service (POTS) to deliver POTS, plus a second and third line.

The SuperLine Integrated Access Device (IAD) is the size of a PC modem. You plug your POTS line into one jack and a POTS extension into another. Plug phones, modems, or fax machines into the second and third lines.

Now, telcos can market extra phone lines again. For much less than it costs to run copper, they can offer SuperLines.

But does SuperLine work? Well, the three companies announcing it at ComNet were Paradyne, the $200 million broadband access company; AG Communication Systems, the $500 million telephone equipment company; and AG's parent company, Lucent Technologies, the mother of all telephone equipment companies.

Paradyne developed Tripleplay, the technology that carries SuperLine over POTS copper. The company makes SuperLine IADs for homes.

AG Communications developed and makes SuperLine Integrated Access Platforms (IAPs) for telephone central offices.

Lucent markets SuperLine to providers of residential and small-office telephone services. About 100 million U.S. households receive service using Lucent equipment, not counting the 18 million that use AG equipment. And because SuperLine meets telephone industry standards, it can also be deployed in non-Lucent central offices.

The two extra lines provided by SuperLine are digital, crystal clear, and let 56Kbps modems operate at full speed (53.6Kbps). SuperLine's central-office IAPs will detect modem calls and take them around telephone switches directly into the Internet.

Paradyne Vice President Mark Housman says that SuperLine is passing Bellcore TR57 — "the mother of all telco tests." He added that SuperLine is in "final standardization testing" at a major telco that is aiming to deploy hundreds of thousands of SuperLines during 1999. Another major telco will soon start testing.

The market for SuperLines is easily 10 times that for ISDN and ADSL combined. But why do I mention ISDN and ADSL?

Well, there's a SuperLine jack I have not been telling you about. Turns out SuperLine comes with an Ethernet RJ-45 through which Internet packets can be exchanged with the central office at 500Kbps (take note, ADSL fans) without disturbing the three phones on that same POTS line.

Paradyne asks me not to refer to SuperLine as yet another Digital Subscriber Line technology. The business breakthrough is that telco voice people can profitably deploy SuperLines in huge numbers while telco data people wring their hands in Washington.

If telopolies can't figure out how to piggyback broadband Internet access on something like SuperLine, we will likely end up buying POTS from cable companies, who are already piggybacking Internet broadband on digital television.

With AT&T Leading the Charge, It's Full Speed Ahead for CTM Internet Service

June 7, 1999

Cable television modems (CTMs) offer always-on broadband Internet access for less than $50 per month to a rapidly increasing number of our 100 million U.S. homes.

If your home can get CTM Internet service, sign up. The vast majority of the first 1 million CTM users are happy to have gotten rid of their mostly off narrowband dial-up modems. If you can't get CTM service, call your cable operator and demand it. More than 30 million U.S. homes are near ready for CTMs.

If your cable guy can't promise always-on broadband Internet access within, say, two years, pack up and move your home to somewhere serious about the Information Age. Vote with your feet.

My feet have just taken me home from Vortex99 in Laguna Niguel, Calif., where we discussed convergence of the Internet, telephone, and television networking industries. Vortex talks are off the record, so I'll summarize without naming names.

Clearly, the next big step in network convergence is residential always-on broadband Internet access.

There is confusion about the word "broadband." Some include ISDN's 128Kbps. I define it faster than 1Mbps.

There is a question of which will have more impact, the speed of broadband or its being always on.

The CEO of a major telco told Vortex that his company intends to provide the Internet's first mile, last mile, and every mile in between. His new low price for DSL is $30 per month, not counting associated telephone and Internet services. In the last year, his company has deployed half of DSL's current installed base, estimated to be 70,000.

The CEO of a chip supplier to CTM- and DSL-equipment providers says the technologies are equally promising, but CTM standards are further along. Modems that conform to the Data Over Cable Services Interface Specification are already shipping.

The CEO of a major Internet switching-equipment company says last-quarter orders for CTM and DSL equipment jumped 60 percent.

The CTO of a major Internet service provider says CTM deployment is accelerating and has just passed 1 million. That means CTMs are ahead by about a 10-to-1 ratio over DSLs.

To name a name, Leo Hindery, president of AT&T Broadband and Internet Services, spoke at Vortex and again that day on the record for *The Wall Street Journal.* He said AT&T — now merged with TCI, which owns much of @Home, which just bought Excite — will not bundle content with its Internet services. AT&T is furiously investing billions in CTMs, backbones, caching, and navigation software to provide advanced Internet, telephone, and television services.

The chairman of a federal commission with jurisdiction told Vortex that he will not stop AT&T from deploying CTMs for Internet access or insist that AT&T let other ISPs resell its CTM services.

So, with AT&T leading, it's full speed ahead for CTMs.

My conclusion from Vortex99 is that DSLs are being deployed more slowly than CTMs. Why? Because local telephone companies are more secure in their monopolies than cable companies and have overpriced data revenues they'd prefer not to cannibalize.

Even when telopolies deploy broadband, they find their core competencies are not transmission and switching, or billing and support, but lobbying and litigation.

Many readers report they can get DSLs only in locales where CTMs are deployed. DSLs are going mostly to business users at speeds I wouldn't call broadband and at prices much higher than $50 per month — so that T1 services can stay expensive.

With CTMs ahead of DSLs by about a 10-1 ratio, we'll be hearing a lot more about DSL from telopolies. If only they'd invest less energy in capturing regulators, lobbying legislatures, and clogging courts than in re-engineering their central offices for always-on broadband Internet access.

This space for rent

Rebuttal by. . .

I couldn't get anyone to rebut my saying that the Internet is too slow, which is consistent with the STOP button being so prominent in Internet browsers.

— Bob Metcalfe

Internet Collapses

Starting in late 1995, I began to write that the Internet was fated to collapse in 1996. I thought then that packet losses would continue to increase to the point of an event in cyberspace that would make an 8.0 earthquake seem friendly in comparison. Well, total disaster didn't hit in 1996 and I had to eat my words.

So, what happened? Did the problems I outlined in these columns go away? Hardly. There's still a creaky technical infrastructure underlying the Internet, packets take suicidal leaps off of bridges on a regular basis, and ISPs are getting better and better at passing bucks here, there and everywhere. So, I guess you could call me an optimist: If the Internet didn't collapse in 1996, there's always next year.

Predicting the Internet's Catastrophic Collapse in 1996

December 4, 1995

Almost all of the many predictions now being made about 1996 hinge on the Internet's continuing exponential growth. But I predict the Internet, which only just recently got this section here in *InfoWorld*, will soon go spectacularly supernova and in 1996 catastrophically collapse. Here's why there soon will be only World Wide Web ghost pages:

✦ **Money.** Investors poured a lot of money into the Internet during 1995, but very little leaked out. Everyone will realize this suddenly in January when financial results are tallied. A hurried search for greater fools to absorb projected continuing losses won't pan out this time.

✦ **Digital money.** As if to make up for the shortage of real money to finance Internet commerce, several companies have been trying to mint digital money. They have, however, failed to streamline financial activity — there are now more, not fewer, middlepersons. Therefore, transaction costs, at 50 cents each or more, remain way too high. Without efficient micropayments, there will be little Internet commerce, except, maybe, but probably not, some advertising.

✦ **Measurement.** Advertisers only invest the big bucks in measured media, where they can have some inkling of how many potential buyers with what demographics are reading their ads. Even if, as Nielsen just reported, 37 million North Americans tried the Internet in the last three months, we'll discover in 1996 that the vast majority surfed for several hours and then went back to watching TV. After the third major corporation stuffs its Web pages full of dazzling product literature and gets no hits, the Internet's collapse will begin to accelerate.

✦ **Monopolies.** Dazzling product literature and advertising require at least ISDN speeds. But the major corporations upon which we are relying to upgrade Internet access past 28.8Kbps are the local telco monopolies, which like our postal service and public schools have become little more than jobs programs.

The local telcos will escape demonopolization in 1995 and, while they pursue long-distance voice business in 1996, their motivation to lower costs on high-speed Internet access will wither, fatally constipating the Web.

✦ **Security.** Already most TCP/IP networks are not on the Internet but behind security firewalls, in Intranets. In early 1996, another series of major security breaches will drive the rest of the productive Internet to safety and out of reach.

✦ **Compatibility.** During 1996, the war for control of standards will tear the Web. And early initiatives to migrate to Internet Protocol Next Generation will add to a general loss of compatibility. Such losses, including the flight to Intranets, will reduce whatever systemic value was accumulating in the Internet, as governed by the inverse of Metcalfe's Law. (See "Metcalfe's Law: A network becomes more valuable as it reaches more users," Oct. 2.)

✦ **Capacity.** You've read that the Internet was designed to survive thermonuclear war, but it's repeatedly been brought to its knees, its circuits choked, for example, by the reaction to one measly jury verdict in Los Angeles. The Internet is intermittently overloaded, and the TCP/IP architecture doesn't deal well with overloads. Furthermore, the Internet's naive flat-rate business model is incapable of financing the new capacity it would need to serve continued growth, if there were any, but there won't be, so no problem.

✦ **Privacy.** Internet backlash among professional paranoids will break into a full collapse after a series of well-publicized privacy violations instigated by the professional paranoids themselves for our own good.

✦ **Video.** One of two bad things will happen with video over the Internet during 1996. Either the Internet's attached computers, operating systems, and applications software will fail to deliver video, or they will succeed. If they succeed, the packet-punctuated pre-Asynchronous Transfer Mode Internet will fail to carry it. In either case, without video the Internet will lack the energy needed to sustain its current expansion.

✦ **Pornography.** The Internet traffic carrying arguments about pornography on the Internet will during 1996 swamp the actual pornography, so even the most sophisticated Web search engines will too often fail to find any. What quicker road to collapse? So, in 1996, CD-ROMs through Federal Express will emerge as the Information Superhighway. Instead of an Internet brimming with Web pages under construction, too few of us will haunt ghost pages.

I hope I'm not being too negative. Tell me if you think so.

Fuzzy-Headed Anarchy Will Lead the Way to the Internet's Total Collapse

February 26, 1996

"Question authority" is not the silliest bumper sticker I've ever seen on a Volkswagen stopped at a traffic light. Sillier would be, for example, "Save the Earth," because bumpers come with internal combustion engines. But now, worried about the Internet's impending collapse, I've got a new bumper sticker in mind for my Volvo: "Question Anarchy."

Cyberspace gurus tell us the Internet is not simply a computer network. It's biological, exponential, chaotic, resilient, decentralist, anarchic. Nobody's in charge, and ain't that just profoundly dandy.

Well, it's time to reconsider this bumper-sticker notion and see the Internet for what it is, a network of computers, increasingly important but verging on collapse.

Midcoast Internet Solutions, in Owls Head, Maine, recently sent me a message explaining why my 56Kbps Internet service had been out one morning. The outage, Midcoast wrote, was out of their control. In fact, it could only be blamed on a provider to the provider of my Internet provider. Such buck-passing is a consequence of anarchy, and it's for the birds.

David Garrison, president of Netcom On-Line Communication Services Inc., told customers on Feb. 8 that "service has recently become an issue for most Internet providers, and [Netcom] anticipates a bit of a bumpy period...several unrelated instances of network problems...included two separate cases of flooding in the northeast region, which took out a primary as well as backup routes."

When I tried to reach Netcom on the World Wide Web, I got, "Netscape is unable to locate the server www.netcom.com. The server does not have a DNS entry...try again."

Last week I introduced you to John Quarterman's fascinating Internet Weather Reports. I've since asked him about worrisome trends in his Internet "storms." I was surprised, after seeing all the statistics he's been gathering, that he was unprepared to talk about trends.

Quarterman quickly pulled together some delay trend data and commented, "I don't see any trend of imminent demise in this data — if anything, the opposite: gradual improvement."

But the data was for only one month, January 1996. Quarterman is now off examining trends back to 1993.

Actually, the Internet is not all that anarchic. Our National Science Foundation did not simply walk away when it privatized the backbone. It established, among other things, a Routing Arbiter, which collects data on how Internet backbones are operating.

If the Internet has any central consciousness, this is it. The Routing Arbiter tracks packet delay, loss, and routing "flaps."

Browsing the data, I was astounded to see the high percentages of packets lost over the Internet's backbone circuits. At times of peak loading, they move up into the double digits, well above 10 percent. Even without trend data, I can tell you that losing one packet in 10 is no way to run a TCP/IP network. Performance degrades rapidly when packets are lost. Such losses can lead to retransmission gridlock — not minute by minute here and there, but collapse all day all over.

Why do we only get reports of positive Internet trends, like numbers of domains, hosts, users, and bytes transmitted? Am I worried unduly by the few statistics I've dug up on packet delay, loss, and flaps? Where is the trend data? Would whoever the Internet's leader is please set our minds at ease? Let's all "question anarchy."

Numbers Add Up to Intoxicated Internet Hangover?

March 11, 1996

Perhaps you are back for new evidence of the Internet's coming catastrophic collapse, or to see whether I've finally recanted the unpopular prediction made here in December. (See "Predicting the Internet's catastrophic collapse and ghost sites galore in 1996," Dec. 4, 1995.)

Well, this week the collapse is foreshadowed in market research I've extracted from International Data Corp., InfoWorld's sister company, of which I'm a director.

At the end of 1995, IDC analyst Frank Gens polled many of his 300 colleagues in 40 countries before predicting that during 1996 the Internet will move from "intoxication" to "hangover."

He ventured that 20 percent of Fortune 500 companies' commercial World Wide Web sites will either stabilize or be closed this year. Gens anticipates disappointing financial results among Internet companies, the Internet stretched to the breaking point, and high turnover among underwhelmed Web users.

Frankly, Gens doesn't paint my picture of catastrophic collapse, but close.

Another Gens prediction is that Internet appliances will arrive in 1996, not for $500, but for $100 to $300. He expects a Sony Playstation with Internet access for $249. Beyond 1996, he foresees free Internet appliances distributed by on-line services.

Gens, like me, is optimistic about the Internet in the long run and subscribes to the IDC Internet Commerce Market Model. It predicts that in the year 2000, more than 200 million Web users will conduct between $150 and $200 billion of Internet commerce. This is up from 8 million active Web users in 1995, which in turn was up from 1 million in 1994.

It's fair to ask whether these predictions are optimism or cluelessness, and, oh, by the way, where is my collapse? Out of its model, IDC produces an index of commercial opportunity on the Web, for estimating returns on investments in Web pages.

The IDC Web Index is roughly total Web hours divided by total Web pages times transaction activity.

Each of the Index's major metrics is in turn dependent on a spreadsheet of parameters, such as numbers of personal computers, modems, average Web hours, and what IDC calls its Surf-to-Buy Ratio — the fraction of users actually buying on the Web (19 percent in 1995, climbing to 24 percent in 1997).

Well, does the IDC Web Index indicate Internet collapse in 1996? Not exactly. IDC uses the terms "shake-out" and "backlash" to describe a modest decline of its index at the end of 1996.

The decline is due to the growth of Web pages exceeding the growth of Web users, "a classic scenario of a start-up market, where pent-up demand generates investment in capacity that comes on-line just as early market growth cools."

The IDC Model and Index are fascinating attempts to escape the cluelessness that enshrouds commerce on the Internet. I'm sure IDC is in for considerable debate.

For example, when IDC says $200 billion of Internet commerce will be conducted during the year 2000, what do they mean? Is it just counting transactions fulfilled over the Internet using some form of micromoney, such as the purchase and delivery of a software component? Or transactions ordered over the Internet but paid and/or fulfilled off-line? Or transactions begun during on-line browsing but completed off-line? IDC answers all of the above — which is, I think, too broad.

When IDC divides Web hours by Web pages, are they coming up with any useful measure, or does commercial activity not care if there are gazillions of Web pages that hardly anybody visits? Should pages for the Index include just Home pages — published URLs — or should it count all reachable pages?

Finally, IDC's bottoms-up estimates of Web hours begin with the huge database that IDC has on the installed base of PCs.

What if $100-to-$500 Internet appliances start taking off during 1996?

They would make no difference during the collapse, but at those price points, IDC's numbers leading to Web hours would be gross underestimates.

With Your Help, I'll Document This Year's Internet Collapses

April 1, 1996

Many still faithfully deny that the Internet will suffer catastrophic collapses this year, but I'm ready to start counting collapses, and you can help.

John Quarterman has been counting on the Internet since 1991. (See "Up next, Internet weather forecast calls for traffical depressions and storms," Feb. 19, page 57.) For example, he "pings" thousands of Internet sites worldwide every four hours and then counts and times their responses.

Quarterman graphs these times in his Internet Weather Reports. The delays Quarterman averaged worldwide in 1995 — 431 milliseconds — were down 30 percent. This good news does not support theories of collapse.

But on the other hand, Quarterman's data have spikes. Some clearly mark the Internet's rush hours, daily and weekly. Some are random, severe, and unexplained. Quarterman tells me, "This data does not disprove your [collapse] theory."

Now, about Internet anarchy, many of you responded with outrage when I said question it. (See "Fuzzy-headed anarchy will lead the way to the Internet's total collapse," Feb. 26.) You accused me of inviting government intervention, like if only I would shut up, our governments might slumber. Give me a break. I'll tell you exactly which organization should get its Internet management act together, and it's not the Federal Communications Commission.

The Internet Society is where to organize the management of Internet operations worldwide, and to drive the tracking, policy development, and engineering that would have averted the collapses I've been whining about since December. The society has the Internet Engineering Planning Group (IEPG) for just this purpose. Problem is, the IEPG is not taken seriously enough. I just read the IEPG's latest reports of Internet traffic problems.

They were dated — uh-oh — March 1994.

The IEPG seems to have at least one active subgroup, the North American Network Operation Group (NANOG), which just met and will again in — uh-oh — May.

The right network problems, including outages crossing over into collapses, are being discussed in NANOG forums. And NANOG seems not to be grabbing hold and getting them handled — alas the collapses.

NANOG discussions are full of foreboding. They enumerate "routing pathologies" — unresponsive routers, loops, flaps, bad routes, flutter, skipping, increasing diameters (some now greater than 30 hops), and outages (some now greater than 30 seconds). And the trends are not good.

There is still no system of traffic-based settlements among cooperating Internet Service Providers (ISPs).

What's worst at NANOG is the declining goodwill between competing ISPs. While Internet loads increase, ISPs argue without supervision in the dark. They don't often report their outages to one another, and never to us.

Right here, at NANOG and I hope the IEPG (if we are still interested in a global Internet), is where anarchy must be questioned. Right here is where enlightened self-interest, competition, cooperation, practicality, learning, and leadership will pull the Internet out of its coming collapses.

So now you are hereby invited to join me in counting the Internet's collapses.

Why? Because when customers organize their complaints, suppliers who need to cooperate often do.

Next time you lose use of the Internet, please let your ISP (and me) know.

When your Internet access comes back up, collect as many facts as you can, put the word "collapse" in your e-mail subject field, and send me a copy of your collapse report. I'll count them.

Netcom-Cisco Outage Could Foreshadow Much Bigger Collapses Ahead

July 8, 1996

When a tropical storm grows large enough — winds exceeding 75 mph — we call it a hurricane and give it a name. It's time we do something similar with Internet outages.

Borrowing a threshold used by our Federal Communications Commission in the reporting of telephone outages, when more than 50,000 people are denied their Internet access for more than an hour, let's call it an Internet collapse and give it a name. Let's call the threshold a 50Kx1 collapse, or a 50 kilolapse.

Then we can say that, two weeks ago, the Internet suffered a 400Kx13 collapse, or a 5.2 megalapse. Beginning in the afternoon of June 18, the 400,000 customers of Netcom On-Line Communication Services Inc. experienced not just the usual worsening afternoon Internet brownout but lost their Internet mail and Web access for 13 hours. (See "Netcom service forced into 12-hour shutdown," June 24.)

Netcom says that this 5.2 megalapse was triggered by an engineer incorrectly typing an ampersand into a router made by Cisco Systems Inc. This typo was followed by "a flood of non-Netcom BGP [Boundary Gateway Protocol] routes being introduced into our OSPF [open shortest path first] network backbone. This led to a chain reaction of routing protocol fluctuations, which in turn overloaded a majority of the gateway routers on the Netcom WAN. Our network support staff diagnosed the problem early and worked through the night rebuilding the routing tables of our hub and POP routers."

So let's name this the Netcom-Cisco Ampersand Collapse.

Netcom CEO Dave Garrison apologized to his customers on KGO talk radio in San Francisco. He explained that the collapse was caused by human error. He admitted that the Ampersand Collapse had overwhelmed Netcom's telephone support. He promised to meet with Cisco, maker of most of Netcom's 100 routers, about preventing future outages.

Interviewed by *The Boston Globe,* Garrison explained the Internet is growing rapidly and there is plenty of room for competition. Then he said, "Internet companies face ruthless competition and don't have billions to spend on reliability upgrades."

Uh-oh, this despite Netcom's trademarked slogan: The Network Works. No Excuses.

Now, to err is human, and Internet fogies ask us to accept this latest megalapse as nothing new, no big deal. But Garrison's upcoming meeting with Cisco is important. Cisco should continuously improve the software with which its routers are programmed so that catastrophic human errors are less likely.

Ed Kozel, Cisco's chief technology officer, writes that "network routing is quite susceptible to human error... complete flexibility is driving routing architecture development... in recent years a lot of work has gone into creating interdomain routing firewalls and untrusted routing gateway functions, the result being that, in general, routing misbehavior is usually confined to a specific domain."

So we should be encouraged that the Netcom-Cisco Ampersand Collapse did not escape Netcom and go Internetwide, this time.

While Netcom and Cisco are at it, they should find a way to make Internet error messages more informative. Throughout the Ampersand Collapse, Netcom customers were told that their user names and passwords were incorrect, their calls were failing, their network connections were lost, or nothing at all as their starting session screens hung.

Now why has Netcom not offered each of its 400,000 customers a refund for the access lost during the megalapse? Let's see, that would be, say, half a day out of 30, or typically 33 cents each. Seems only fair.

The Netcom-Cisco Ampersand Collapse and other major outages should be prominent agenda items at upcoming meetings of Internet service providers.

Unfortunately, my favorite of such meetings, those of the North American Network Operators Group (NANOG), are not likely to take systematic outage analysis seriously. As one NANOG wag put it, "This is the 'Net, people, deal with it."

What's needed is for NANOG to deal with it. Another NANOG participant minimized the Netcom-Cisco 5.2 megalapse with this arithmetic: Since the Internet has 60 million users, the Netcom outage inconvenienced far fewer than 1 percent — some collapse. He has a point. There is ample room for much bigger Internet collapses ahead, maybe eventually some gigalapses.

Another Way to Collapse: Too Many Domain Names

September 9, 1996

All hell is breaking loose over Internet names. The number of Internet domain names is now more than half a million. Name lookups, which fetch Internet addresses on-the-fly from Web hyperlinks, are taking longer and failing more often, and the phrase "unable to locate server" is popping up on PC screens more than ever.

Furthermore, registering a domain is no longer free, and the best vanity names, scooped by speculators, have gotten quite expensive — into six figures I hear.

Trademark disputes over Internet names are now enriching lawyers. You may lose the use of your domain name without notice or recourse. Alternative Domain Name System (DNS) providers are threatening to divide the Internet. And entirely new naming systems are being proposed and (of course) bitterly debated.

As I said, all hell is breaking loose over Internet names. The Internet's DNS has served us well for over a decade. Since April 1993 when there were 9,000 domains, the registry of names has been kept by Network Solutions Inc. (NSI). It's not easy being Network Solutions, winning awards from one side while getting attacked from the other.

The DNS is a distributed database, with servers at each Internet service provider (ISP). But to resolve names, these servers often need to refer up the DNS hierarchy. The root server at NSI is receiving resolution requests at rapidly increasing rates, now in the hundreds per second.

Yes, I know, the Internet was designed to survive nuclear war, but its DNS is bogging down. Let's hope that NSI will scale up the DNS quickly enough, but if not, well, as I've been warning you since last year, the Internet might suffer collapses — DNS collapses.

NSI has a monopoly on Internet name registrations, and so when it started charging to cover costs, there was incoming fire from those who think the Internet should be free, or at least cheap. Then NSI compounded its problems by actually trying to collect on DNS invoices. NSI had some database problems.

And many ISPs were caught collecting registration fees from users but failing to forward them to NSI. A high point of sorts was reached the day that NSI wrongly deregistered msnbc.com.

And now NSI finds itself lost in the murky law surrounding trademarks in cyberspace. "Murky" means big bucks for lawyers. NSI used to give domain names out first come, first served. Then, when threatened with legal action by trademark holders, they made a policy giving preference to those with federally registered trademarks. So now they're getting sued by holders of so-called common law trademarks. NSI has even attracted the oversight of its very own Domain Name Rights Coalition.

Some folks have decided to break NSI's monopoly more directly. They have developed their own DNS and are offering an entirely new domain name space.

It really is time to break NSI's monopoly. A more respectable revamp of the DNS is being proposed by Internet pioneer Jon Postel at the University of Southern California. Postel is proposing the establishment of registries for new international top-level domains (iTLDs). The current TLDs — including .com, .edu, .gov, and .net — would be extended to nontrademark three, four, or five alphanumeric iTLDs beginning with a letter. Postel is proposing that registration, annual, and percentage-of-income fees be collected to pay for the new registration authorities.

Of course, I have a different way of thinking about all this. The trend is away from users seeing IP addresses, DNS names, and URLs. Search engines should lead us directly to what we're looking for just by clicking. I wonder, would it work to go from search results directly to hidden IP numbers, thereby skipping most if not all DNS lookups? In any case, we won't be seeing DNS names so often in the future, and their trademark values will likely decline.

In the meantime, all hell is breaking loose over Internet names. Let's watch with fingers crossed against the collapse of Internet DNS.

Internet Is Collapsing; Who's Going to Be Caught?

November 18, 1996
The Internet might possibly escape a "gigalapse" this year. If so, I'll be eating [my column] at the World Wide Web Conference in April. Even so, Scott Bradner should still be concerned about the Internet's coming catastrophic collapses.

Collapses are widespread and prolonged Internet outages, which, when catastrophic enough, get named and tracked much like tropical storms.

To size an outage, multiply the number of users times their hours of denied access. A recent BBN Corp. "kilolapse" lost thousands of user hours. An ampersand mistyped into a router deNetted 400,000 Netcom users for 13 hours — a 5.2 "megalapse." Another botched router update deWebbed 6.2 million America Online users for 19 hours — a catastrophic 118 megalapse.

Now don't you be confusing megalapses with the Internet's bogging down.

Members of the World Wide Wait Watchers Club do this. They complain about waiting too long for downloads, too often hitting their stop-loading buttons, and too seldom getting better service by changing Internet service providers (ISPs). To them, the bogging down and collapses are the same thing — a pain.

To work around the bogging and collapsing Internet, many have been building intranets. Even the universities that built the Internet are angling for their very own private new one. When will our thousands of uncooperative ISPs, who count on luring users from their collapsing competitors, learn why airlines don't compete by claiming their airplanes crash less? Among the causes of Internet collapse are traffic jams. Of course, this automobile analogy forgets that when Internet bridges are gridlocked, packets (unlike cars) get dumped into the river. The 10 percent packet losses that caught my attention last December now sometimes exceed 40 percent.

Internet retransmission protocols, as widely implemented, multiply packet losses, slow downloads, and often sneak away leaving inexplicable error messages. There's a danger of regenerative retransmission collapse.

Overbuilding the Internet to overcome its architectural problems is decreasingly an option. Financial incentives for adding capacity are weak — ISPs struggle to make money. Despite all that dark fiber, actual circuits are harder to come by. Installation delays on 45Mbps backbone circuits, for example, are now stretching out toward 180 days.

Let's be concerned that large portions of the Internet might be brought down not by nuclear war but by power failures, telephone outages, overloaded domain name servers, bugs in stressed router software, human errors in maintaining routing tables, and sabotage, to name a few weak spots.

Because the Internet's builders believed that it defies management — it's alive, they say — they punted, leaving no organized process for managing Internet operations. Where are circuits inventoried, traffic forecasts consolidated, outages reported, upgrades analyzed and coordinated? As my programming friends would say, the Internet Engineering and Planning Group and the North American Network Operators' Group are by most accounts no-ops — they exist, but they don't do anything.

But the Internet is not alive. It's actually a network of computers. And somebody, hopefully cooperating ISPs, should be managing its operations.

The Internet Engineering Task Force now seems to be coming around. It just reorganized itself to create an Operations and Management (O&M) Area. Scott Bradner should be reelected to lead O&M and to organize ISP processes for cooperative operational management.

Now, some say I'm a control freak, and we should let competition in the free market save us from Internet catastrophe. Excuse me, but pundits whining their concerns, buyers getting informed, and competing service providers better organizing their cooperations are all good examples of exactly how this free market thing actually works. If we get ISPs cooperating on operations soon, maybe our growing governments and their telephone monopolies won't need to step in to save the Internet's day.

Are Your Internet Packets Heading for Unstable Horizon?

November 25, 1996

A television producer posed me atop Treasure Island overlooking the San Francisco Bay Bridge. Her camera aimed down past me at the bridge's commuter lanes, all clogged with cars stopped bumper to bumper. We were dramatizing traffic jams on the Internet.

I told her camera what I've been telling you since Ethernet's first "collisions" in the early 1970s: Packets are just like cars. Packets can get caught in traffic jams and nowadays often do, which is why we're all revving up for the Information Superhighway.

Glancing down in midsentence at the bay beneath the bridge, I saw suddenly that to understand today's World Wide Wait, I'd have to admit that Internet packets are not really all that much like cars.

When packets find themselves in Internet traffic jams, they don't lip-sync golden oldies until eventually getting to work late for a meeting. When packets get stopped in traffic on an Internet bridge, they, unlike cars, are summarily dumped into the bay without even getting a chance to call in sick on their cellular phones.

When an Internet protocol family doesn't hear that its packet has arrived safely at work, members don't worry. They just wake up another copy of their lost packet, hand it lunch, and send it off toward work again.

For Internet packets, every day is like Bill Murray's *Groundhog Day*.

Now, although slow servers are much to blame for bogging down the Internet, lost packets are high among the Internet's dirty little secrets.

A year ago I uncovered evidence that packet losses along some Internet routes during rush hours were hitting an outrageous 10 percent. Hey, even packet losses below 1 percent can halve your Internet throughput.

Today, packet losses too often reach 20 percent, 40 percent, or 80 percent during some of the Internet's more gridlocked 15-minute intervals. At those rates, Web downloads are not just slow, but they often hang with inexplicable (if any) error messages.

So, let's expand my simplistic formula for Internet delay: $D=H*Q*(R+P/C)/(1-L)$.

D is for delay, H for hops, Q for queues, R for routing, P for packet length, C for circuit speed, and now L is for the percentage of packets lost into various bays along the way.

Note that as packet losses (L) approach 100 percent (1.0), packet delays (D) ramp to infinity. (See "Cisco's tag-switching technology may be the answer to Internet jams," Oct. 7, page 48.) John Quarterman has long been publishing measurements of delay that seem to refute my infamous predictions of Internet collapse.

Quarterman reports the good news that the Internet's average delays, as measured to 4,500 sites every 4 hours, have in fact over the past few years been trending down. But note that his gorgeous graphs do have many colorful spikes, each evidence of poor response and an opportunity for collapse.

I've asked Quarterman why even his long-term averages show frequent periods of major packet loss. And I've asked him how he computes his averages when many sample delays are infinite.

Stay tuned.

So here's something else to fix in the Internet: packet loss accountability.

How many of your packets get through? When you abort an interminable Web download, was it because some packets got dumped into a bay somewhere? Internet service providers are already counting packet discards in their routers; how about some loss reports along with their bills? Now it's great that TCP/IP, like Ethernet, backs off as traffic increases.

Backing off keeps networks stable. Lost packets are Mother Nature's way of telling your software to let up off the gas before driving the Internet down.

But beware of our latest crop of Internet opportunists offering software that helps you flood the Internet to make up for lost packets.

These products increase rather than decrease packet rates as losses mount. They start the painful downloading of every Web page in sight while you are figuring out which ones you actually want. If too many people start using such irresponsible software, the Internet could go unstable and — dare I say it again — collapse.

I'll Eat My Column, but Was Prophetic

December 23/December 30, 1996

Let's go back to my infamous column here on Dec. 4, 1995. Was I right about the Internet collapsing this year? And in particular, was I right that CD-ROMs sent through Federal Express — instead of the bogging Internet — would be this year's Information Superhighway?

OK, so last December I predicted that Internet stocks would collapse in January: "A hurried search for greater fools to absorb projected continuing losses won't pan out this time." I was wrong, greater fools were found, and they lost big.

Last year I also predicted that "we'll discover in 1996 that the vast majority [of new Internet users] surfed for several hours and then went back to watching TV." This was sarcasm.

I predicted that "the local telcos will escape demonopolization, ... their motivation to lower costs on high-speed Internet access will wither, fatally constipating the [World Wide] Web." I was all too right about the telcos' escaping demonopolization.

I predicted that "another series of major security breaches will drive the rest of the productive Internet ...out of reach." The major breaches did not occur, but the flight from the insecure, unreliable, and bogging Internet to private intranets for employees accelerated. And now people are even building private extranets for customers.

I predicted that "early initiatives to migrate to Internet Protocol Next Generation [IPNG] will add to a general loss of compatibility." IPNG migration failed to get started in 1996, so losses of compatibility lie ahead. Now IPv6 is suddenly called "research."

I stated that "the Internet is intermittently overloaded, and the TCP/IP architecture doesn't deal well with overloads." Well, it was undeniably the World Wide Wait during 1996, due mainly to slow servers and, as I was to discover later, lost packets.

I stated that "the Internet's naive flat-rate business model is incapable of financing the new capacity it would need to serve continued growth" and predicted it would change. To say the trend is toward flat-rate pricing, just because America Offline is doing it, is to debunk global warming during winter.

I predicted that "without video, the Internet will lack the energy needed to sustain its current expansion." Today's continuing expansion apparently does not rely on what most people would call video.

I predicted that "the Internet traffic carrying arguments about pornography on the Internet will during 1996 swamp the actual pornography." This happened.

And with the Communications Decency Act now at the Supreme Court, the problem will only get worse for you porno hounds.

And I predicted, as my parting shot, that "in 1996, CD-ROMs through Federal Express will emerge as the Information Superhighway." Let's dwell on this snide and unlikely prediction, which surprised even me by turning out to be more true than false.

According to a study of 2,000 randomly selected U.S. households, the number of households with PCs grew from 35 percent to 36 percent during the first half of 1996. Odyssey, in San Francisco, found that households with online services, including the Internet, grew more rapidly — from 11 percent to 14 percent — during the same period. But the penetration of CD-ROMs grew faster still, from 15 percent to 20 percent.

Do CD-ROMs get used? The average nationwide hours per week of usage for personal purposes is 107.5 million hours for CD-ROM versus only 87.4 million for online time.

And what about satisfaction? About 68 percent of CD-ROM users said they are very satisfied, while only 52 percent with online services they use at home said they are satisfied.

Or, as Odyssey President Nick Donatiello summarizes, CD-ROM has greater market penetration than online, it's growing faster than online, it's used more, and consumers are more satisfied with CD-ROM than with online. I rest my case.

Next week, having not learned my lesson, I'll sketch next year's progress on the Internet, the bogging and collapsing of which will get worse before it gets better.

Pundit's secret bared: giant panda bear...

Rebuttal by Vint Cerf

Vint Cerf is Senior Vice President of Internet Architecture and Engineering at MCI WorldCom and "Father of the Internet." Vint started working on the ARPAnet in 1968 at UCLA, contributing to the design of its Host-Host protocol. He then went to Stanford where, together with Bob Kahn, he designed the TCP/IP protocols and the basic architecture of the Internet. Currently he's working with the Jet Propulsion Laboratory on the design of an interplanetary Internet.

It would be easy to describe Bob Metcalfe as a loud-mouthed, publicity-grabbing, grandstanding pundit, who is less interested in facts than the sound of his own voice (or the look of his hot air in print). As I say, it would be easy.

But it would also be wrong. Oh yes, he's been dead wrong on a number of points; the most visible was the utter failure of his prediction of a gigameltdown on the Internet in 1996 (and again in 1997). It just didn't happen. And, to be fair, he consumed his words in a blended concoction in a public forum. It was, of course, just another grandstanding publicity stunt of the kind that have become a trademark, but. . .

The trouble with discounting Bob's rants as mere public relations gambits is that he's often found the heart of serious problems. Like a cartoonist who uses exaggeration for attention-getting emphasis, he draws them to our attention in the most hyperbolic fashion. I've learned to filter these features of Bob's ravings, and, frankly, find much to command my attention in his observations.

His concern about Internet capacity and fragility is worthy of our attention. The system isn't infinitely scalable in its present form and several incidents with the root domain server databases, with various routing table corruptions, and with congestion at various points and times in the global network suggest that the engineers of the Internet really do need to start paying more attention to these matters. Internet operators need to give guidance to vendors as to what functionality is needed in routers. Internet operators need to work together to improve our collective ability to deliver quality service. The multicast and broadcast applications that emerge in video and audio forms need new internal network facilities that are not widely available. Internet telephony brings its own set of challenges to the table: technical, regulatory and economic.

In one of his most recent diatribes, Bob weighs in on the difficulty of getting high-speed local access to the Internet. He rightly focuses the spotlight on monopoly controls over local loops and the difficulty this poses for any significant advancement of high-speed access. We need technical and regulatory options here. Real competition in local loop use is needed, but absent. Alternatives to local loops, such as cable and wireless (no pun intended), must be pursued.

So, what to make of this ranting gasbag named Metcalfe? Turn up the filters, tune in, and listen. You may not like the way he phrases it, but he's actually got some very important things to say, and he isn't afraid to say them.

Finally, in real life, this pundit is really a big, cuddly panda bear, but he's too chicken to admit it in public.

Vint Cerf

Camelot

February 1998

Making ISPs Accountable

Entrepreneurship, on the face of it, is a wonderful thing. But if you've followed the explosive growth of ISPs over the last several years, you might have noticed, as I did, the lack of accountability and quality of service in this brave new breed of entrepreneur. Built on a bogging backbone and mired in a confusion of telepoly tariffs, the proliferation of thousands of ISPs is, at best, a mixed blessing.

In the land of POP, SLA and ISP, performance and reliability seem to be obscure myths, and investment in equipment upgrades a budget line item nobody will approve. See how your own experience with your ISP compares with my assessments collected here.

Meet Jason Philbrook, Our Next Internet Service Provider

April 24, 1995

Jason Philbrook, like many other Maine natives, has five jobs. He hauls lobsters with his dad just off Owls Head near our summer home. He sells and services PCs with his mom, a town selectwoman. He's a nature photographer.

He's a sysop for a one-line bulletin board system with 200 midcoast callers.

And this summer, after computer classes let out at Worcester Polytechnic Institute in Massachusetts, just like every other college sophomore I know, Philbrook is planning to start his own Internet service company.

Philbrook's business plan is confidential, but I can tell you it does have a spreadsheet with positive cash in the first year, and a list of potential customers collected during a year of selling his BBS.

Philbrook's current BBS is a 286 running Wildcat, from Mustang Software Inc. in Bakersfield, California. He swears by Wildcat, and so, apparently, do many other sysops — this month Mustang was the first BBS company to take its stock public. I wonder what their first business plan looked like.

About 100 of Philbrook's current callers pay for e-mail service. They take turns dialing into his BBS modem to exchange messages once a day through the Internet. I would go crazy with the busy signals and two-day turnaround, but his callers have little money and few choices, two conditions that Philbrook's new Internet service company aims to improve.

Two weeks ago, Philbrook got himself written up in the local newspaper. They reported that Midcoast Internet Solutions (MIS) would soon offer Internet users a toll-free dial-in shell service, Slip/PPP, and continuous direct access. Two days later, Philbrook had messages expressing interest from a dozen midcoast Mainers.

Using Netscape from my office in Boston, Philbrook hyperlinked to the Home page on his Web server in Worcester, and from there to a state-maintained map of the Internet in Maine. The map revealed Philbrook's opportunity — a lack of toll-free Internet access along the midcoast. And what few Internet access points exist are governmental/educational, not for profitable use, and therefore not competitors.

I hate to rain on parades, but I had to tell Philbrook what I saw as three big risks. First, despite the promising response to his early publicity, there might still be too few midcoast people willing to pay him enough to provide his service — especially if they can sneak their way onto a free state-supported system.

Second, like some of its biggest competitors, MIS might have trouble supporting a profitable number of customers who have paid to have their high expectations met, especially since Philbrook will return to Worcester in September.

Third, a big risk for MIS is that it might soon face serious competition from companies like America Online, AT&T, IBM, MCI, Microsoft, Performance Systems International, Sprint, UUNet, the cable television companies, the local telephone companies, and all the other Internet service companies now being started by college sophomores. Philbrook didn't flinch.

So I ask Philbrook how he will offer me toll-free access from Lincolnville to his Internet router way over in Owls Head. Easy, smiles Philbrook. Because Camden is a local call from both Lincolnville and Owls Head, a friend in Camden will order up a phone with call forwarding. Philbrook will then call the friend's house in Camden and be automatically forwarded toll free to Owls Head.

This hack reminds me of just how bent our telco regulatory system is, but I won't get started on that again this week.

Philbrook plans to provide Internet service on a Pentium running LINUX, a shareware Unix clone with devotees even more passionate than OS/2's. Philbrook says he's the only one he knows who hasn't built his own Linux kernel — his customers prefer long periods of uninterrupted service.

Now, if you think I've told you all this just because I find Philbrook's enthusiasm exciting, or because Wildcat and Linux are worthy of your attention, fine. But I must disclose that Philbrook has promised a lobsta dinna if I sign up for his service.

Reevaluate Your ISP Contract in the Face of the Internet Crisis

April 29, 1996

The Internet hasn't collapsed quite yet, as far as I can tell, but now suddenly there's loose talk that it might. Bio-anarchic ideologues are digging deeper into denial as the Internet's bogging down worsens, outages multiply, and the popular press, smelling blood, moves in.

Meanwhile, I've turned cheerfully to preparations for the post-collapse industrial-strength Internet. For example, I've been reading the hilarious pre-collapse access contracts that many of you are still signing with our nation's 1,447 or so Internet service providers (ISPs).

If today's ISP contracts are anything they are short, and yet they still somehow manage to deny at length that there are any guarantees on your use of the Internet. These contracts invariably deny ISP responsibility for damages due to interruptions of your Internet access. They sometimes warn against using the Internet for unlawful purposes. Some reserve an ISP's right to terminate your service immediately, with or without reason. And all limit ISP exposure past restoration of Internet access. And aside from raw speed, they just don't get around to mentioning the qualities of that access.

Today's ISP contracts say why the Internet has outgrown its 20-year old architecture to become a house of cards. Or, to put it in bio-anarchic terms, today's ISP contracts are defects in the Internet's DNA. The question is, do we sit through the Internet's collapses, faithfully letting natural selection improve the ecology, or do we inform the Internet's genes directly that they have crawled up out of the National Science Foundation's (NSF) primordial ocean and now must survive upright on commercial dry land? Unfortunately, your ISP contract is similar to the contract your ISP has with his ISP, all the way on up to the big ISPs, the several Network Access Providers (NAPs) anointed by NSF to run the Internet's backbones. Trouble is, your ISPs guarantee you what their ISPs guarantee them, which is doodley-squat.

Before we recover from the Internet's bogging down, frequent outages, and coming catastrophic collapses, we must begin reengineering the Internet by upgrading the current best-effort ISP contracts — yours with your users, between you and your ISPs, among ISPs, all the way on up to the NAPs. When you start insisting on contracts that assure value for money, just you watch, ISPs will start insisting on the same from one another.

In short, ISP contracts should specify qualities of service. They should specify minimums for availability, throughput, delay, and probability of packet delivery. Such qualities should be monitored by you and your ISP. Yes, this will require some new software, in routers and on your desk, so we'd better get writing it.

ISP contracts should also specify the qualities of service that ISPs buy on your behalf, say of the ports per dial-in user or the bandwidth of long-haul lines carrying the total projected traffic of their users. Contracts might well offer assurances about the capacities and redundancies of lines to specified destinations. Hops to your important destinations must be capped, for sure.

And ISP contracts should specify variable fees for service. These should be based on metered usage between you and your ISP and "settlements" among ISPs and NAPs. Unfortunately, metered service and settlements are ideologically opposed by the Internet's ruling bio-anarchic intelligentsia.

In case you've been wondering, the reason we must suffer through the Internet's coming collapses is to discredit this ideology and, shortly thereafter, dump this intelligentsia.

There is some small progress to report, and it's from UuNet Technologies Inc., the major ISP I hassled here a few months back. (See "Up next, Internet weather forecast calls for traffical depressions and storms," Feb. 19.) UuNet is now offering a "burstable T1" service through which its customers pay in tiers for their actual average usage of T1 lines to the Internet. A small, but coming, thing. Please let me know of other progress on ISP contracts.

The first Boardwatch Magazine Directory of Internet Service Providers lists our 1,447 ISPs and their 5,400 telephone numbers. Consider joining many of them and discussing their contracts at One ISPCon (formerly One BBSCon) in San Francisco, Aug. 8 to 10.

To break from reading ISP contracts, I read your Internet outage reports, thanks. Please keep them coming. A hundred of you will soon report the first really big Internet collapse.

Smaller ISPs Must Join to Fend Off Monopolies and Collapses

August 26, 1996

On Aug. 7, I arrived in San Francisco to attend a convention of Internet service providers (ISPs). Boardwatch Magazine Editor Jack Rickard was letting me keynote again. This time I was ready to wrap up ISPCon with a defiant defense of my predictions about this year's Internet collapses.

Well, just my luck, that first day of ISPCon became Black Wednesday for the world's largest ISP, America Online. All of AOL's 6.2 million subscribers lost their Internet services for 19 hours — on my Internet outage scale that's a 6.2-million-times-19 collapse, or a 118 megalapse. The "America Offline" story broke that afternoon on *InfoWorld Electric*, and the next morning it topped *USA Today*'s front page, above reports of life on Mars.

AOL chief Steve Case should not have tempted fate on Black Wednesday by opining that AOL would someday be as reliable as electricity. Just as ISPCon was winding down on Saturday, much of the western United States lost its electricity.

About 2,000 ISPs, ISP wanna-bes, and hangers-on like me showed up for ISPCon's 120 sessions, 100 product exhibits, and four days of schmoozing. Rickard is now in contact with more than 3,000 ISPs in North America.

ISPs are an important new category of vendors to *InfoWorld* readers. And as vendors, ISPs should be interested in a recent QuickPoll in which 65 percent of responding *InfoWorld* readers said they were unsatisfied with the Internet's reliability and performance.

ISPs seem to think of themselves as a community of hub, router, switch, and circuit customers, and not as vendors themselves of Internet services. For example, the ISP contracts you are signing, as I wrote here on April 29 (see "It's time to re-evaluate your ISP contracts in the face of Internet crisis"), are laughably lacking in accountability. It's major progress that AOL is refunding its subscribers for Black Wednesday — unlike Netcom, which only a few weeks before refused refunds following its 5.2 megalapse. (See "Netcom-Cisco outage could foreshadow much bigger collapses ahead," July 8.) Rickard says of the Internet: The world bought the demo; now it's time to build the next-generation, industrial-strength Internet.

A big question at ISPCon is whether there will be another ISPCon. On one hand, the number of ISPs is growing rapidly. ISP franchisers were working the crowd at ISPCon with great success. On the other hand, the top 10 ISPs, mostly huge telephone companies, did not show up at ISPCon. Independent ISPs fear that telco monopolies will give Internet service away free to promote their voice services. As

Microsoft is now teaching Netscape, free is a price with which it is very hard to compete.

My advice to ISPs is to organize. ISPs large and small need to work together to manage the Internet toward increasing reliability and performance. It's too late to avoid this year's collapses, but better late than never. ISPs should look into the new ISP Consortium at www.ispc.org.

ISPs should also organize to develop a louder voice among various intruding government agencies. The Telecommunications Act of 1996 is law, the Federal Communications Commission is pounding out its 80 consequent rule-makings, and thereafter our 51 Public Utilities Commissions (PUCs), with the help of telco lobbyists, will be rationalizing their monopolies with self-serving notions of the public good. ISPs, beware PUCs bearing universal service.

Many ISPs don't think the Internet will collapse — "it's alive!" They remind me snidely that the Internet did not collapse during the Olympics, as I had warned. Some are still betting I'll be climbing down early next year from my predictions, or trying to weasel out of them. Perhaps.

But for now, I'm predicting the Internet will suffer gigalapses before Dec. 31, outages nearly 200 times bigger than the Netcom-Cisco Ampersand 5.2 megalapse, and nearly 10 times AOL's Black Wednesday 118 megalapse.

Growing complexities in Internet routing and vulnerabilities in peering among ISPs are sufficient to make the chances of gigalapses this year quite high. It will be a very long time before electric utilities envy the reliability of the Internet, this despite the fact that, as you have so often read, the Internet was designed to survive a nuclear war.

ISPs Add Stripes, Dots to Differentiate in Darwinian Market

January 13, 1997

There are now 3,068 Internet service providers (ISPs) listed in North America.

That's a doubling in the past seven months. The average ISP has annual revenues of $637,572 and 13 paid employees, and it provides 199 dial-up telephone ports to 1,844 Internet users.

These facts and my key fact of the week are found in Boardwatch Magazine's — better late than never — Fall 1996 Directory of Internet Service Providers.

Order the 340-page directory for $10 at www.boardwatch.com, which also offers an ISP locator service. The Boardwatch Directory is recommended not just for its 11,500 listings of ISPs near you but also for editor/publisher Jack Rickard's analysis of the ISP industry.

So far, the closest ISPs have gotten to coordination is listing themselves in Rickard's directory.

My key fact of the week is that there is no meaningful notion of an "average" ISP. ISPs are speciating rapidly in the face of expanding opportunities and growing evolutionary pressure.

Some ISPs are lowering prices to gain market share, others are raising prices to cover costs, some are discontinuing unprofitable services, and others are beginning to pretend they have earnings — even if only before interest, taxes, depreciation, and amortization. And many, the likely survivors, are creating entirely new services.

It's survival of the fittest at the ISP corral. If you're not satisfied with your current ISP, then improve the breed by selecting a new one.

While collecting nominations for the 1996 *InfoWorld* Internet Plumbing Award, to be announced Jan. 27, I spoke with master plumbers about ISP speciation.

Robert Berger is chief technical officer of InterNex Information Services, in Santa Clara, Calif. InterNex has avoided providing modem dial-up service to individuals. Berger plumbs for businesses with no less than ISDN pipes.

InterNex has evolved into Web hosting, software downloading, and secure transaction services.

Milo Medin is technology vice president of @Home, in Mountain View, Calif. @Home doesn't offer dial-up Internet service but does offer access through cable television networks. Medin said that before millions of users can come onto the Internet through multimegabit cable modems, something must be done about the poor performance through today's bogging backbones and slow servers.

So @Home is building its own backbone network and is installing Internet services at cable head-ends. It's caching data for cable customers so they won't end up operating at dial-up speeds.

Rodney Jaffe is chief technical officer of Genuity, in San Francisco. In Genuity, we find an entirely new genus of ISP.

Genuity has an international DS3 (45Mbps) backbone to connect its data centers in Chicago, London, Los Angeles, New York, Phoenix, San Francisco, and Washington. These are colocated with the Internet's major network access points (NAPs). Internet users connecting to the servers of Genuity customers are routed with Genuity's Hopscotch technology to the data center that is "closest" when considering 'Net topology, backbone traffic, and Genuity server loading.

It will be interesting to see back-end ISPs such as Genuity and InterNex coevolve with front-end ISPs such as @Home. Genuity and @Home are complementary but only if @Home focuses on serving millions of cable modem users and Genuity focuses on serving large sites hoping to attract the hyperlinks of those millions. Now Genuity and @Home interconnect through NAPs, but they may later peer bilaterally (connect directly), avoiding and mitigating NAP congestion. Or, they may choose to fight it out over who will provide caching services — Genuity on behalf of servers versus @Home on behalf of clients, or both, or neither.

Think about all the caching mutations we're seeing on the 'Net. There's caching in the operating systems of servers. There's caching at Genuity's data centers. There's caching at @Home's head-ends. There's caching in individual Web clients. Can't wait to see who'll cash in on caching.

Service Agreements with ISPs Would Make Them Accountable for Outages

June 2, 1997

The letters "SLA" take me back 20 years to the days of Patricia Hearst and the Symbionese Liberation Army. Then it was mostly left-wing fanatics running amok. Today, outside Peru, those running amok are mostly my people — right-wing fanatics. And now SLA stands for Service Level Agreements.

SLAs were the big issue during a recent visit from Visual Networks, a private company in Rockville, Md., that has about 100 employees. Visual's 1996 sales were up 3,233 percent to $10 million.

Visual's various hot products contain analysis service elements (ASEs). They are bought by interexchange carriers (IXCs), which are long-distance telephone companies; by local exchange carriers (LECs), which are local telephone monopolies; by competitive access providers (CAPs), which are local telcos trying to give LECs a run for their monopolies; and by Internet service providers (ISPs), some of which are IXCs, LECs, and CAPs. But most interestingly, ASEs are bought by the many of you who are corporate network managers.

ASEs monitor transmissions across 56Kbps, 64Kbps, fractional T1, and T1 circuits. They analyze protocols for leased-line, frame-relay, Asynchronous Transfer Mode, and Internet traffic. Visual says that during the past two years, it has delivered about 7,000 ASEs — half to corporate network managers, half to T1 circuit providers — mostly for frame-relay networks, which are increasingly used for Internet services.

Visual's software collects data from a network's ASEs and displays reports so managers can visualize what's going on among their routers and circuits.

Take, for example, the Internet access an intranet gets through an ISP. Say you're normal and are being ripped off on a T1 line by your LEC. You paid $3,000 to get the T1 line installed, eventually, and now you pay $500 per month — maybe 10 times what it's worth. Visual's ASE is a $3,600 box that sits between your 1.5Mbps T1 service unit and your router.

ASEs use SNMP to tell Visual's access management software whether your pricey T1 circuit is available. They also indicate frame error rates and delays, packet retransmission rates and delays, and how your Internet traffic breaks down by protocol and by user. You can save maintenance calls with better diagnostics, plan future capacity better by watching traffic patterns, bill back costs based on traffic per user, and log data for verifying ISP performance against your ironclad T1 Internet SLA.

Trouble is, of course, most of you don't have ironclad SLAs with your ISPs.

There is an international standard, G.821, for deciding whether your expensive T1 line is available. Visual will monitor conformance to that standard.

However, Visual complains, there are no standards for Internet SLAs. There is no general agreement on when an Internet connection is up, let alone performing acceptably.

Custom SLAs are now proliferating. Expect standard SLAs to emerge, perhaps through IOPS.ORG, the ISP operations cooperative whose formation was celebrated in this column last week.

Internet SLAs are becoming an urgent matter. Consider the major Internet "incident" on April 25. Reports vary, but from zero percent to 40 percent of traffic was lost for zero to 7 hours that business day. Some of you have written that I ate my *InfoWorld* Internet collapse column too soon.

The April 25 incident was doubly disturbing. First, unlike the Netcom, America Online, and BBN megalapses of last year, this time bad routing information escaped the offending ISP, infected other ISPs, and eventually appeared at the Internet's major exchange points.

The April 25 incident was also disturbing because hardly anybody complained.

Apologists for the ISP "community" say the incident wasn't noticed because of the Internet's resilience and because of effective cooperation among ISPs during the emergency. Other reports suggest that Internet users accepted as normal whatever lack of access or slowness of response they experienced during the morning of April 25. Users simply decided to hit stop and try again later without complaint, as usual. Few of those so inconvenienced knew that others — perhaps millions — were experiencing similar difficulties at the same time.

My hope is that we'll soon have standard Internet SLAs and widespread accountability such as that provided by Visual Networks. Only then will Internet reliability and performance trends turn up — and with them, our sagging expectations.

How One Unregulated ISP Is Making a Killing Surfing the Absurd Telopoly Tariffs

July 28, 1997

In April 1995, Jason Philbrook, a sophomore at Worcester Polytechnic Institute (WPI), took a bus into Boston to show me how he planned to become an ISP. I don't generally read business plans, but Philbrook had grown up in Owls Head, Maine, just down the road from our summer home. And he promised me a lobsta dinna.

I ended up writing a cautionary critique of Philbrook's plan. (See "From the Ether," April 24, 1995.) I warned him that midcoast Maine might have too few people willing to pay for Internet access, especially because the University of Maine was very effective at providing it free to various hangers-on. I warned him that if he returned to WPI in the fall, he might have trouble meeting the expectations of paying customers. And I warned him that he would be facing some formidable competition from America Online, AT&T, Microsoft, UUNET, local telephone companies (of which there are 18 in Maine), cable TV companies, and other start-up ISPs.

Undeterred, Philbrook opened for business in June 1995 as Midcoast Internet Solutions (MIS).

Today, MIS' 2,800 customers pay $20 per month for e-mail, as much as 5MB of Web pages, and as many as 30 hours of 33.6Kbps access and 50 cents per hour thereafter. At these prices, MIS' customer list grows by 50 to 100 names each month.

Philbrook, who has not yet returned for his junior year at WPI, now employs nine people (including his mom) in two offices and six points of presence (POPs).

Philbrook relies mostly on two of the 18 telephone monopolies that divide Maine. Nynex is the big one, and the other is my local telopoly, which also happens to be both an ISP and my local cable-TV monopoly. A lot of what Philbrook does is surf the absurdities of their telopoly tariffs.

For example, calls from Lincolnville, Maine, to Camden, Maine, are free, and from Camden to Owls Head are free, but calls from Lincolnville to Owls Head are not free. So MIS keeps a phone at a customer's house in Camden that does nothing but call-forwarding to Owls Head. This gives Lincolnville customers toll-free access to the MIS POP in Owls Head, which by car is 40 minutes away. Philbrook says this is common practice among ISPs and, although absurd, is perfectly legal.

Probably because Maine has so many telcos busily not competing, our intrastate long-distance telephone rates are some of the highest in the nation. So MIS needs six POPs to cover the midcoast toll-free.

The Rockland, Maine, POP is two 19-inch racks in a computer-store basement. About 100 telephone pairs come in from a nearby telco central office. The lines each cost $20 per month.

MIS uses Centrex hunt groups of 23 individual analog telephone lines. MIS does not use 23-channel Primary Rate Interfaces. Why? Because ISDN is tariffed at a rate three times higher than plain old telephone service, not counting ISDN's penny-per-minute usage charges.

MIS' Rockland POP also has 100 modems, a couple of remote-access servers, and an Internet router. Rockland is interconnected with MIS' other POPs and upstream to the Internet using 1.5Mbps T1 service, T1 frame relay, or 56Kbps frame relay from Nynex.

One of MIS' POPs is in Damariscotta, Maine, near MIS' office there. The office goes via Nynex 56Kbps frame relay to Owls Head, a half hour up the coast, and then via Nynex T1 from Owls Head back down to Damariscotta. Because staying within Damariscotta keeps MIS under Maine tariffs, Philbrook says, our local telco wanted two months delay, $1,000, and $200 per month for 56Kbps to go just 3 miles. No, thanks.

This same local telco competes with Philbrook as an ISP over his service area with not six but one POP. It does this because the telco can use its own T1 lines to forward all calls toll-free from among its central offices to its one POP.

When the telco does this, by the way, it gets 24 circuit-switched calls per T1. When Philbrook uses remote-access servers and routers to do the same thing, he gets 200 packet-switched calls per T1.

Philbrook is looking at starting another company — a regulated telephone company — that can sell services to his unregulated ISP. That's how he might get packet-switching equipment into central offices and get "coppertone" for megabit Digital Subscriber Lines.

I remembered Philbrook taking the bus to see me in Boston two years ago. Now, by surfing the absurd tariffs of telopolies, Philbrook has 85 percent of a market that is 5 percent penetrated. He is growing profitably at 33 percent per year. And he has a shiny red Jaguar coupe, but notes that it's used — unlike the next one, I suppose.

Public ISPs Now Number 4,500 — Many of Which Are Looking to Buy Or Be Bought

April 20, 1998

The news from last March's ISP conference, ISPCon in Baltimore, is that, despite my repeated worryings about an imminent consolidation, the number of ISPs is still growing.

There are now more than 4,500 ISPs in North America. And they're mostly wondering whether to buy or be bought by one another, or better yet by somebody big and clueless.

So says Jack Rickard, champion of small ISPs.

Rickard is publisher of *Boardwatch*, a monthly magazine serving 28,000 readers, mostly ISPs. He also publishes *Boardwatch*'s quarterly 500-page *ISP Directory* for 110,000 readers.

Now, when Rickard says there are 4,500 ISPs in North America, he isn't just estimating. He has their addresses and phone numbers. But after ISPCon, Rickard is worried his directory isn't keeping up. He estimates he has missed 500 ISPs.

And the 4,500 counts only public ISPs. Rickard says ISPCon is also for the many ISPs in corporate IT departments. The "opportunities" you face in supporting your company's users on the Internet have much in common with those faced by public ISPs.

Rickard says an ISP shakeout is not imminent. Many ISPs are buying and being bought, but the barriers to entry are low, hope springs eternal, and more are starting up. Rickard says the number of ISPs is still growing, despite consolidation. Growing more slowly, but growing.

The limiting factor is people, Rickard says. Money is not enough anymore. ISPs have become the first line of computer technical support. It's hard to find people who can explain to new Internet users how to run Windows and turn their printers on before connecting to the Internet, and you know how easy that is. That's why the big and clueless are buying into small ISPs.

Of course, ISPs also face having to make investments in expensive equipment that does not plug and play nor scale very well. ISPs charge $10 to $30 per month per subscriber, which sounds pretty good against one employee per 1,000 subscribers. However, ISPs have to overpay telopolies for transmission services and upgrade equipment every 14 months.

This is why when ISPs report financial results, they often talk about EBITDA, or earnings before interest, taxes, depreciation, and amortization. EBITDA is all the money you've made, not counting all the money you're losing.

One amazing story Rickard tells is about an ISP that just got a $175 million equipment line of credit from Northern Telecom (Nortel). Nortel is clearly buying into ISP growth. This ISP has huge equipment-upgrade needs, but what's amazing is that, although profitable, it cleared $28,000 on annual revenues of only $1.8 million. Compare that to $175 million.

And it's not just Nortel that's trying to buy into the ISP business. Even the big three — Compaq, Intel, and Wal-Mart — are wheeling and dealing. Credit lines, private labels, and affinity marketing are everywhere.

Rickard's paying readers are mostly ISPs, but he risks measuring Internet service providers against one another. His backbone comparisons, although well-received among Internet users, drove ISPs crazy. Now he's comparing call-completion rates. Next, customer satisfaction. Is Rickard biting the hand that feeds? Perhaps this is why Rickard drives a Hummer.

Rickard is watching incumbent local exchange carriers (ILECs) — telephone monopolies — expanding into Internet services. I asked Rickard whether he would agree that ILECs should not be allowed to offer Internet service.

Rickard, like me, is a big fan of free markets. But, like me, he overcomes ideological recriminations after noting that ILECs are government-created monopolies. He agrees ILECs should not be ISPs.

There are two ways to have a robust Internet. One is to have a few big ISPs, preferably one big ISP. That way, reliable Internet service can be offered end to end from a single big Soviet-style one-stop shopping telecommunications provider. It can provide local, long-distance, and cellular telephone services on the same bill, and generously subsidize Internet access for rural inner-city schools, by overcharging ... you.

The second is to have a robust Internet with many competing ISPs cooperating to provide inexpensive and rapidly evolving service.

Rickard and I prefer fierce ISP competition, but like democracy, it's a jungle out there.

The Internet Needs to Get Its Act Together — IOPS Is Helping, but Has More to Do

February 1, 1999

People don't ask anymore if I invented Ethernet. Sometimes they ask if I'm that handsome devil of an NFL coach, Bill Parcells. More often they ask, snickering, whether the Internet has collapsed yet. Very funny.

Yes, I worried in 1995 about the Internet's unreliability, poor performance, and lack of security. I warned that the Internet was suffering ever-larger outages, the biggest of which I called "collapses." And then I predicted that during 1996 the Internet would suffer a "gigalapse" — the loss of 1 billion user hours in a single outage.

Well, the largest reported Internet outage during 1996 was a 118-megalapse — an outage of 118-million user hours — one-tenth of my prediction. So, violating a basic rule of punditry, I admitted I was wrong (about the gigalapse) and literally ate my *InfoWorld* column at the International World Wide Web Conference in April 1997.

Isn't it time to let bygones be bygones? I didn't even lie under oath or anything.

It was clear in 1995 that the Internet was getting so important that, especially if it gigalapsed, our Federal Communications Commission would have to ask its regulated telephone monopolies to make the Internet's trains run on time.

Telopolies running the Internet would be almost exactly like foxes guarding the henhouse, except that foxes are smart and agile.

There is, in fact, a Network Reliability and Interoperability Council (NRIC), which has advised the FCC since 1992 on telephone networks. AT&T CEO Michael Armstrong now chairs the NRIC.

So I set out to save the Internet from the NRIC. I started looking for a forum in which ISPs could themselves coordinate Internet operations.

Too bad the Internet Society is focused on "standards, issues, and education," not operations. Too bad the Internet Engineering Task Force is focused on architecture and standards, not operations. And too bad the North American Network Operators Group — with the right name, charter, and a fine group of participants — has all the due process of a lynch mob.

So, I pinned my hopes on IOPS.org, founded (as I ate my column) in April 1997 to focus on Internet operations. IOPS has as members about a dozen of the largest ISPs. These are ANS (purchased by WorldCom), AT&T (hoping to buy TCI, which owns most of @Home), BBN (now GTE), Earthlink (Sprint owns 27 percent), GTE (may soon be Bell Atlantic), MCI (now merged with WorldCom), Netcom (soon Mindspring), PSINet (IXC owns 20 percent), Sprint, UUNet (now MCI WorldCom), Agis, Epoch, Exodus, IBM (sold operations to AT&T), and Icon (now Qwest).

Well, I just attended an IOPS meeting in Reston, Va., and yes, its members have been very busy … merging. Executive Director Ira Richer says IOPS has accomplished more than is appreciated. I say IOPS has accomplished much less than necessary.

What's necessary is getting the Internet's act together on actionable reliability and performance metrics, outage reporting and response, security attacks, and routing robustness. IOPS has barely started on these.

IOPS has yet to get moving on the operational technicalities of the year-2000 problem, peering, settlements, quality of service, the Internet Corporation for Assigned Names and Numbers, direct access using cable modems and Digital Subscriber Lines, and deployment of IPv6 before the Internet runs out of addresses.

IOPS needs more participation from its members. It should involve qualified people from more of the thousands of smaller ISPs. And it needs to take on more operational challenges.

Ominously, NRIC now appears bent on expanding its charter from telephone to cable, wireless, satellite, and Internet networks. IOPS should preemptively volunteer to be NRIC's Internet subcommittee. If IOPS doesn't, somebody else will.

My ISP Is into Linux and Wireless Technology, but Not Inflated Internet Stocks

January 7, 2000

Jason Philbrook is my Internet service provider in Maine.

In April 1995, Philbrook was a sophomore at Worcester Polytechnic Institute. His secret weapons were Pentiums running "shareware" called Linux. And he had a business plan for becoming midcoast Maine's first ISP.

Being a pundit, I don't read business plans. But Philbrook's father is a lobsterman out of Owls Head, where we summer. And he offered me "a wicked lobsta dinna."

I worried that Philbrook would find few people in Maine willing to pay for Internet access, that he would not support them satisfactorily from his dorm, and that he would soon be squashed by the big national ISPs.

By June 1995, despite my worries, Philbrook left college, founded Midcoast Internet Solutions and signed me up as a customer.

By July 1997, Philbrook had 2,800 customers, nine employees, six points of presence (POPs), 85 percent of a market only 5 percent penetrated, profitable annual growth of 33 percent, and a used red Jaguar.

Today, Midcoast prospers. It looks messy, but it's in new digs, offers local V.90 access to 4,500 customers from Bath to Belfast, and doubled its revenue during 1999.

Midcoast's financials are private, but Philbrook has replaced his old Jaguar with an older one — a 1969 E-Type — and a sporty new Saab.

What are Philbrook's secrets? He still uses Linux, by Red Hat, in which he owns stock. He offers two dial-in numbers, one for each of the slightly incompatible V.90 modems people use a lot. Midcoast makes a profit after installing customer PCs onto the Internet for free. And Philbrook helps out in surrounding communities.

Midcoast depends on Bell Atlantic for telephone facilities. Philbrook says that the monopoly is behaving itself, except he just requested five new ISDN Primary Rate Interfaces and has to wait an estimated 60 days for installation.

Philbrook's long-range plan is to expand V.90 only in territories already served, to focus on developing access alternatives, to provision wireless access for other ISPs, and to become a competitive local exchange carrier (CLEC) offering Internet telephone services.

Midcoast will soon offer Digital Subscriber Lines. My access will go up in speed six times and down in cost four times — can't wait.

But the big news at Midcoast is wireless. Philbrook already has nine radio towers and over 70 wireless customers. They get 1Mbps Internet after paying less than $1,000 for installation and $50 per month, plus $8 per month for each additional computer. The service is fast, cheap, and rock solid, Philbrook says.

Philbrook's hardware is from BreezeCOM. It is IEEE 802.11 Wireless Ethernet in the 2.4-GHz band. (Note: 2.4GHz is a carrier frequency, not a bandwidth, not a bit rate.) Philbrook is as enthusiastic about BreezeCOM as he is about Linux, which is very.

Midcoast uses omnidirectional 2.4-GHz antennas to offer two-way 1Mbps wireless access within 15 miles line of sight. Directional antennas replace T1 for hauling traffic back to Midcoast's POPs. And soon Midcoast plans to carry voice over IP (VOIP).

But Midcoast is not yet a CLEC. Philbrook says Midcoast's application was submitted six months ago. He'll probably need a lawyer.

Philbrook rattles off competitors who have been "consolidated." These competitors were poorly run companies that had to sell out cheap, he says.

However, Midcoast is profitable and growing, so Philbrook rejects the low offers he receives monthly. He is open to selling, but for the right price, and suitors bearing inflated Internet stocks need not apply.

The Sky is falling...or is it?

Rebuttal by Sky Dayton

Sky Dayton is the founder and chairman of EarthLink, Inc., and currently incubating Internet startups as co-founder of eCompanies.

Bob, thanks for asking me to write a rebuttal to your columns about ISPs. I'm really good at writing them, like the 1000-word rebuttal I had to crank out in a hurry in 1996. That was when our phones at Earthlink started ringing off the hook because some lunatic had predicted the Internet was about to collapse. Of course, that lunatic would be you, Bob (not that I knew you then).

At the time, EarthLink was just a tiny company compared to today — not more than a few hundred employees. And, as if I didn't have enough to do managing our explosive growth, I had to field calls from investors and members in a state of panic over this imaginary Internet crash. "The guy who invented Ethernet says the Internet is going to melt down; the sky is falling; the world is coming to an end!"

I should have started a side business selling bomb shelters and freeze-dried food. Instead, I had to explain to callers carefully why the world wasn't actually coming to an end, calm their nerves, and do some serious handholding. Your pronouncements created a lot of jitters. Finally, after answering a few hundred e-mails, I figured the best thing was to write a rebuttal and post it on the EarthLink Web site to assuage everyone's fear.

I still have it — and my predictions seem to have held up better than many of yours. My rebuttal pointed out that the Internet is like a system of roads and bridges; if there's a traffic jam in one place, there are always alternate routes you can take to get around it.

The Internet is also a self-healing entity. It wasn't built like one big federal highway program, with one group laying down all the roads. Instead, it was as if thousands of entrepreneurs went out, bought cement machines, and started pouring their own roads. The result is so many points of redundancy that the Internet can never fail, unless something really cataclysmic happens.

Bob, you're a Libertarian, aren't you? You should have known all of this. Entrepreneurs are the world's greatest natural resource. Which brings us to another one of your predictions regarding ISPs. You somehow found yourself in the herd chanting that independent ISPs wouldn't survive and would be gobbled up by telephone companies. It never happened. Today, little EarthLink is larger than the ISPs of all of the local telephone companies combined. Now here I can't blame you for starting a stampede, only for joining it, and running off a cliff like everyone else.

In 1995, you pointed out that there were already a thousand ISPs. The same herd chanted that there would be a big consolidation, ending up with just three or four giant ISPs. In fact, five years later there are over 10,000 local ISPs.

Sorry, Bob — wrong again.

It's pretty obvious why small ISPs survived, and big ones, such as EarthLink, flourished. Handholding, the human element of the Internet, has become essential to people. A basic market need combined with low barriers to entry has given rise to thousands of local ISP businesses, most of which are profitable, solid enterprises. A few, such as EarthLink and MindSpring, achieved scale and grew from local to international businesses. They didn't gobble up the little guys. The little guys flourished right alongside them, in the same way specialized retail boutiques still live a good life on the same block as Wal-Mart.

The reason there are still so many ISPs is the same reason your ISP in Maine, Jason Philbrook at midcoast.com, is still there to help you out. When he agreed to buy you a "lob-sta dinna" in exchange for reading his business plan for a local ISP in Rockport, Maine, he was onto something.

Just as I knew when I started Earthlink, an ISP is more than a mere connection to the Internet. Unlike plain old telephone service, an ISP offers a human relationship, a friendly voice on the other end of the line ready to guide you through this brave new world. Our favorite question to quote from new members at EarthLink is, "Okay, I'm on the Internet; now what do I do?"

So the world didn't end and ISPs multiplied and flourished.

Bob, do me a favor: Now that I'm busy as heck at eCompanies starting another new bunch of businesses, if you get in the mood to make predictions, just ask Jason and me to write them for you. Then you can save us the time spent mollifying our investors, and calming the nerves of terrified Internet users. And, with any luck, we won't have to write any more rebuttals.

Crypto, Privacy and Censorship

Put politicians, telephone company monopolies, and
lawyers in the same room and what do you get? No,
there's no punch line. The joke is inherent in the question. The
feeding frenzy over privacy, security, and freedom of speech
online threatens to create a dizzying tangle of laws, acts and
lobbyist agendas. As always, less is more, and the more the
government can keep its nose and our money out of the
debate, probably the better.

In the columns gathered here, you'll find out why decency and
censorship are not synonymous, why lawyers are like
hammers, and why demonopolization is good and
deregulation isn't.

Our National Information Infrastructure Agenda

October 4, 1993
President Clinton and I have a lot in common. We are Eastern-educated, 47-year-old pale males with families, and both of us have many new and exciting ideas about how to spend my money.

One exciting idea we share is networking our nation, and just released for comment is Clinton's agenda for constructing "an advanced National Information Infrastructure (NII), a seamless web of communication networks, computers, databases, and consumer electronics that will put vast amounts of information at users' fingertips." Amen.

With NII, the agenda begins, people can live anywhere and telecommute. The best schools can be available to all. And services that improve health care and respond to other social needs can be available on-line when and where you need them. Private-sector firms are already deploying NII today, the agenda observes, and so government doesn't have to spend all that much money on NII.

Amen. If only Clinton's NII agenda had ended right there.

But the agenda goes on to say that there are essential roles for government in constructing NII. Among other things, the government should promote private-sector investment through appropriate tax and regulatory policies; ensure security and reliability as well as nationwide access to NII; commit government research to help the private sector develop technologies and applications for NII; provide access to government information, including getting the whole bureaucracy up on e-mail; and turn the federal government into a leading-edge NII technology procurer.

The agenda says Washington needs to provide a little catalytic action to get the Internet to go commercial. What's a little catalytic action? The agenda says $40 million in FY94 for research on NII by (of all people) the Department of Energy. And then $50 million for National Telecommunications and Information Administration (NTIA) grants to demonstrate the application of NII for nonprofits. Maybe it's because I'm a net supplier of money to the Feds, but this looks like a lot of it to me.

But wait, there's more. First, another $600 million for the Defense Advanced Research Projects Agency (DARPA) Technology Reinvestment Project (TRP) to cover many NII proposals. Then, another $1.1 billion for continuing the High-Performance Computing and Communications Initiative. In Washington terms, all told, not much, really, something less than $2 billion per year — a nuclear submarine or two.

I think the agenda tries to reassure taxpayers by quoting Vice President Gore's National Performance Review that "electronic benefits transfer" through NII will save $1 billion over five years just by distributing food stamps electronically. I'm not reassured.

The agenda calls for the establishment of the Information Infrastructure Task Force (IITF), headed by Commerce Secretary Ron Brown and not to be confused with the Internet Engineering Task Force (IETF). The IITF will be guided by the new United States Advisory Council on the National Information Infrastructure (USACNII, I guess), which for some reason will be separate from the High Performance Computing Advisory Committee. USACNII will consist of 25 senior-level individuals representing "business, labor, academia, public interest groups, and state and local governments."

To me, that's a funny list. I'll take a professor or two, but aren't public interest groups just lobbyists, and by labor do they mean the guys who insist on a fireman at every packet switch?

I even have a couple of problems with the business category. First, every time I ask an NII advocate about who "business" or "industry" or "the private sector" is, I get a list of computer and communications companies that would like to sell NII, not buyers of it like you. And, second, to give them proper weight on the list, various industries should be listed separately — manufacturing, aerospace, agriculture, construction, health care, finance, and so on — any one of which is at least as important as the professors and PIGs.

Now, don't be put off by my reactions to Clinton's NII agenda. Keep in mind that I'm now reading Ayn Rand's *Atlas Shrugged* for the sixth time in 30 years.

Get a copy of the NII agenda from, and return comments to the NTIA NII Office, 15th Street and Constitution Ave., Washington, DC 20230.

I'm adamant that you get involved because it is you, dear *InfoWorld* reader, that the NII should serve first, especially if Clinton plans for us to end up with any wealth at all to redistribute, electronically or otherwise.

We Need Decency, Privacy on the Iway — but No Lawyers

March 20, 1995

Reports of a pending Communications Decency Act in the United States Senate got Ed Foster and me cranking up recently to do another of our subscription-canceling column debates. I was preparing to applaud Senate bill S.314 as work by the new Congress on civilizing cyberspace, work long deferred by lily-livered liberals. Ed would be condemning S.314 as an attack on free speech by righteous conservative Republicans. A day later, we learned that S.314 is the brainchild of Sen. James Exon of Nebraska, a Democrat, and that S.314 is identical to provisions of the Telecommunications Reform Act of 1994, killed by Sen. Bob Dole, a Republican.

Ed and I received S.314, thanks to the Internet, and then read it — which was hard because it is written in legalese as a series of edits to the Communications Act of 1934. We both concluded that it really is a bad idea to use fines and prison terms to encourage Iway service providers to read all your personal electronic messages just to be certain they are decent, whatever that means. I bet you agree.

Now, killing Exon's decency bill will not, I hasten to add, leave our Iways decent, whatever that means. In our house, we don't let kids loose with TV remotes, and after seeing some of the stuff flying around the Internet, we shouldn't let them loose with Web browsers, either. Is somebody going to fix this before too many more millions are spent putting schools on the Internet? Rest assured that there is no chance S.314 will pass, especially with the Electronic Frontier Foundation (EFF) and others arguing so strongly against it.

Speaking of EFF, I am sad to report that EFF is now suing the American people — our representatives, anyway — to lift current restrictions on the export of encryption technology. To be more exact, EFF is helping a cryptologist named Daniel Bernstein with his lawsuit against, among others, our Department of State, Arms Control and Disarmament Agency, Department of Defense, Department of Commerce, and National Security Agency, as well as Warren Christopher, William Perry, and Ronald Brown. I'd suggest letting up on Perry — he's the one with F-16s.

The Feds have for some time said that encryption technology is critical to our national security and have therefore restricted its export or disclosure. These restrictions are complicating efforts to bring privacy, authentication, and payment systems into global information infrastructure.

To be clear, I agree with EFF that all remaining restrictions on the export of cryptography should be removed. It's like what is often said about gun control laws: Encryption export restrictions inconvenience everyone but the bad guys.

But I wish EFF had not chosen to sue us.

After years of redirecting tax receipts into legal services and after years of distracting our secretaries of State, Defense, and Commerce, EFF will lose this suit. Substitute "nuclear weapons" for "encryption technology" in this discussion and you'll see why the Feds, even if they must limit speech, should be able to make the kind of restrictions they have for encryption. The restrictions are counterproductive — they hurt exports, they slow the economic development of cyberspace, and the bad guys will encrypt anyway. But, this should be fixed without the undue processes of law — perhaps in the executive branch, perhaps in Congress, but not in courtrooms.

EFF board member John Gilmore disagrees, saying that years have already been wasted trying to get the administration and Congress to eliminate export restrictions. Some restrictions have been relaxed. Despite this, Gilmore says, the State Department and NSA remain firm with the president against Commerce, EFF, and me on this issue.

In defending EFF's new lawsuit, Gilmore says, "We have only one branch of government left before our only alternative is civil disobedience and/or armed revolt." I would add that if we don't get our way with armed revolt, we do have the freedom to hold our breaths in large numbers until we turn blue.

Let's pass a Communications Act of 1995 that uses plain language to break communication monopolies while bringing decency and privacy to the Iways.

Decency Without Censors?

May 1, 1995

I'm sure all the brains on the Iway can work this out: Sen. James Exon's proposed Communications Decency Act is now before Congress, which has the Internet intelligentsia back into its normal mode — apoplectic.

But I dare say Exon has a point. Before many more schools are put on the Internet, something should be done about the foul language and dirty pictures.

Search the newsgroups for various mentions of Exon's bill. You'll find yourself in the boys' locker room at the ACLU.

I ran across one freedom fighter throwing himself down in front of the censorship tank by repeatedly writing Exon after the word (expletive deleted).

Oh, for the good old days when fanatics used to set themselves on fire.

Here on March 20 (see "We need to have decency and privacy on the Iway — but no lawyers"), while arguing against Exon's Senate Bill 314 as then written, I failed to distinguish decency — which Exon and I demand — from censorship, which you and I abhor. As I've had to write since then in answer to many excited responses, decency is being able to turn kids loose on the Internet without previewing their every hyperlink. It's being able to cruise the Internet without pornographic billboards in your face. It's having nonviolent recourse to harassment. It's life, liberty, and the pursuit of happiness.

Censorship, on the other hand, is keeping you from saying whatever you want among consenting adults. It is the American Way to demand a lot of decency and accept very little censorship.

The much-improved S.314 is still an incomprehensible update of the outmoded Communications Act of 1934. (Read it at the Electronic Frontier Foundation [EFF], which still opposes S.314.) Thinking highly of the EFF, I asked what they propose instead of S.314. Turns out that the EFF has thought little about decency beyond stopping Exon. Perhaps EFF thinks that parents can follow their kids around all day, or that porno is good for them. Can't stop there.

So, how can we have Iway decency without censorship? Here's what I suggest. In short, paraphrasing Voltaire, I disapprove of what you say and will defend to the death my right not to listen to it.

First, let's not fall for the argument that in cyberspace we have to derive from scratch all the social structures of the modern world. Let's take the debate about what's obscene on-line and reduce it to a previously unsolved problem — what's obscene in the real world. This is S.314's complicated job. Right away, today's familiar degrees of sex and violence would not be legal on easily accessible Web pages. The equivalent of porno billboards would be prohibited, some magazines would end up on high shelves, explicit sex would be moved out of family viewing hours, and so on. Realistically, pornographers would be somewhat inconvenienced. I would, of course, continue arguing for protection of speech among consenting adults.

Then, while that debate rages, we computer geniuses could have better ideas, develop standards, and write software to make it easier for Iway travelers not to find what they don't want. For example, let's have browsing software for kids that allows hard-wired hyperlinks and lists of domains to which subsequent hyperlinks will be allowed or blocked.

After that, let's return to the law and put in those very few principles needed to enable our better software. For example — and I'm sure the EFF could improve on this — we might insist that hyperlinks be encoded with something like parental guidance ratings. Iway travelers might need the encryption-based equivalent of driver's licenses to go certain places in cyberspace. For instance, maybe you should have to be carded to enter sadomasochistic chat rooms.

Stepping back, I must say that S.314 is not nearly the most important issue in Washington's ongoing rewrite of the Communications Act of 1934. Especially if you are fanatical about speech, you should want competition in communications.

Internauts are not yet appropriately apoplectic about how special interests are preserving much of the regulation now enforced by bureaucrats and their helpful lobbyists in Washington. Why are we not watching gavel-to-gavel coverage of hearings on telecom deregulation, including S.314?

`Godless Far Left' Takes Correct Stand on Decency, Encryption

April 15, 1996

The sixth conference on Computers, Freedom, and Privacy (CFP96) brought together 400 people ardently debating the implications of the Internet for freedom of expression and personal privacy. It's just not fair to say that all of us attending CFP96 last month were Luddites, socialists, anarchists, cyberpunks, terrorists, child pornographers, and lawyers. Actually, a few of us weren't lawyers.

Now, some of my best friends are lawyers, and I can tell you that lawyers are just exactly like guns. There are way too many of them. They do a lot of damage. The Constitution protects our right to have them. And until you need one, they are best kept, like F. Lee Bailey, locked up.

Lawyers are also like hammers, but I'll come back to that later.

Issues discussed at CFP96 included cryptography for confidentiality and authentication, crime and law in cyberspace, falsifying electronic evidence, global freedom and privacy, limiting on-line speech, copyright and freedom of expression, electronic money, criminalization of unauthorized encryption, controlling controversial content, and liability issues for system administrators.

Much to the credit of its organizers, led by MIT Professor Hal Abelson, who is not a lawyer, CFP96 sessions were wonderfully put together, with admirable ideological balance, admirable at least for a conference in Cambridge, Massachusetts.

The grossly outnumbered were people who took seriously their responsibility — despite hissing, heckling, and hectoring — to achieve balance among more than just one constitutional amendment at a time.

No surprise, the big issue at CFP96 was the Communications Decency Act (CDA), passed with the new Telecommunications Act of 1996. CDA criminalizes the knowing transmission of indecent materials to minors. The issues have to do with what is meant by words like knowing, transmission, indecent, materials, and minors. For some reason, all these words have entirely new meanings on the Internet — hence the Gold Rush in what they call CyberLaw.

The general feeling at CFP96 was that the CDA should be struck down by the Supreme Court. The CDA would inconvenience adults in the exercise of First Amendment rights. The CDA would fail to control our wonderfully uncontrollable international Internet. The word "indecency" is poorly understood in law and could easily turn out too broad, especially if in November the wrong people win, namely "religious far right Republicans." Holding my nose, I found myself agreeing in the end with "godless far left Democrats" that the CDA needs at least some debugging.

The other big issue at CFP96 was the effort to decriminalize unauthorized encryption. Some law enforcement and national security officers want to restrict strong encryption so that they can continue to wiretap bad guys (and gals).

The general feeling at CFP96 was that criminalizing encryption violates privacy rights and wouldn't work anyway — the technology is already out of the bag. In the end, I found myself agreeing that when it comes to encryption — and a lot of other things — our various governments should just leave us all alone.

Not leaving us alone have been a growing number of Beltway lobbyists falling all over themselves to fashion the Internet according to the ideologies of whoever will pay the piper. Now, as announced at CFP96, the Internet also has its own bicameral, bipartisan Congressional caucus. I urge you to get involved. No matter what you think about lawyers and guns, the first principle of winning a gunfight is, have a gun.

Lawyers, especially civil liberties lawyers, are also like hammers. To them, every problem, even the Telecommunications Act of 1996, is a nail. Truth be known, the CDA is mostly a distraction from bigger problems in the Telecommunications Act, bigger problems that also threaten our civil liberties.

This Telecommunications Act, made by telco lobbyists while the Internet was in a black-and-blue snit over the CDA, is not increasing competition in local telecommunications like it was supposed to. The ink isn't even dry and the huge local telco monopolies are already rushing to buy up their competition — cable companies and one another.

Next year, we'll need the Telecommunications Demonopolization Act of 1997. This year, our only hope is our Justice Department antitrust chief Anne Bingaman, who is out hiring 50 more lawyers. Annie, get your gun!

Be a Cryptomaniac on the Internet and Help Set Long-Overdue Standards

June 24, 1996

Everything on the Internet should be strongly encrypted all the time. Everything, strongly encrypted, all the time. Now we do have this debate raging between those defending privacy on the Internet and those with responsibilities in law enforcement and national security. Our FBI and National Security Agency want to continue listening in on the electronic communications of criminals and terrorists. So, they've been restricting the use and export of encryption technologies.

Well, on the one hand, I think of my FBI and NSA as being made up of good guys wearing white hats, enforcing laws, defending national security, protecting my family and property. But, on the other hand, I abhor monopolies, especially governments run amok, as they are wont to do. I know from long experience how monopolies grow toward complacency, incompetence, and eventually corruption and coercion, especially when they have M-16s at their disposal.

In the case of encryption, I finesse my ambivalence by accepting the fact that the crypto is out of the bag. A major report has just been issued by the National Research Council saying what's long been obvious, that encryption should be unrestricted because it is needed by private citizens and businesses to defend themselves against criminals and terrorists.

If the arguments for decontrolling crypto sound to you like those for decontrolling guns, you've been paying attention. Crypto export is now restricted under, yes, munitions control laws. Forgive this paraphrase of our much-maligned Second Amendment, but what most of us are now saying is, Being necessary to the security of a free State, the right of the people to keep and bear crypto shall not be infringed.

Legislation is now pending — the Promotion of Commerce On-Line in the Digital Era (Pro-CODE) Act of 1996 (S.1726) — that would eliminate federal crypto regulation. This bill would go as far as preventing the feds from setting standards in encryption.

The "fight to free crypto" is about to be won, which is great, except, get this, federal regulation of cryptography has not been the main reason we don't use it on the Internet.

In 1973, I sounded an early, and perhaps the first, warning about the Internet's lack of security. Ever since, we've had our heads wedged on Internet security, feds or no feds.

Security, until now, has neither been interesting enough to Internet developers nor worth the trouble to Internet users. There are no standards. Encrypting is inconvenient, especially when you count distributing keys. Crypto slows things down and is expensive. And nothing that we've sent so far over the Internet has been so valuable as to justify all that inconvenience and cost.

Although there's no shortage of crypto products for protecting the privacy and establishing the authenticity of Internet communications, hardly any of us uses them, not even those freely available over the Internet, such as Pretty Good Privacy. Heck, we aren't even careful in our use of passwords.

Using strong encryption in all Internet products all the time will force the overdue emergence of standards. We need finally to work out some crypto standards — without or with (contrary to Pro-CODE) the help of the National Institute of Standards and Technology.

Using strong encryption all the time will lead to its perfection, lowering cost while increasing performance. Using encryption on everything all the time will drive the underlying mechanisms out of sight, saving us from the "implementation-independent" add-on kludges that make encryption so intolerably hard to use today.

Using strong standard encryption routinely on all our Internet communications will save us from underestimating our security risks. And using crypto all the time will make it much harder for anyone to find, let alone read or tamper with, those few communications that actually require strong encryption.

For a long list of cryptographic products, see a survey maintained by Trusted Information Systems Inc., in Glenwood, Md. Become a cryptomaniac today.

Don't Let the Name Fool You: Beware the Internet Protection Act of 1997

August 25, 1997

IPA97 was filed on July 31 to "ensure that the development of the Internet and interactive computer services is unfettered by Federal and State regulation." The House immediately referred IPA97 to its Commerce Committee, and Congress adjourned the next day.

Next week, Congress comes back from summer vacation to consider yet another proposed Internet law, H.R. 2372. Because laws often seem to accomplish the opposite of what their names imply, I'm worried about the name Congress has given this one: the Internet Protection Act of 1997 (IPA97). I'm also worried because two staff members at our Federal Communications Commission sought me out recently at the National Press Club, in Washington, to call my attention to IPA97. And I'm worried because they asked not to be identified.

Introducing IPA97 in the House was Rick White, a Republican representing Washington State's Microsoft District. White was joined by five co-sponsors, including "Your Cajun Ambassador to Congress," Billy Tauzin. Tauzin chairs the House Commerce Subcommittee on Telecommunications, Trade, and Consumer Protection, on which White serves.

White also leads the Congressional Internet Caucus. In March, he filed the Internet Tax Freedom Act (H.R. 1054) which got various hearings and referrals but was not passed. So maybe there's nothing to worry about. On the other hand, White is from what might also be called Washington State's US West District.

Now, it's hard to read acts of Congress, which suit their authors and other lawyers, but I think this one, as now written, would set U.S. telecommunications regulatory policy in favor of private initiatives over government regulation. It would reserve such regulation to Congress, not letting the FCC and our 51 state public utilities commissions (PUCs) set rates, services, and technical specifications for Internet access, software, and services. Not a bad start.

The FCC and PUCs would be allowed to prohibit subsidization of Internet services from telephone revenues and to prohibit favoritism by telephone monopolies toward affiliated Internet services. The FCC would be allowed to establish rules that protect national security, law enforcement, and network reliability, which is an exception large enough to drive a government agency through.

For example, when the Internet suffers that gigalapse I've predicted, the FCC could step in to regulate Internet service providers.

IPA97 goes on to offer something really wild that it calls "deregulatory leverage." If an Internet service begins to compete with a regulated telopoly service, then that regulated service would be deregulated. This would be really interesting in the case of Internet telephony.

My major worry about IPA97 is that it might make the same mistake as the Telecommunications Act of 1996, which pushes for the deregulation of telopolies when it's demonopolization that we need. The only thing worse than a few, big regulated telopolies is fewer, bigger unregulated telopolies.

Another worry about IPA97 is that it may be playing right into the hands of the telopolies. Telopolies favor shifting regulatory authority from the FCC to the 51 PUCs, each of which will tend to side with the telopolies against small competitors that can't afford big campaign contributions and against large long-distance companies that generally are from out-of-state.

Another worry about IPA97 is that it talks about Internet services as if they are separate from telephony. In fact, a large fraction of today's Internet costs are paid by ISPs to the telopolies, which enjoy no competition and are already ripping off Internet users by factors approaching 10.

Now, I don't suppose it's a coincidence that on Sept. 18 the United States Telephone Association (USTA), which I vilified here two weeks ago, will be holding a luncheon discussion at the National Press Club about whether to regulate the Internet.

The USTA's announcement begins by reporting how the Internet is stressing telephone networks and then asks whether the Internet should remain "a government-free zone." No secret which way the $100 billion USTA is leaning. We Internet enthusiasts should show up at the USTA's luncheon after reading IPA97 on the Web. We certainly don't want the USTA to have too much say about how IPA97 gets rewritten in the coming months.

TRUSTe Uses Consents and Disclosures to Protect Privacy on the Internet

November 10, 1997

Life is easy for people who have just one bete noire and a trusty silver bullet.

There are, for example, people whose bete noire is censorship and whose silver bullet is the First Amendment. For others, the Second Amendment is a silver bullet — no pun intended. And there are many whose life is all about this week's subject — privacy — as if nothing else matters.

Problem is that privacy conflicts with other important rights, such as freedom of speech. This conflict is prominent in the sad story of Princess Diana and, closer to home, in the proliferation of "spam" — unwanted e-mail on the Internet.

Many of you report what I'm experiencing: Half my e-mail is spam, jubilantly exercising its freedom of speech. And it's not a good omen that much of the spam I'm getting touts new spamming services.

Many Internet users are upset about spam and want something done. I fear we will rush to legislate spam away and end up with defective law such as the overturned Communications Decency Act.

Last week, Esther Dyson and Susan Scott invited a bunch of us to discuss privacy over lunch in Boston. Dyson writes the Release 1.0 newsletter and is my second-favorite technology pundit; Scott is executive director of TRUSTe.

TRUSTe, formerly eTRUST, is a nonprofit initiative to establish trust in electronic communications by creating infrastructure for online privacy. TRUSTe was formed by the Electronic Frontier Foundation, which Dyson chairs, and CommerceNet.

TRUSTe is focused on publisher disclosure and consumer consent through "trust marks." Seeing the TRUSTe mark assures consumers that a Web site discloses and stands behind its policies on what personal information it collects and how that information is used. Click on the mark at TRUSTe's Web site to see a sample of such a disclosure.

To display the TRUSTe mark, sites negotiate a disclosure statement with TRUSTe and pay a fee of between $500 and $5,000. When Web visitors click on the mark, it displays the site's particular privacy policies.

TRUSTe is new, and its first mark assures only disclosure. A site can use the current mark to disclose perfectly putrid privacy policies.

Representatives of the World Wide Web Consortium (W3C) at MIT were also at Dyson's lunch; W3C has a Platform for Privacy Preferences Project (P3P), which is working to automate checking of your preferences on privacy policies against those disclosed by the sites you visit. With P3P you could, for example, be warned by your browser if you happen upon a site that collects e-mail addresses for promotions.

The difficulty in all this is that privacy and freedom of speech must be balanced carefully. This raises hell from people for whom privacy or freedom of speech is their silver bullet. Let the flaming begin.

What is spam? If you send a bunch of e-mails, they're probably protected speech. But if someone else does, it's definitely spam.

I get spam from nice people who think it's not spam because they're nonprofit organizations. I get spam from nice people who think it's fine to put me on their Christmas lists or invite me to their parties. I get spam from nice people who think that if they are only e-mailing me, it's not spam, because spam is only sent in bulk. And I get spam from slime balls who don't mind wasting my time in finding a few prospects for highly questionable products.

At the TRUSTe lunch, Dyson gave us copies of her new book *Release 2.0: a Design for Living in the Digital Age*. I recommend the book, which touches on TRUSTe. But hey, was Dyson spamming us with her book at lunch?

Anonymity is big among privacy paranoids, who want anonymity protected at all costs. On the other hand, much spam comes with fake return addresses, making it nearly impossible for a recipient to get off an undesired list.

Anonymity is low-grade privacy and should be avoided. E-mails without valid return addresses should be marked so I can filter them automatically. This would be progress on the spam front.

Now, my silver bullet for the bete noire of Internet mail — spam — is e-postage. (See "Internet groupies blast my mailbox, but I still say e-postage is a good thing," Feb. 17.) If a little e-postage were paid for each copy of e-mail, spam would drop to tolerable levels.

Freedom of speech should be protected, but free speech is a nuisance.

The view through the rear-view mirror

Rebuttal by John Perry Barlow

John Perry Barlow is the co-founder of the Electronic Frontier Foundation, an organization that promotes freedom of expression in digital media. He currently serves as Vice-Chairman of the EFF, Mr. Barlow is a retired Wyoming cattle rancher and a former lyricist for the Grateful Dead. He has been a contributing writer for Wired, and his articles, such as "Declaration of Independence of Cyberspace," have earned him the title of "the Thomas Jefferson of Cyberspace" from Yahoo! Internet Life Magazine.

Rebuttal: Our national information infrastructure agenda

The view through the rear-view mirror is always interesting, especially when it's a kind of rear-view telescope that can see all the way back to 1993.

Of course, a lot has changed since then. Most of the bold administration initiatives Bob was fulminating against have fallen on the ash heap of Grandiose Stupidity, and appropriately so.

Instead, Al Gore, the self-proclaimed Father of the Internet, has spent his time on initiatives that would have killed the Internet if the Net was not so resilient and he was not so incompetent.

Instead of building the Information Superhighway — a term used by no one today but the impossibly clueless — Gore and his administration have devoted their time, energy, and money to stopping privacy and commerce online through their battle against crypto imposing censorship by supporting the Communications Decency Act all the way to the Supreme Court restricting expression to all but the large institutions that claim to "own" most of the Internet with a series of hideous copyright laws that mainly serve to perpetuate the distribution dinosaurs in publishing and other media.

The administration's actual contributions to The Great Work, whether by funding or policy, have been modest indeed. They have supported the National Computational Science Alliance, but only in the tens of millions. They have failed to actually deregulate telephony. They have invested much energy into lopping off the arms of the doomed Microsoft octopus — but so what? The Net has continued to grow like kudzu — and on its own — in spite of their best efforts to turn it into a huge government project.

Probably the only thing the administration has accomplished is the thing Bob feared most. They have placed a great deal of control in the hands of Internet stakeholders, by which they mean private commercial institutions, wresting that control from ordinary netizens.

And they still don't quite understand that the Internet is a global, rather than an American, undertaking.

Rebuttal: We need decency, privacy on the Iway — but no lawyers

I'm pretty sure that Bob Metcalfe doesn't take drugs, which leaves me without an explanation for this column. It is a marvel of self-contradiction.

For starters, it is rife with defamatory snideness toward the Electronic Frontier Foundation, an organization whose goals he supports. He even accuses us of suing him, along with all other Americans, in our support of the fairly obvious proposition that an encryption algorithm is a form of expression.

This view, by the way, has so far prevailed in court. In December of 1997, despite Bob's certainty of its futility, our suit on behalf of Mr. Bernstein won in the 9th Circuit Court of Appeals. Since then, the government has all but conceded by its failure to appeal.

Further, it is widely believed that the court's relaxation of restrictions on crypto had much to do with this victory. In other words, we achieved many of Bob's goals, even though we did so by means he found odious. (We have yet to receive a thank-you note from him.)

I also must point out that we were suing the United States Government. I'm baffled that anyone as intelligent as Bob still equates our government with the people of America. He must be the only one left.

As it happens, we have turned to the courts solely because the judiciary is the only branch of government that has shown a general willingness to understand technology and resist public hysteria.

Thus, as Bob predicted, Congress did pass the odious Communications "Decency" Act by a wide margin — though his prediction gave us far too much credit in claiming it might do so because of our opposition. Later, when we took it to the Supreme Court, it was squashed nine to zip. Even under the leadership of my favorite oxymoron, Justice Rehnquist, reason prevailed.

Perhaps the most astonishing assertion of this column is Bob's remarkable equation of cryptography with nuclear weapons. Given the choice between being threatened by a nuclear weapon or a malefactor armed with strong encryption, I'd take the latter every time.

Rebuttal: Decency without censors?

This one was a real howler at the time. It's even funnier now.

The most darkly amusing irony here is that the EFF did decide to create something like Bob's suggested digital smut-screens. We promoted the creation of the PICS standard, hoping that such a tool might resist governmental censorship by restoring parental control over what children could view on-line. Since then, PICS has shown itself remarkably effective in endowing such parents as the governments of China, Singapore, and many of our united states with the power to censor what adults, as well as children, can have access to.

Of course, these Big Daddies have not simply restricted access to the sort of thing Bob abhors. Because PICS was designed to enable highly adaptable filtration, most of the filters that have been created for it blank not only pornography, but also anything those in authority find threatening. The new PICS-enabled Great Wall of China restricts access to such

Continued

(continued)

offensive sites as CNN. Further, most of the filters that are sold to American parents, such as Net Nanny, not only block pornography sites — generally inefficiently, because these sites proliferate faster than the filters can add them — but they block such smut zones as the ACLU, the National Organization for Women, and, of course, EFF.

The fact is that Bob is wrong in suggesting that the only way to prevent children from viewing pornography is to place them under constant surveillance. There is another method that is far more effective, efficient, and responsible. The best way for parents to keep their children away from pornography is for them to shoulder their parental duties and to teach their kids to find pornography as detestable as they do.

As to the provisions of the Telecommunications Reform Act (into which the CDA was embedded) that would have increased competition in telecom, those provisions are still intact, and almost entirely unenforced.

In other words, Bob got what he wanted — and then didn't. Be careful what you wish for.

Rebuttal: `Godless far left' takes correct stand on decency, encryption

At last, Bob has written a column with which I can agree (almost) wholeheartedly. That is probably because it seems to be written in one voice. Inner Bob, The Suit, has started to exhaust himself with the exertion required to be consistently wrong.

It is certainly true that it would be better for commerce, security, privacy, and just about everyone but the ironically named Mr. Freeh if encryption were the standard instead of the exception in Internet traffic.

If encryption were the standard, far fewer traditional organizations would waste the billions they spend on private networks and firewalls. Far fewer individuals would be wary of putting their credit cards online. It would be a Good Thing. But it's not going to happen for a while.

Two problems remain.

First, the U.S. Government, while relaxing its opposition to strong crypto somewhat, has not given up altogether. In fact, the Pro-CODE legislation, which Bob was sure would pass did not, largely as a result of Administration opposition. Also, there is the adoption of the recent Wassenaur Agreement. This privately negotiated agreement bound most industrial powers to restrict the use of strong cryptography. It was, most agree, the direct result of bullying by the most paranoid entities of our government: the NSA and the FBI. As long as this agreement stands, and as long as these forces continue to hold the White House hostage, it's highly unlikely that the encrypted Internet Bob and I long for will ever exist.

The second problem is the messy method the Internet Engineering Task Force (IETF) uses to adopt standards. Even such politically uncontroversial problems as expanding the address space of the Internet can result in years of wrangling by the members of the IETF. Imagine the prolonged donnybrook that would have to precede the adoption of an

Internet-wide crypto standard, especially given the "long list of cryptographic products" Bob mentions that would be vying for the honor of ubiquity.

For once, I'd say Bob is being more idealistic than I am. And that's saying something.

Rebuttal: Don't let the name fool you: Beware the Internet Protection Act of 1997

Indeed, there was good reason to be somewhat concerned about the Internet Protection Act of 1997, only bits of which actually passed. As originally written, it would have given the telcos a lot of freedom to prey upon their smaller, weaker competitors.

But of course, just as Bob was wrong about the coming "Internet gigalapse," he also failed to see the emergence of two fearsome new creatures in the paleolithic Internet jungle: The Cable Internet Provider, such as Time-Warner, and the Telco Internet Provider, such as MCIWorldCom. These creatures are quite frightening and monopolistic in their behavior. And they are kicking the bejesus out of the dopey old telcos.

But so far, even in the absence of something such as the Internet Protection Act, the government has made no effort to regulate Cable and Telco Internet Providers.

Probably because it doesn't know how.

I think it's unlikely that the government will learn. That's because commerce is naturally smarter, quicker, and more adaptable than government. And we live in times when it's very good to be smarter, quicker, and more adaptable.

Still, I'm not terribly concerned. Just as we once worried about living in a world controlled by an IBM that seemed immune to governmental regulation, we are probably shortsighted in worrying about a world ruled by Time-Warner, AT&T, and MCIWorldCom.

Instead, we are living in a world where power can shift very rapidly, and nothing lasts very long. For the foreseeable future, the greatest regulatory force will be the sudden emergence of new technologies and entities that unseat the existing monopolies. At least that's where my faith resides, at present.

Rebuttal: TRUSTe uses consents and disclosures to protect privacy on the Internet

Of course, Bob is right in his assertion that there are neither simple problems nor easy answers to them. He asserts this even as he is wrong in proposing what he imagines to be an easy answer toward the end of this column: e-postage. (Who would collect this postage? By what authority? What would become of the vast wealth generated from it?)

For years, I have wrestled with the necessary tensions between the need to let information flow freely and the need to restrict some of that flow in the interest of privacy.

Continued

(continued)

After long, hard thought, I still don't have a perfect solution (although I am enough the advocate of free speech that I oppose restrictions on spam, despite my loathing for it. Besides, I am a spammer myself. I regularly dispatch electronic outbursts to about 900 friends, of which Bob is one. I've never heard a complaint from him, nor any of the rest of them.)

Therein lies the problem. One man's spam is another's preferred way of getting information. Like practically everything else having to do with information, value is deeply subjective. Regulation is almost always sweepingly general and, indeed, regulators pride themselves in being scrupulously impersonal.

When EFF proposed TRUSTe, we imagined that it would provide a kind of *Good Housekeeping* Seal of Privacy that requires only full disclosure of an institution's privacy practices. We thought we were creating a kind of natural, market-based regulation. Now, I'm not so sure. Increasingly, it appears quite easy to disguise malignant practices behind bland statements of policy. Furthermore, few consumers seem to pay much attention to these statements.

As is often the case, I think that spam directed towards me is a problem I must address, rather than hoping that someone else will do it for me. This is actually not so difficult, and though it requires an effort I'd rather not expend, doing it myself is preferable to having someone else do it for me.

My e-mail software permits me to filter incoming e-mail. It turns out that there are not that many telltale signs of spam (such as the appearance of "!!!" or "$$$" or "(<number string>)" or phrases like "accept credit cards," "E-Mail Advertising," "Find out anything about anyone," and so on). After examining a lot of spam, I set up a filter that looks for these few signs and consigns their accompanying messages to the bit-void.

It was a nuisance preparing this filter, but freedom of expression, and the ability to receive the spam I welcome, is certainly worth going to a little trouble.

The Billings Client-Server Patent and Undue Processes of Law

I f you've ever read my columns (and if you've gotten this far in this book you've read quite a few) you know I have the most sacred respect for lawyers, and in fact our entire adorable legal system. The Billings suit, in which a fellow named Billings accused Novell and Bank of America of infringing his patent for . . . well, basically the whole of client-server technology, is a marvelous example of that legal system at its finest. Throw in our U.S. Patent system and its complete ignorance of the world of software and you have a real bureaucratic waste of time and money.

The lawsuit immortalized in these articles started in the early '90s and still isn't over. Only the U.S. legal system could keep my seven-year-old articles as in vogue as the day they were written!

The Undue Process of Billings versus Novell

March 22, 1993

To the best of my recollection, your honor, I got the call from an attorney in Los Angeles recruiting me to be a paid expert witness in 1991. His client, the American Academy of Science, said I am world renowned in distributed data processing and just right for its lawsuit. He added that the Academy of Science — not the big one in Washington, but the other one, in Missouri — was suing Novell Inc., my former arch competitor, and wouldn't I really want to testify? After I turned him down twice, the attorney threatened that I could be subpoenaed. I said bye, hung up, and had my phone disinfected.

On the afternoon of December 14, 1992, I took a call at InfoWorld from a Leonard Holahan of American Energy Research, in London. Holahan was calling on behalf of a colleague in hydrogen energy research, a Dr. Roger E. Billings. Holahan wanted to direct my attention to the plight of Dr. Billings, who was being forced to sue Novell for infringing one of his many patents.

Holahan said *InfoWorld* should cover this lawsuit as other notable newspapers had. I said we focus on PC products and a hydrogen lawsuit seemed a bit off our beat. Holahan persisted, saying that other computer publications had courageously picked up this story, despite the fact that Novell is a large advertiser — as it surely is, he reminded me, in *InfoWorld*.

Holahan faxed me press clippings in which many people expressed concern that Novell's NetWare infringes on the Billings patent — U.S. Patent 4,714,989.

Billings has generously donated this patent to the not-for-profit American Academy of Science, which is seeking 8 percent of Novell's NetWare revenues and damages, more than $600 million. It turns out, Billings admits, that he retains a 45 percent financial interest in the donated patent, which multiplication will reveal is no small change.

Holahan, who has not responded to questions about his financial interest in the Billings patent, faxed more clippings when Novell announced its planned acquisition of USL in January. I also have copies of letters written by Billings himself to journalists asserting that Novell stole his ideas and that thereafter a "powerful unknown financial entity" had driven his company to close.

Intrigued, I asked Holahan for a copy of the Billings patent. Somehow, only a small piece of the front page appeared, though none of the other materials got hung up on the fax. Smelling a rat, your honor, I got a complete copy myself.

The Billings patent, "Functionally Structured Distributed Data Processing System," was originally filed in 1982, abandoned twice, refiled in 1986, and finally issued in

December 1987. The inventor is the same Billings who is now president and chairman of the International Academy of Science, which is also in Missouri.

This is what Billings claims he invented: "a plurality of independently operating user station processors for servicing users, a data center for storing data to be processed by the user stations, and a communication network for coupling each user station to one or more data centers. The data center includes its own processor and mass storage devices for managing a database of data for the user stations." In short, Billings claims to have invented what most of us now call client/server computing.

Being a world-renowned expert in this field, I assure you that Novell — not to mention almost every other computing company — would infringe the Billings patent if it were valid. And I am willing to testify that it most assuredly is not.

Your honor, if Billings did think up distributed database systems independently in 1982, which I doubt, then it was after phenomenal bad luck in not seeing a huge body of freely available scientific and product literature — "prior art" — that reaches back to the 1960s. It took me 10 minutes on the phone with the library to find such prior art. So why didn't the U.S. Patent and Trademark Office find prior art?

Billings says he is familiar with the paper I found, "Separating Data from Function in a Distributed File System," by Israel, Mitchell, and Sturgis (CSL report 78-5, Xerox Palo Alto Research Center), published five years before the earliest Billings patent filing. But he says it is not related to his patent. I'd say he is looking through $200 million glasses.

In closing, your honor, we have again caught our legal system in the act.

Lawyers routinely exploit the undue processes of law to pick deep pockets, and there is no justice in that.

If you happen to have any prior art on user stations accessing data on a server, let me know so I will be ready with a truckload if asked to testify in Billings vs. Novell. I'd gladly do it for free.

Billings Must Be Stopped, and You Can Help

April 26, 1993

If Dr. Roger Billings wins, settles, or even loses his patent infringement lawsuit against Novell, he may be after you next. But don't worry, I've got a plan.

Recall my column some weeks ago about Billings, head of the International Academy of Science (in Missouri), who has a patent that claims he invented network file service — if not all of client/server computing — in 1982. To repeat my unpaid expert opinion, the Billings patent, No. 4,714,989, "Functionally Structured Distributed Data Processing System," is grossly invalid. File service was old hat in, yes, 1972.

InfoWorld readers have sent me a stack of references to file service products from Datapoint, Nestar, and Convergent Technologies, and to academic papers on many variations of file service dating back into the early 1970s. The earliest so far is from Professor David J. Farber, now at the University of Pennsylvania, who sent "The structure of a distributed computer system — the distributed file system," published in the 1972 proceedings of the International Conference on Computer Communications.

(No, Dr. Billings, I will not fax it to you.) I've heard from lawyers in Texas defending California's Bank of America, the second defendant named in the Billings lawsuit. They sent me a list of BofA's many NetWare networks, for which Billings hopes to collect royalties. So you probably don't have to worry right away about being sued by Billings, as he seems now to only be going after one carefully chosen user of NetWare in one carefully chosen state.

Sorry, but knowing this, and after meanderings like the following, I now believe that Billings is just jerking me around. For example, on the phone to my research assistant Anne Ryder, Billings said he is familiar with the 1978 Xerox paper that I say is prior art (beating his patent filing by three years), and he fully discounts it. But then, in a following fax, he said he has not seen the Xerox paper and asked me to fax him a copy. If it discloses his invention, he says, "I will immediately drop the lawsuit against Novell and the Bank of America with a long letter of apology to Ray Noorda."

As if I were Billings' private research and fax-back service, I sent him the Xerox paper — which he might easily have found in 1982. He has since called to say the paper (surprise!) has nothing to do with his patent.

I faxed Billings eight other references to prior art, which he has thus far not responded to in writing. He is now calling me and, because I refuse to talk with him, is upset — which has now become my major reason for not talking with him.

Billings vs. Novell might get to a California jury in 1994. If the jury doesn't like BofA or companies from Utah, it could decide that Billings invented file service and award the large sum Billings is seeking. It's unlikely, but that would be the end of life as we know it.

Or, after lots of expert testimony like mine, the jury could confirm that the patent is invalid and that Novell infringed nothing. Yes! But what if the jury sees things less clearly and says that Novell did not infringe Billings' patent, which it interprets as covering database management systems instead of file service systems? This verdict would be terrible because then Billings could easily turn on Apple, IBM, Informix, Microsoft, Oracle, Sun, Sybase, and all their customers.

My real fear, and one you should share, is that the suit will not go to trial.

Instead, I fear that Novell will make the business decision to settle with Billings, paying him some millions rather than continue to fund its defense and risk an unfavorable jury verdict.

This would give Billings a war chest with which to launch a legal campaign to collect hundreds of millions of dollars in license fees from the rest of you.

Please, Mr. Noorda, stand your ground — millions for defense but not a penny for tribute!

All this trouble started when the U.S. Patent and Trademark Office wrongly issued the Billings patent in 1987, five years after the application was filed.

Turns out, there is a way to ask the Patent Office to reconsider. Novell's lawyers know about this but are not pursuing it. They tell me that anyone can, after paying a fee, submit previously undiscovered prior art to get a patent invalidated. The file on the Billings patent is reportedly thin — the departed examiner, perhaps waiting for me to fax it to him, found little prior art.

Now, will all of you stand by while poor little old me and the good Professor Farber collect the prior art, put up $1,000, and go off to Washington? Or, can we get help from some major U.S. corporations (and their patent counsel), which have much more at stake? You know who you are and how to contact me.

B of A Caves in to Billings NetWare Extortion

October 25, 1993

The Bank of America, threatened with the sudden loss of 150 NetWare-based banking systems, just paid $125,000 to Roger Billings, holder of a bogus 1987 patent on what he lately calls network file service. Now it's clear how Billings plans to extort his claimed $3.5 billion in royalties.

You can hope the Billings patent will soon be invalidated, but given our self-servingly dilatory court system, don't hold your breath. In the meantime, Billings intends to pick off network systems suppliers and their users one by one. You may be next. Lawyers advise that you should all let Novell handle this matter and stay out of it. But I urge you to reject this advice — which will in the long term only enrich the lawyers — and unite now against Billings.

I warned about Billings' lawsuit against Novell and BofA here on March 22, April 26, and May 31. After that last column, Billings visited me and explained, in his undeniably charming way, how disappointed he is that I, of all people, am arguing that a legitimate inventor should not profit from his work.

I counter, in my undeniably charming way, how outraged I am to hear him claim that in 1982 he invented distributed file systems. Most of them were invented in the 1970s.

Shortly after Billings visited us here at InfoWorld, Anne Ryder in my office received a call from a man who said he had been approached about an investment in the Billings lawsuit. He was told that I had changed my expert opinion about the Billings patent being grossly invalid. No. The patent was twice correctly rejected and then wrongly issued by our litigation-generating Patent and Trademark Office, which miraculously failed to find the mountains of prior art that Billings somehow failed to submit.

I once planned to submit prior art to the PTO and ask that the Billings patent be invalidated. Billings even taunted me with a check for $1,000 to pay the fees required by the PTO for help in doing the job it should have done in the first place. Lawyers have repeatedly advised me against this tactic.

Anyway, as BofA counsel tells it, Billings first claimed that 1,500 bank systems infringed his bogus patent. After court arguments, he narrowed his claim to 150 infringing systems and he offered a secret settlement for $150,000. BofA countered with an offer of $125,000 with no admission of infringement and no secrets. Billings accepted. BofA found $125,000 a low price to pay to end the nuisance of continuing litigation — and for peace of mind.

Last spring I was reassured that Novell had indemnified BofA, as it would any NetWare user, against infringement of the Billings patent.

Apparently, now this indemnification is insufficient. The peace of mind that BofA sought was from the threat that if the Billings patent were upheld, a court injunction could force BofA to suddenly stop using its network systems. Gulp.

Billings plans to pursue users of products that infringe his patent.

Anyone may obtain a voluntary license.

Of course, Novell and NetWare users are not the only ones whom Billings threatens. Those now letting Novell carry the water on this lawsuit should note that Billings intends to pursue licenses with other suppliers of network operating systems, network database management systems, network applications software, and file servers.

Billings wrote me with the extortionate phrasing that got to the bank's lawyers. "Some may choose not to purchase a license, which would put us in a position of having to seek legal remedies. Licenses which require legal action will be priced higher.... If we are forced to proceed all the way through trial, we will have no choice but not to grant a license at all."

How will Novell now strengthen its indemnification so that other NetWare users will not find themselves vulnerable to extortion when Billings turns on them? In what form might Novell get help from other distributed file and database system suppliers so that it will not find itself eventually alone also having to cave in to Billings? I'm one of the few people left who is not a lawyer, but I suggest that what's needed here is some sort of class action lawsuit against Billings seeking declarative relief.

Washington Grinds Down New Patent Chief

May 9, 1994

Bruce Lehman is Commissioner of our U.S. Patent & Trademark Office (PTO). In December, he ordered an unprecedented reexamination of the infamous Compton's multimedia patent. When Lehman opened the reexamination to "prior art" from third parties, his PTO discovered belatedly that there really was quite a lot of work done on multimedia prior to Compton's patent filing in 1989. So then, much to the disappointment on all sides of lawyers itching to litigate their kids through college, patent examiners rejected Compton's 41 ridiculous claims. Thank you, Commissioner Lehman, my hero.

After January hearings in Silicon Valley on software patents, Lehman said he planned to clean up the "indefensible mess." He talked about granting patent monopolies from dates of filing instead of from abusively delayed dates of issuance. He talked about opening up the currently closed reexamination process. And he talked about inviting opposition to patents out of court by publicizing applications before issuance — with "high likelihood" by year's end. So, I called Lehman to ask him to reject my favorite bogus patent.

Novell is still in court defending against the man whose 1987 software patent — U.S. Patent 4,714,989 — says he is entitled to hundreds of millions of dollars of royalties on file service, client/server computing, and/or, in the words of his bogus patent, networked data centers. This despite the 400 items of prior art Novell has collected — items that have yet to be considered by PTO examiners. The lawsuit grinds expensively toward a trial in September at which opposing paid expert witnesses will duel, not at the PTO, but in front of a jury of our nonexpert peers.

Lehman's Washington office took my call and, at the appointed hour, I was shocked to be put right through to him. He was impressively forthcoming with direct answers to my hardest questions. And so, even with two strikes against him — he's a patent lawyer and a Clintonista — Bruce Lehman moved from hero to god. He is apparently a really good guy, which makes what's happening to him all the more tragic.

Lehman tells me that our 200-year-old patent system is making a mess of software, and it's easy to explain. There are too few examiners for the growing number of patent applications, fewer still who know anything about software, and they have no reasonably complete collection of prior art outside the patent system, which is where almost all software is. These are the problems that Lehman now says he must solve first. I argue, but hmm, priorities, OK, fine.

Beginning to sound harried, Lehman tells me how a typical PTO examiner is paid $72,000 annually, plus $8,000 for software knowledge if any, plus another $8,000 based on how many patent decisions are made each year, one way or another.

Lehman says he needs to attract more software expertise, and to reward quality, which means, he says, exhaling, he must now contend with the examiner's union.

Uh-oh.

Lehman says that the PTO operates on fees paid by inventors for the handling of pending applications and issued patents. He says that he could solve our problems if only he could get back the $20 million in PTO fees that Congress carts off each year for other purposes.

Gasp.

What about the plan to open patent exams to submissions of prior art from third parties? It's off. Japan does this to keep its markets closed, Lehman explains, and so we can't.

What? What about the plan to open up the currently closed and practically inoperable regular reexamination process? Revealing some frustration, Lehman says it's over in OMB. Other Major Bureaucracy?

Sigh.

What about a special open reexamination of U.S. Patent 4,714,989? Sorry, gotta run. Lehman says he can't just go around ordering open re-exams because, well, the PTO needs the fees it collects for its (rarely used) closed re-exams.

Huh? I'm worried about Commissioner Lehman, not because I failed in one phone call to get him to strike down the bogus file service patent, but because it's clear Washington is grinding my hero down. I'm worried that, in his weakened condition, Lehman might catch Potomac fever, for which they tell me the only known cure is embalming fluid.

Rebuttal X 2

Comments from the U.S. Patent Office and a Novell Spokesperson

This series of articles has two rebuttals, in the form of interviews dating from 1998. The first is from Richard Malsby, Director of Public Affairs of the US Patent Office; and the second from a Novell spokesperson.

Richard Malsby, Director of Public Affairs, US PTO

Q: (to the US Patent Office) What's happening with the Billings patent?

A: All I can tell you is that the matter is still before the Patent Appeal Board and since it is I can't really comment any further on it, nor would it be appropriate for the Commissioner or anyone else here to do an interview as long as this is a matter that is pending before us administratively.

But the more important thing, I think, is to remind you that this whole business of issuing patents for computer software is a case battle that we lost — the courts ruled that we had to issue patents for computer software. It's always been historically the Patent & Trademark Office's position that they were not patentable, but that was court decision, the highest court in the land, and so we are simply bound by that. So it is quite a moot point about what the Commissioner or anybody else may think about it.

A Novell corporate spokesperson

Q: (To Novell) What's happening with the Billings patent litigation?

A: The situation has not changed appreciably. In September, 1994, the judge in Federal District Court in San Francisco, where Billings was suing Novell and Novell was counter-suing, put a stay on the Federal Court Action pending a ruling by the Federal Patent Court.

The Patent Board rejected the validity of the Billings patent in '95, and Billings appealed to the Board, as is his right. That second appeal is still pending (in review). Nothing will move forward in the case until that case comes through.

If his patent is invalidated, Billings would then have to appeal to a higher Federal Court if he wants to go further. If his patent is held to be valid, the lawsuit will proceed in the Federal District Court in San Francisco, where the question will be, has anyone violated Billings' patent?

The most likely scenario: The whole thing will drag along for years before it's resolved.

The Dark Spam Tunnel

I hold out hope that, somehow, advertising on the Web will flourish and make the Internet affordable, while nasty spamming will fade away like Pet Rocks and disco. Since spamming is most often used to advertise, these hopes might seem at cross-purposes, but I hope not. If the world follows my advice (and it should), spam buttons, e-postage and editors online will save the day.

Of course, this discussion requires that I walk the fine line between disparaging an annoying form of communication and promoting freedom of speech. Even the most adroit pundit has been caught on the horns of that dilemma. See how you think I fare in this series of columns that deal with spam and advertising online.

Advertising Can Save the Internet from a Utopia Gone Sour

May 30, 1994

Laurence Canter and Martha Siegel are the Arizona lawyers who recently rose to national prominence thanks to their advertising on the Internet.

Well, Larry and Martha got ink, not for their advertising, exactly, but for the death threats they received in response. Their ads, which were posted indiscriminately on thousands of Internet newsgroups, apparently broke the precious concentration of a good many Internauts with no sense of humor. And for this breach of "Netiquette," poor Larry and Martha found themselves surrounded by an Internet lynch mob.

After posting their advertisements, Larry and Martha received thousands of flaming messages, which is par for the Internet. But then the flamers started pressuring the providers of Larry and Martha's Internet access to get them off the Internet. Next, the lawyers' voice-mail system and fax machine were spiked by Internet hackers. And then came the anti-Semitic hate mail and death threats.

The lynch-mob response to Larry and Martha's Internet ads is evidence that the Internet, after 25 years, is just another Utopia that has finally gone sour.

After worrying about this for a week, I have come to the following contrarian conclusion: Paid advertising, mostly as we have come to know and love it since the early settlement of Madison Avenue, can save the Internet.

Paid advertising will save the Internet in two ways. First, advertising will make the Internet sustainably inexpensive, like today's newspapers, magazines, TV, and radio — a prospect that should excite universal-access advocates. Second, advertising will provide practical incentives for attracting the attention of Internet citizens to the information they need.

The fact is, the Internet is now large and rapidly outgrowing its quaint Netiquette. The Internet is running up against new limits — not on computing power, not on bandwidth, but on the attention span of its citizens.

It's time the Internet got itself some editors — like the editors of *InfoWorld*, who collect, filter, analyze, and present information for their readers. (*InfoWorld News and Reviews* are already available on the Internet via the Internet Shopping Network. Editors attract readers. And the attentions of these readers are valuable assets that require major investments and continuing maintenance, but which can be — get this — profitably sold.

Who pays editors? Sometimes their readers do. But mostly it's advertisers paying on behalf of the readers whose attention they want to buy. For example, TV and radio broadcasting, and increasingly even public broadcasting, are almost 100-percent advertiser supported.

Newspapers and magazines get twice as much support from advertisers as from their readers directly. Telephones are supported fully by their users, but of course, telephone companies have no editors to pay.

It's also time the Internet got itself some publishers — like me during the day — who can afford to pay their editors by carefully selling the hard-earned attentions of their readers to advertisers. Of course, should such attentions be abused by polluted editorial or irrelevant ads, then, this still being a free country, readers can be relied upon individually or in large groups to take their attentions elsewhere.

Martha and Larry might not have been able to post their ads so widely if there had been someone to charge them for the privilege of posting them. If newsgroups were edited, Larry and Martha's ads would, in most cases, have been edited out. In this post-Utopian Internet, Martha and Larry would have found indiscriminate advertising on newsgroups unaffordable.

Inevitably, Martha and Larry are intent on pressing their legal rights to break Internet Netiquette. It turns out that, despite all the bad will they generated, their offending ads worked, getting a reported 20,000 leads for almost nothing, thanks to the Internet's current unsustainable (if not free, then flat) pricing schemes. Not only will Martha and Larry advertise impolitely again, they have started a business, predictably called Cybersell, to help others do the same.

Until editors and publishers take their familiar places on the Internet, and advertising is introduced to fund and filter the free flow of information, we can expect a spiraling of abusive ads in our newsgroups and lynch mobs for the likes of Larry and Martha, which is no way to live. Or would you prefer the government handle it?

Book on Iway Advertising Is Evil — Don't Even Buy to Burn

February 20, 1995

Laurence Canter and Martha Siegel are the Phoenix lawyers who won Iway infamy last year by indiscriminately posting advertisements on 6,000 Usenet newsgroups — newsgroups, it turns out, that were mostly (no surprise) uninterested in immigration lottery services. They've since found the nerve to get out and exploit their infamy by publishing an evil book, *How to Make a Fortune on the Information Superhighway.*

You know I'm a big fan of freedom of speech (especially mine) and that I would not deny their right to publish their book, but I'll tell you flatly the book is evil. I would recommend burning it, except you would have to buy one first.

Last year in this column I came quite close to defending Canter and Siegel. (See "Advertising can save the Internet from becoming a Utopia gone sour," May 30, 1994) The poor things had spammed Usenet and, as a result, were buried in Internet vituperation — electronic mail bombs, fax floods, death threats, and Internet disconnection. I was appalled at the lynch mob. I enumerated lessons about online speech and advertising. I, too, got buried in Internet nastygrams.

Canter and Siegel do read my columns, and much of the book reeks of them. It actually quotes me once, but instead of expressing gratitude for my defense against the mob, the book snidely takes one of my sarcastic quips entirely out of its context. Foul.

Like most How-to-Make-a-Fortune books, Canter and Siegel's is quite simply a rip-off. It purports to reveal in full what your average fortune-hunters need to know to buy a PC and connect to the Internet. According to the authors, "Geeks" use too much jargon, and it's all very simple, actually. Then come two pages on the computer revolution (computers can't really think), two pages on IBM versus Macintosh (buy DOS), and a page on memory (4MB is good, 8MB better; if slow, buy more).

The book pretends to puncture our geek obfuscation shield by explaining in just 15 pages how to connect to the Internet. But why then a mean and condescending chapter on how, in the end, Canter and Siegel had to hire their own geeks? With what products will you make a fortune on the Iway? Canter and Siegel's secret: "Give them something they want, and they can make you very rich." For example, advice on love and relationships, flowers and romance, cyberscalping tickets, things for the dorm, food and recipes, government publications, and red-light districts. This book is not worth the air it displaces. Foul.

But the real evil starts when Canter and Siegel show us how few scruples it takes to advertise on the Internet. They offer four pages of tables to compare the costs of advertising in television, radio, newspapers, magazines, and the Internet. Taking $1,000 per month to be on the Internet and dividing by 30 million users, they get Internet advertising page impressions at $.0333 per thousand users per month. This number is lined up against, for example, *People* magazine at $24 per thousand readers per month. But there aren't any Internet pages that more than a tiny fraction of Internet users read every month. Foul.

Canter and Siegel have discovered that it's easy with robot mailers and vacation responders to reach hundreds of thousands of Internet users with any random advertising message. Never mind that the vast majority of those so "spammed" are inconvenienced and turned off by the intrusion. Never mind that valuable Internet resources are cynically misappropriated. Never mind that this book sets back the Internet's economic development by giving online advertising a bad name.

Canter and Siegel are like those early North Americans who discovered that when they jumped out from behind just the right bush, they could stampede a thousand buffalo over a cliff and with a clear conscience save themselves all the trouble of hunting.

One last atrocity: Canter and Siegel disparage the Internet's "front men," including Vint Cerf. They say Cerf owns CERFnet, an Internet access provider, and that the father of the Internet has an unseemly conflict of interest. CERFnet is the California Education and Research Federation network and is not owned by Vint Cerf.

A better name for this book would be Geeks in Shysterspace.

E-Postage Would Fund the System, Stop Spammers

January 20, 1997

Thanks to the many of you who invested the cost of an e-mail to write Editor-in-Chief Sandy Reed in support of my year-end bonus. And thanks even if you demanded that this column be discontinued because I failed to kill myself after not being entirely right about the Internet's collapses in 1996.

Now notice that all those e-mails you sent, and Sandy's confirmations, were carried by various Internet service providers for no extra charge on top of a flat monthly fee; they were free. Starting work on my 1997 bonus, this week I would like to sketch some arguments for why you should really want to pay postage on each of your e-mails.

Proponents of flat-rate pricing and free e-mail argue that the Internet would not have taken off if people had been asked to pay for what they used. Maybe, but the Internet has now taken off. It must soon lift its landing gear and do whatever else planes do to sustain flight.

Proponents of free e-mail note that Prodigy tried charging for e-mail, and all that got them was sued. Of course, not charging for e-mail didn't help Prodigy much either.

Proponents of free e-mail say that Internet usage will be retarded if people are asked to pay for what they use. OK, this is likely true, and, therefore, "e-postage" may even be beneficial.

Usage of our postal services, long-distance telephones, automobiles, food, and water, although perhaps retarded, has all been managing to grow substantially despite their consumers having mostly to pay as they go. And many of the exceptions, such as free water in California, are problems.

You really deserve improved e-mail service. This can be had over time if carriers cover their costs. Paying e-postage for what you use of e-mail is the best way to cover costs. Competition among e-mail carriers will over time drive prices down, getting us to universal service at just about the perfect time.

We should probably pay for each message we send based on how big it is, on how many copies we're sending, and on how far it's being sent. We should probably pay extra for special services such as urgency, acknowledgment, storage, privacy, and authentication. We should be able to send e-mails collect and bill them to willing third parties.

Some say it would cost much more to charge for e-mail than it costs to provide it. Even if this were true, so what, and as we grow out of ASCII e-mail, this won't be true for long.

Too bad the Internet's designers had no apparent interest in economics and left money out of e-mail standards. Internet servers exchange mail around the world without asking the obvious questions such as, "How much should who pay for this message?" Unfortunately, even if this question were being asked today, there are no micromoney systems in place to handle the required small exchanges of value: no coins for stamps. So paying e-postage will have to wait for micromoney and the upgrading of e-mail to work with it.

Too bad we're going to have to wait a long time to pay Internet e-postage. Free e-mail will tend to be worth every penny paid for it. And too bad, because e-postage is the ultimate solution to unwanted e-mail, most of it poorly targeted advertising or "spamming."

Think of all the mail you'd receive through the United States Postal Service were it not for the cost of paper, printing, and postage. The root cause of spam on the Internet is that there is no paper, printing, or postage. With e-postage, anybody sending you e-mail has to pay for it.

Now a mail server that is seeking to forward e-mail to your mailbox server could be asked to describe each message intended for you.

Your e-mail "acceptance" agent could compute incremental e-postage based on that description. This way, you could set the price that advertisers could choose to pay for your time to read (or subsequently discard) their messages.

With e-postage, there would be pressure on spam and just enough over time so as not to require any major overhauls of the United States Constitution and its First Amendment.

Is anybody at the Internet Engineering Task Force (IETF) working on e-postage? No? Hello, earth to IETF; come in, please.

Groupies Blast Mailbox, But E-Postage Is a Good Thing

February 17, 1997

On Jan. 27, *The New Yorker* carried a piece about letter bombs. The piece concluded that "the only mail that poses no threat is [e]-mail ... it can't kill you." Well, maybe. You should read the e-mails I got in response to my Jan. 20 column about "e-postage." (See "E-postage would not only help fund the system, but it could stop spammers," page 44.) All I suggested was that we should pay for e-mail — per copy, per byte, per mile, per whatever — to allow competing carriers to cover the costs of improving services and to deter junk e-mail.

Many of the e-mail bombs I received came from the Internet's intelligentsia — the Internetgentsia — still in its continuing snit about clueless newbies invading cyberspace.

The word "newbies" is, of course, the IPonics name for those who weren't developing protocols during the 1960s when the intentions of the Internet were set in stone, don't recall the first e-mails sent from BBN in the 1970s, or don't even know SMTP from POP3. And yet these newbies dare persist in their opinions about the future of the Internet.

The Internetgentsia would prefer to guide our exploration, settlement, and development of cyberspace. We're talking (in IPonics again) about an Internetgentsia that says "information wants to be free," that the Internet is "alive," and that its traffic is (oh my God) "fractal." We're talking about an Internetgentsia that holds 'Netiquette on a par with, if not superior to, English common law.

The Internetgentsia wants to determine how we'll live virtually in cyberspace, although it knows less than nothing about and eschews (God bless you) real economics, politics, culture, and the fundamentals of personal grooming.

Many readers wrote in outrage about how badly they need e-mail. If they had to pay anything for e-mail — anything! — they couldn't afford it. The neediness, outrage, and entitlement expressed were no doubt heartfelt. But arguing against socialism's idea that heartfelt need is a valid claim would get us into political economy, and so I won't.

Many readers argued that e-mail is not free but covered by flat fees of one kind or another. Flat fees will persist but only where they can be high or offset by advertising. Light users of e-mail will eventually tire of subsidizing heavy users. They will force carriers to let them pay only for the e-mails they send.

Many argued that e-postage accounting systems would end up costing most of what e-mail costs. A frequent example was the cost of telephony, for which accounting was estimated to be as high as 80 percent of all costs.

I doubt such numbers, but they made me think of all that concert organizers do to sell tickets to public events and exclude people without them. Very few people crash events, so why not save all those sales and security costs by asking audiences to pay performers when they get a chance? Many argued that e-postage would not stop junk e-mail — postage has not stopped junk mail through the U.S. Postal Service. But we would receive much more junk mail if paper, printing, and postage were free. And we would receive much less if postage covered mailing costs. Charging e-mail senders for costs incurred creates the right backpressure, not to stop spamming entirely, but to deter it to an acceptable level.

Many argued that e-postage can't be implemented. They wrote that the Internet is insecure and does not have a system for micropayments. Well, I've written about that, too. But the Internet needs and will eventually have security, micromoney, and e-postage — change to buy stamps.

Many argued that e-postage would require further Internet intervention by governments, especially the Postal Service. If so, then I agree we should drop this e-postage idea at once.

Now please rush me reports about the increasing burdens of carrying e-mail, especially the new forms beyond ASCII — "push" in IPonics — or about services that are beginning to charge e-postage.

If you'd like to advertise how very much you need free e-mail, please do not post your pleadings to me. I consider them spam, violations of 'Netiquette, which would force me to retaliate or do whatever else the Internetgentsia would have us do to handle such real-world misbehaviors without e-postage.

CyberGold Spurns Spam by Paying People to Read Ads on the Internet

October 13, 1997

CyberGold is a Berkeley, Calif., start-up that pays you to spend what little remains of your life reading ads on the Web. Founder Nat Goldhaber says that CyberGold "values your attention."

Now, if futurist George Gilder is right, CyberGold is onto something. At his Telecom conference last month, Gilder pointed out the Information Age is defined by two major limitations. The first is the speed of light — 300 million meters per second, and, if we're to believe Einstein, there's no getting around that.

Gilder's second limitation is the span of human life. Time is what we have too little of. It is not acceptable to keep people waiting online anymore. So many Web pages, so many e-mail messages, so little time.

Which brings us to "spam" — unsolicited bulk e-mail carrying unwanted ads. Many of us are now getting mostly spam e-mails.

Many of us don't care that spam steals scarce Internet resources — nobody seems to pay for those. Many remain hostile to my brilliant idea of charging e-postage to cover e-mail transport costs and to deter spam. (See "E-postage would not only help fund the system, but it could stop spammers," Jan. 20.)

What bothers most of us about spam is that it steals time from our short, miserable lives. Just deleting unread spam consumes more attention than many of us can afford.

Pretty soon we're going to snap and pass laws aimed at eliminating spam. The first few laws will be stupid if not downright dangerous, but we'll get it right eventually, and e-postage will emerge.

The purveyors of spam — damn them — know more about the Internet than they do about advertising. They don't know that extending the reach and frequency of advertising not only annoys innocent bystanders, but is inefficient and self-defeating (see TV, now in decline). They don't seem to know that finely targeting audiences and valuing their attention is what good advertising is about (see *InfoWorld*).

The editors of *InfoWorld* like to think of advertising as a necessary evil. They think — bless them — that you read the magazine despite the ads.

However, most *InfoWorld* readers, because they are so well selected, read *InfoWorld* and other trade publications in part because of the ads. After all, the ads are mostly about products they are interested in buying.

Making ads relevant to readers is one way of getting them read. Another way is CyberGold, now up and running on the Web.

Again, CyberGold arranges for advertisers to pay you for the scarce time you spend reading their ads.

CyberGold began with a chicken-and-egg problem. It needed advertisers who were willing to sign up to pay Web users to read ads, and it needed Web users willing to sign up to get paid. CyberGold is now counting its chickens.

For example, if you signed up and listed my name as a referral, this put $1 into my CyberGold account.

Goldhaber says that 100,000 people have signed up and the number is growing by 30 percent to 50 percent per week.

Goldhaber says CyberGold now has 25 paying advertisers and 25 more in negotiation. Some show you their ad, ask a few questions to confirm that you read it, and then let you click on CyberGold's logo to collect. CyberGold keeps track so you won't get paid for reading the same ad twice.

For example, I added $2.50 to my CyberGold account by expressing interest in a subscription to *Wired* magazine. When I returned to CyberGold to again express my heartfelt interest in *Wired*, I wasn't even shown the *Wired* offer.

You can see the status of your CyberGold account anytime, and it's fun to watch the money pile up at the speed of light.

You get to direct money accumulating in your CyberGold account in several ways. You can, in preparation for the hereafter, donate the money to a worthy cause. You can convert CyberGold into CyberCash. Or, you can move CyberGold into your bank account.

CyberGold's Goldhaber says we should stay tuned for upcoming exciting news on other ways to spend your CyberGold. I say you might as well register for CyberGold.

There's a Bright Light and a Sendmail at the End of the Dark Spam Tunnel

July 27, 1998

Spam is in the eye of the beholder.

Like the time I received e-mail inviting me to Earth Day. Being pro-pollution, I wrote back asking them to stop spamming me. Earth Day responded by saying their invitation was not spam because, well, they're nonprofit.

Some see spam simply as unsolicited bulk electronic advertising — a clear violation of some part of the Constitution. But I see spam as unwanted e-mail of all kinds, in many shades of gray, evading blanket prohibitions.

Advertising facilitates economic, political, and social activity, so we can't just criminalize unsolicited bulk e-mail. The growth of I-commerce depends on our doing something, but not too much, about spam. Unfortunately, zealots are threatening spam legislation on a par with our recently overturned decency legislation.

There are three things we should be doing about spam, none of which will eliminate it entirely.

First, we should reduce anonymity on the Internet. Anonymity has important uses, but it shouldn't be so convenient for polluters of our e-mail streams.

Second, we should be getting better at filtering our e-mail. The solution for indecent Web pages is not prohibition, but better filtering — ditto for e-mail.

And third, we should be paying electronic postage to compensate competing carriers of evolving e-mail. Postage and Bright Light are getting us two-thirds the way into spam-filtering heaven.

Sendmail is a 17-year-old start-up in Emeryville, Calif. At its recent inception, Sendmail boasted an installed base of about 750,000 or 75 percent of Internet e-mail servers.

Sendmail's founder is Eric Allman, who has been leading the Sendmail consortium since 1981. His company's product, sendmail, is the SMTP software that has been carrying most Internet mail ever since. Allman has now joined with CEO Greg Olson to continue offering sendmail as the free "open source" mail software that it has been for 17 years, plus now in commercially supported for-profit binary versions.

Sendmail 8.9 comes with 13 new anti-spam tools. For example, mail relaying is now off by default. Network managers can choose to forward the e-mail of specified users, but not anonymous spam.

The sendmail release can also validate the sources of incoming e-mail by looking them up through the Internet's DNS. This helps thwart spammers who fake source addresses to dodge unsubscribe requests, penalizing them with disconnection by their ISPs or, in some states, litigation for theft of services.

Olson estimates that Sendmail 8.9 can be used to cut spam by as much as 90 percent at e-mail sites with determined and astute network administrators.

Bright Light is a new company working with Sendmail and other mail software suppliers. CEO Sunil Paul, formerly of America Online, sees spam as a mutating virus.

Senders of bulk unsolicited e-mail change their attacks as measures are taken against them. Bright Light will offer a service that gathers alerts from ISPs, your companies, and its own probe e-mail accounts. When a new attack is detected, say by the receipt of unsolicited mail at a probe mailbox, humans will analyze the attack and distribute new filtering parameters to mail servers.

Sendmail offers ubiquitous spam filters, and Bright Light offers a service for tuning them. But the next big anti-spam step remains to be taken. Internet users should have tools to filter out what they individually behold as spam.

Users should be able to keep lists of senders from whom they will or will not accept e-mail. And after reading e-mail, I'd like to hit a forward, reply, file, delete, or spam button in my e-mail client. If my eye beholds spam, hitting the spam button would file it for use in future prosecutions, ask my server to filter all future e-mail from that sender, and notify the sender, using a new mandatory anti-spam protocol, that I am to be removed from that list.

Is the Internet Engineering Task Force refining such a spam-control protocol? After it becomes mandatory, I promise not to use it against too many of you, mostly just those who still insist the Monty Hall Paradox is a 50-50 proposition.

If Unwanted E-Mail Is in the Eye of the Beholder Then I Want a Spam Button

August 3, 1998

Last week I argued that spam is in the eye of the beholder. However, judging from your many responses, my notion of spam — unwanted e-mail — is atypical.

Unlike most of you, my e-mail address is passed in print weekly to close to a million *InfoWorld* readers. And since I ask you to respond to my columns, I can't very well call your e-mail, even the hateful ones, spam.

By the way, I do still read your e-mail myself (thanks), but can no longer answer all of them (sorry).

The big responses I've enjoyed recently were to my columns breaking the news that the National Education Association is a union (see "CTC98 promises to teach our educators a thing or two about the Internet," July 20), suggesting that e-postage would deter spam (see "There's a bright light and a sendmail at the end of the dark spam tunnel," July 27), and solving the old Monty Hall Paradox (see "Microsoft, government got you down? Try these mind puzzles for a lift," June 8).

There are many of you who still insist that the Monty Hall Paradox ends up 50-50. I've asked you to stop e-mailing me until you've played the Paradox with an ace and two deuces. I now behold your continuing incorrect puzzle proofs as spam.

Speaking of puzzles, here's another, sent to me by Hal Becker, an alert reader whose e-mail is definitely not spam. You have two glasses, one half full of coffee and the other half full of tea. You pour some of the coffee into the tea and mix thoroughly. Then you pour the same amount of the mixture back into the coffee. Now, which of the two liquids is diluted more by the other, the coffee or tea?

Please send me your solutions. (Solutions. Get it?) Eventually, many of you insisting the tea is more diluted will send me too much e-mail, and I'll have to declare it spam.

Which will get me in big trouble with the Coalition Against Unsolicited Commercial Email (CAUCE). CAUCE uses the word spam to mean bulk unsolicited commercial e-mail (UCE). CAUCE would probably not agree that spam is in the eye of the beholder. It probably finds that unsolicited e-mail is OK from nonprofits. Maybe CAUCE would accept unsolicited e-mail from unprofitables?

Last week, I argued that blanket prohibitions against bulk UCE go too far, and yet not far enough.

Blanket prohibitions against UCE go too far in that advertising is a facilitator of economic, political, and social activity. Criminalizing UCE would slow the civilization of cyberspace.

On the other hand, criminalizing UCE does not go far enough. There's much spam that is not UCE. As I am fond of saying, spam is in the eye of the beholder.

Some spam is pretty easy to behold these days. It begins with a completely dumbfounding announcement like "This is not spam." A sure sign.

And then follows what spammers take for Netiquette.

"We had reason to believe you solicited a message from us. We would not want you to receive our mailings if you don't want them. If we've contacted you in error, we're sorry, which should just about cover it.

"If you insist on us not sending you more e-mail, type lower-case Remove in the subject of a reply. Don't reply to this message, but send Remove to our Webmaster, whose really long address is below. Be sure your reply-to address is exactly the address to which we sent this e-mail. Follow up three days later with an identical e-mail, so we can be sure you really want out of the mainstream.

"The Internet being what it is today, our e-mail server may not be always up, so be prepared to try again. We reserve the right to send you future e-mail on different subjects. We also might send you e-mail on the same subject with a different return address, in which case no harm done, just simply repeat the above procedure. And now on to our exciting offer."

When I get what my eye beholds as spam — single or bulk, solicited or un, commercial or non — I want to push my spam button once to get that spam filed for future prosecutions, to get my mail server blocking e-mail from that sender, and to get a message sent according to a spam protocol demanding that the sender cease and desist.

Several other alert readers have suggested the spam button should feed a collaborative filtering process so that all my friends on the Net could be saved the trouble of receiving the spam again.

Dealing with spam by pushing one button in less than a second would go a long way toward not making a federal case out if it.

Is anyone working on getting me my spam button? And if that's too hard, which is more diluted, the coffee or tea?

Spam: Shoplifting your time and mine

Rebuttal by Seth Godin

Seth Godin was the founder of Yoyodyne, Vice President of Direct Marketing at Yahoo!, and the author of "Permission Marketing". He holds a B.S.E.M.E. in the Philosophy of Computers from Tufts University. Seth now writes, and develops businesses.

I need to start by saying that Bob and I violently agree about almost everything. I was proposing many of the things he wrote about years ago, years ago. I was hooted down by the same intelligentsia when I proposed, more than four years ago, that commercial e-mail carry a distinctive symbol in the subject line, making it easy to filter. What can I say. . .he's a visionary.

That said, I'd like to add my thoughts about spam, which I hope will be particularly relevant to those who think that it's a small nuisance, and that a minority is making too big a deal out of it.

Spam is like shoplifting.

In small amounts, shoplifting can bankrupt no business. The shoplifter gets something worth a few bucks and the store has a tiny loss. No big deal. It's certainly not worth putting people in jail over. I mean, hey, it's a victimless crime. It costs too much to enforce, it ruins the life of the shoplifter, and the cost to society for building and maintaining all those prisons is too high.

But. . .what happens when 100 people shoplift from a store? Or 1,000? Well, a few things happen. The first thing is that the rule of law and civility breaks down. When you can steal with impunity, it makes it more likely you'll succumb to the temptation to perform other victimless crimes.

Worse, the store goes out of business. Or raises its prices so that other customers pay the price for the deeds of the few shoplifters.

In societies where shoplifting is abhorred or patrolled closely, just about everyone benefits. Stores are more profitable. Prices are lower. People don't have to wonder how they're secretly being taxed.

Well, not to belabor the analogy, but the same is true online. No single piece of spam could rob me of so much time that I'd really notice it. And one more piece of Internet traffic doesn't really increase the cost of servers and pipe.

But the problem with spam is that it's digital. And free. So small malfeasance becomes large. One hundred spammers soon become one million spammers.

The prisoner's dilemma is no dilemma here at all. The morally suspect businessperson who sees an opportunity for short-term profit at the expense of the rest of us will take that opportunity, if she can get away with it.

Smart marketers are discovering that mailing with permission, in effect earning the privilege to market to consumers, is far more effective than spam. But the lazy operators left in the market are always looking for a shortcut, and spam certainly appears to be one.

Which brings us to Bob's imperatives on spam. YES, we need better filters, and centralized ones certainly make sense. YES, we need smarter e-mail systems so that setting up filters is easier. Even more important, we need to educate consumers to NEVER respond to spam. Except to eliminate the brand from your shopping list and the stock from your portfolio. Once the market punishes spammers for their actions, they'll stop.

I don't think we need legislation to stop spam, except for a requirement that any business include its name and address and phone number in every e-mail it sends. The market has the will to stop this problem. Now we need the tools.

The Pay-As-We-Go Internet

You might have noticed that you can't take a really deep breath these days without running into e-commerce this and e-business that. Any coincidence that back in 1993 I was saying our priority for the Internet should be to make it useful in commerce? Probably not. But in this series of columns, in which I'm either the Rush Limbaugh or Howard Stern of online commerce (you decide), you'll read about my longstanding support of privatizing and commercializing the Internet. Along the way I espoused measured use pricing (Metcalfe Meters — catchy, isn't it?) and suggested that Novell just go out and start its own darn Internet.

With the caveat that my Pay-As-You-Go Internet idea is probably about as popular as the Edsel, read on!

Internet Must Go Commercial — and Do It Right

September 6, 1993

Perhaps you have stayed away from the TCP/IP-based Internet because it's mostly for academics and Unix. Perhaps TCP/IP sounds to you like an admission of damning drug test results. But now the Internet reportedly connects 20 million computers and is doubling that every year. So your DOS and Macintosh PCs are probably already on the Internet, and if not, they will be soon.

The Internet has, since 1969, been a research project, funded through the Department of Defense's Advanced Research Projects Agency (ARPA) and the National Science Foundation. In its first generation, the Internet was called ARPAnet, and it connected mainframes and minicomputers cross-country at 50Kb per second.

In 1983, a new generation of network protocols, TCP/IP, was installed on the ARPAnet mainly to interconnect proliferating megabit-per-second LANs of Unix workstations. In this second generation, ARPAnet became Internet, and since then it has proved a very good model for how workstations and PCs should be networked.

The newly formed Internet Society projects — with tongue in cheek, I assume — that the Internet will connect every human on Earth by 2001. Well before that date, however, the Internet will outgrow TCP/IP. So new protocols are being developed for the Internet — its third generation. The next-generation Internet might become a part of what the Clinton administration calls a national information infrastructure.

Cutting over to this third-generation Internet is going to be a big deal, so let's take more time to get it right. I don't mean that the Internet should become "infrastructure" — a code word that many Internauts (but few Clintonistas) take to mean "funded by the government." I mean that the third-generation Internet needs to be designed for commercial use so it can help make the world go around.

To make the world go around, networks joining the Internet need blocks of addresses for their attached computers. Today, the Internet is running out of these free addresses. The society is considering several schemes for enlarging the addresses used in the Internet. By the time a scheme is chosen and a migration plan worked out, software in tens of millions of computers and the switching systems between them will need to be upgraded. This huge cutover would be rivaled only by Great Britain deciding to drive on the right side of the road.

But Internet needs to upgrade more than its addresses if it is to be used commercially. The next generation should be capable of, among other things, fully exploiting Asynchronous Transfer Mode (ATM), serving individual users via ISDN, and billing for measured use.

The Internet Society is working on ATM, sure, and is close to working out a way to carry Internet packets in ATM cells. This is a mandatory migration tool, but the theory of ATM is that short fixed-length cells are needed for voice and video applications. Carrying long variable-length packets through an ATM cell-switching fabric is, well, the worst of both worlds. I think the third-generation Internet must exploit ATM with cell-based protocols, operating systems, and applications.

Another requirement for the third-generation Internet is that individuals, not just institutions, be allowed to subscribe. The society should be sure its new protocols support personal use, and they should exploit ISDN. ISDN won't replace high-speed Internet trunks, but it will greatly improve personal Internet use from small offices and home offices. And ISDN has something else that the Internet needs: measured usage billing.

There are many arguments in the Internet community about why usage billing is really not needed. For example, everyone should be entitled to use the Internet free. Or, the costs of counting packets are comparable to the costs of carrying them and should therefore be avoided. I'm sorry, but no.

To go commercial, measured usage billing is essential. Price is the time-tested coordinator of supply and demand. Internet carriers must be able to settle with one another for traffic carried on behalf of each other's customers. And end-user billing, as offered by ISDN, is needed. A commercial Internet must be able to bill for usage by kilopackets and kilometers — say, in mega-packet-meters (a unit that I yearn to have named after me when I pass on). If we still want our government to pay the bills for certain Internet users, then it can.

On Surfing the Internet, and Other Kid Stuff

November 1, 1993

As the Internet enters its 25th tax-supported year, I say it's done already.

It should be privatized. Let's clear the way in cyberspace for a new generation of entrepreneurs. I'm with Bill Gates, who recently said in a San Francisco speech that the National Information Infrastructure (NII) shouldn't cost taxpayers another red cent.

Many Internauts say commercializing the Internet would destroy it. That it's too fragile to endure free markets. That the profit motive will lead to exploitation of the information have-nots. That the future of our democracy depends on federally funded information interstates with mandated universal access and guaranteed freedom of speech. That surfing the Internet is fun, fun, fun — please, Daddy, don't take the T-bird away.

So we Internauts, port and starboard, have quite an argument going. You can join us by reading the new Clinton NII agenda.

Whenever they catch me talking up commercialization, my many friends in the Internet bureaucracy ask whether I've been on Mars. They point out that most traffic on the Internet is already commercial, so what am I worried about?

Well, I worry that Intercrats have been colonizing the Beltway since the 1970s. That those directing the Internet's evolution do seem naive about, unprepared for, disinterested in, and sometimes ideologically opposed to commercializing cyberspace. I worry that unbilled commercial traffic will soon bring the Internet to its knees. I worry about Interprises now starting up as if their packet plumbing will grow with them, and as if federal support for NII will not, with all the good intentions in the world, pave their information superhighway to hell.

Frankly, commercial traffic notwithstanding, what we're seeing is still amateur night on the Internet. I see today's many new Interpreneurs sitting brightly behind just so many lemonade stands in cyberspace.

At Interop I met Bob Berger, who is ramping up to sell Integrated Services Digital Network (ISDN) access to the Internet. I get 50Kb per second (Kbps) of Internet at home via ISDN, but I want 500Kbps. So I visited Berger at his start-up, InterNex. Berger showed me how to surf cyberspace with freeware such as Fetch, Gopher, and Wide Area Information Servers (WAIS), and how to hang 10 with Mosaic over the World Wide Web.

Even lemonade stands charge by the cup, but companies such as InterNex are willing to sell you flat-rate Internet access. Your backbone transmissions, no matter how many or how far away, are free, or should I say paid for by somebody else. My main worry is that this mysterious somebody else will figure things out eventually and pull Berger's plug. Or that new mysterious somebodies will not sign up when more capacity is needed. Or that the eternal mysterious somebodies — taxpayers — will be asked, as usual, to pay an ever increasing bill.

By the way, if you are already FTPing the Internet using Unix or Windows on your PC, or using a Macintosh, you must try Mosaic. Get it (again) absolutely free via anonymous FTP from ftp.ncsa.uiuc.edu. Once you do get it, maybe you will see why I worry that accelerating unmetered use of Mosaic might soon bring the Internet to its knees.

A day after Berger got me on Mosaic, I met another fascinating Interpreneur, Tim O'Reilly, whose publishing company just introduced the Global Network Navigator (GNN). It's based on the free use of Mosaic clients and GNN's own Web server. GNN offers news, an Internet magazine, a catalog of Internet information resources, and (get this) a separate marketplace icon behind which paid advertising quietly awaits your perusal.

GNN subscriptions are (what else?) free, and O'Reilly hopes that advertising will someday pay his bills. O'Reilly's view is that advertising, just as long as it stresses providing reliable information instead of getting attention, will be able to play an important role in commercializing the Internet.

He's right, of course, but he can expect a lot of hate electronic mail from surf city.

In case you're not directly on the Internet, you might be interested in the Public Dialup Internet Access List (PDIAL). My 48Kb copy came back within 5 minutes and without an invoice. Which mysterious somebody can I thank for its delivery? Unfortunately, PDIAL is not only delivered for free, but it is also maintained for free. Which explains, I suppose, why PDIAL is 3 months old and does not yet list InterNex. You get what you pay for.

Commercializing the Internet with NetWare

December 20, 1993

Every time I talk about commercializing the Internet, I get waves of outraged leftist e-mail from various tax-supported enclaves across America. It's great — I've become the Rush Limbaugh of the information infrastructure.

And now I've got a really big idea for commercializing the Internet, an idea that probably isn't really mine and doesn't have to involve the Internet. I got this idea after seeing Novell make some moves; it all added up.

The Internet, which uses the TCP/IP family of internetworking protocols, is now a big piece of our information infrastructure. It already has 10 million, 15 million, or maybe 20 million users exchanging however many Internet packets. The Intercrats don't keep track, which is why we need to transform the Internet from a tax-supported hobby for an aging academic elite into a robust, commercially managed platform from which to launch economic growth. Is this Limbaugh, or what?

Here's my idea: Novell should organize its many commercial partnerships into a for-profit NetWare Internet. The old TCP/IP Internet could then be left, providing universal access to the academics and the miserably needy in cyberspace. Is this still Limbaugh, or have I crossed over into Howard Stern?

I caught up with Novell's executive vice president Richard King and ran this idea by him. Although he didn't quite admit that my idea is his, I was reminded of some facts. Fully two-thirds of computers on LANs run NetWare.

There is major overlap between these 30 million and the far fewer computers on the TCP/IP Internet. Novell has been revamping NetWare so that LANs can be tied together across enterprises. All that's left to do is to connect NetWare LANs among enterprises, and voila! — a commercial NetWare Internet.

There is the question of protocols. TCP/IP is a family of WAN-optimized internetwork protocols that has won out in recent years over Systems Network Architecture, DECnet, and (my favorite) Open Systems Interconnection. The developers of TCP/IP are justly proud.

But NetWare's IPX protocols and TCP/IP trace back to the same early-'70s Stanford seminars. Optimized for LANs, IPX now carries the vast majority of network traffic.

So, since both LANs and WANs are required, would TCP/IP or IPX make the better commercial Internet? Novell has been taking IPX enterprisewide, getting it in shape for this contest. For example, it's a small thing, but "burst mode" was added to improve IPX's WAN performance. A much bigger thing is IPX's new scalable internetwork routing, NetWare Link Services Protocol, which has been added by SynOptics, 3Com, Proteon, Wellfleet, and Cisco Systems, whose routers glue together most of the TCP/IP Internet.

Novell globalized NetWare's e-mail service and added an X.500-like directory service that King says is ready for networks with millions of users. And Novell has a NetWare Network Registry where for $100 and up — on the TCP/IP Internet it's free, of course — you can buy unique names and addresses so your enterprise LANs, and WANs can fit smoothly into a global interenterprise Internet.

Why might these NetWare advancements not be enough for commercializing the Internet? Well, IPX is not "open" like TCP/IP — and you know where that's been getting Unix in its competition against Windows. And who will provide our NetWare Internet's interenterprise backbones and local dial-in access around the world?

And both IPX and TCP/IP need to address security and billing.

King ended our meeting by recalling that Novell bought the TCP/IP expertise of Excelan years ago and Unix more recently. Having shipped hundreds of thousands of units in 1993, Novell is now, according to International Data Corp., the world's largest supplier of TCP/IP. There is even a flavor of NetWare based on TCP/IP instead of IPX. So maybe with our new NetWare Internet we won't have to decide between IPX and TCP/IP. Maybe our commercial NetWare Internet won't start from scratch but will gradually take over commercial uses of the TCP/IP Internet.

King then said exactly this:

"Novell hasn't made any formal announcements in this area, and so it's too early to comment. But, yes, NetWare has an important role to play in intercompany communications in a public network environment."

So, what say you to my (or maybe Richard's) big NetWare idea for commercializing the Internet?

Internet Goes Commercial with CommerceNet

April 18, 1994

Give $150 to a doctor, a teacher, a panhandler, and then watch whether the first thing they buy is a month on the Internet.

Not likely, which proves to most of us outside Washington that the information superhypeway will not find its earliest and best uses in health, education, or welfare. These are areas where the problems are structural and unlikely to be solved with a little TCP/IP or even a lot more money.

Keeping in mind where the money for health, education, and welfare comes from, I say the priority should be on making the Internet useful in commerce.

So happily, last week, Enterprise Integration Technologies (EIT) in Palo Alto, Calif., launched CommerceNet, which, according to EIT CEO Marty Tenenbaum, is "the first large-scale market trial of electronic commerce on the Internet."

CommerceNet will let Internet users browse a hyperlinked web of formatted "pages" containing company directories, referral services, catalogs, and product demonstrations. Users will solicit bids, place orders, collaborate on engineering, coordinate production, and schedule transportation.

CommerceNet promises to streamline procurement, cut costs, and shrink development cycles, first for the electronics industry in Silicon Valley, and then, Tenenbaum says, for a thousand companies by the end of this year, and for a million companies in five years.

CommerceNet sees the Internet as the ideal infrastructure for electronic commerce, except that it is hard to access, hard to use, unreliable, and insecure, and offers no way for anybody to get paid.

So CommerceNet will provide Internet access kits. The low end will use 128Kb-per-second (Kbps) ISDN at $150 per month, including all access, backbone, and equipment charges.

CommerceNet will provide industrial-strength upgrades of NCSA Mosaic clients and Worldwide Web (WWW) servers, including RSA public-key cryptography to handle such heretofore missing Internet services as encryption, user authentication, digital signatures, and time stamps.

CommerceNet will provide, with its partners in the financial services industry, on-line credit cards, debit cards, and checks.

And CommerceNet will provide top-level directories — Mosaic/WWW home pages — as entry points into its electronic marketplace.

Tenenbaum was visibly surprised when I asked about what worries him most. Competition? No. Internet capacity? There will be plenty, somehow. Software bugs? The code has been frozen for days. Unrealistic expectations following last week's launch? OK, yes, there is the problem of "success failure."

Tenenbaum didn't really sound worried about anything, which I found fascinating. He did not, for example, say he is worried about, of all things, money.

Which reminds me of Washington. Remember the Clinton administration's agenda for the national information infrastructure (NII)? You know, the NII that will be built and paid for by private industry, so the feds will only have to spend a mere $2 billion of taxpayer money on it? Well, there is $400 million in a Technology Reinvestment Program, out of which EIT has been granted $6 million over three years to launch CommerceNet, but only if the funds are matched by local governments and private industry. With $12 million, Tenenbaum should have fewer worries than most start-up CEOs.

CommerceNet is on the right track and will make great strides in commercializing the Internet, I'm sure. And they're using Mosaic, which was my choice as Industry Milestone of 1993. So I'm all for CommerceNet, except that I can't get comfortable about the feds being so deep into NII, especially with such large amounts of our money.

What about other companies — those lemonade stands in cyberspace — that also are, for example, planning to harden Mosaic/WWW for commercial use? How will they compete against EIT's taxpayer-supported development? Take Quarterdeck, whose industrial-strength Mosaic is due out by the end of this year.

Quarterdeck knows how to write, test, ship, sell, and support competitive commercial software, so maybe, hopefully, they'll do just fine.

And shouldn't we be concerned that CommerceNet is being funded by the same feds who made OSI their protocol standard while supporting the development of TCP/IP? Who just made the Clipper encryption chip a federal standard — which CommerceNet does not plan to use? And who prohibits export of the RSA cryptography that EIT is planning to use in CommerceNet?

And please let me know what you think about the feds spending so much of our money helping private industry commercialize the Internet.

Internet Commercialization Opens Gateways to Interpreneurs

August 8, 1994

The commercialization of cyberspace is my beat, but I'm told calling it cyberspace is like trying to sell sushi as raw dead fish. There are just too many lefties out there — especially on the Internet — who still think that profit is a four-letter word, when obviously it's got six.

But, I must again say that armies of well-meaning government bureaucrats and their various taxpayer-supported hangers-on are not going to deliver the best possible information superhighway. What the Internet needs now is more competition among greedy entrepreneurs — call them Interpreneurs.

Consider, for example, Steve Kirsch, president of InfoSeek, in Santa Clara, California. After two successful start-ups — Mouse Systems Corp. and Frame Technology Corp. — Steve now has his next $2 million in venture capital. InfoSeek and its investors hope to profit wildly by providing better Internet information retrieval services.

Internet Mosaic users are being offered a free trial of InfoSeek through October 15.

InfoSeek's trial now offers back articles from a collection of 140 computer publications. I typed a few key words and received an ordered list of the 20 most relevant articles. Then, I clicked on my most interesting and got their full text.

InfoSeek will soon add the full text of 6,000 Internet news groups to its collections — the server is already gathering 100MB of news daily. Current issues of *InfoWorld* eventually will be available; back issues, limited to a few months, are available now.

The heart of InfoSeek is a search engine that does not just look for key words, but cleverly uses them to calculate the "relevance" of searched text to your queries. My free demo searches returned articles surprisingly quickly in a rank order of relevance.

InfoSeek is staffed by nine people. Its nerve center is a room, maybe 10 feet by 20 feet. A Sun Microsystems Inc. server sits on a table, under which there is a much larger uninterruptible power supply. Next to the Sun is a redundant array of inexpensive drives (RAID) rack for reliably holding and quickly delivering up terabytes.

One short Ethernet cable connects the Sun to a bread-box-size Cisco Systems Inc. router that, in turn, connects InfoSeek to the Internet via a 1.5Mbps T1 line. A second Ethernet has a hub that connects the Sun to InfoSeek's development computers.

The only thing this cyberspace lemonade stand lacks is a hand-painted sign — "Queries: 5 cents."

Steve doesn't say how much InfoSeek will try to charge subscribers after the free trial period, but in an interview he does let it slip that a single query might cost 10 cents.

The cost of the full text of relevant articles will depend on their publishers. The big concept in InfoSeek's story is that it plans to give away its server software to companies that want to publish collections of their information through InfoSeek.

InfoSeek will add them to its master index, spread subscriber queries across participating collections, merge relevance scores with a secret patent-pending algorithm, and distribute revenues collected from subscribers.

InfoSeek differs some from its most direct competitor, Wide Area Information Servers Inc., in Menlo Park, California. I spoke with WAIS founder Brewster Kahle about InfoSeek. Although WAIS also offers retrieval services across many servers, it does so with less of a commitment than InfoSeek to any one business model or user interface.

WAIS sells server software and generally is not so bent on charging subscribers. Brewster says that even when WAIS servers charge their subscribers, it's usually not by query. But many business models will be used on the Internet, and WAIS is agnostic about them. InfoSeek does not want to be agnostic; it wants to be shrink-wrapped.

Brewster brags that WAIS has been profitable for two years. Most revenues are from sales of server software, and the rest from consulting with publishers about getting their brand-name content out on the Internet.

So, InfoSeek has a formidable competitor in WAIS. WAIS has a head start, already employs a dozen people, and is profitable, which, by the way, is a 10-letter word.

Now, as far as I can tell, nobody is obligated to use either InfoSeek or WAIS.

Steve, Brewster, and many others are free to fight it out in the market, hoping to sell their services at a profit. May the best Interpreneur win.

Don't Leave Your Home Page without It

March 13, 1995

Good thing for you I was working the beach in Barbados last week. Had I stayed home here in Maine, I would have missed reading in the *Daily Nation* that they're digging up the Caribbean to run an information superhighway south from the United States, island-hopping all the way down to Trinidad.

A ship is now unreeling 1,715 kilometers of glass into the Eastern Caribbean at a cost of $60 million. Bandwidth is not quite yet actually free.

Four fibers will carry 7,560 simultaneous digital channels of paid international voice calls, facsimile transmissions, processing information on regional stock market trading, video conferencing, imaging, and credit card verification.

They do a lot of credit card verification in Barbados, which made it the perfect locale for researching this week's column on digital cash and the "micropayment" systems needed for the economic development of islands in Eastern Cyberspace.

I contacted cyberstar Steve Crocker, who recently cofounded CyberCash Inc., in Reston, Va., and asked about digital cash via Internet mail. Steve answered, "There's a natural tendency to list various properties of paper money and then design a digital system with the same properties. Anonymity is one of the more enticing properties. Another is divisibility. It is better to ask what properties are truly important, and what we can do with the new medium."

I'll not take time now on how digital money works. I recommend you read papers from several new companies that have popped up to offer Iway money — for example, Steve's new CyberCash and the older DigiCash Inc., with its U.S. offices in Palo Alto, Calif. Both have canonically named Web pages and Internet mail boxes. We will all soon be converting paper money into various forms of digital money so we can buy things on-line. Better yet, we'll be selling things and converting their digital proceeds into, for example, investigative trips to the Caribbean.

Taking Steve's advice, I propose using digital cash that can be exchanged spontaneously in very small amounts. Having a digital cash standard and associated micropayment systems should help solve three big Iway payment problems and ignite Iway commerce.

The first problem is paying for the Iway itself. Those opposed to paying for metered Iway bandwidth — because they think bandwidth ought to be free — are not so much opposed to metering as they are to high prices. If Internet access were to cost a digital dime an on-line hour, or file transfers a mil a megabyte mile, and if there were micropayment systems available to exchange such small amounts, then I think competitive pricing and metering would work just fine.

Second is paying for intellectual property. We are in a tizzy about copyrights in cyberspace, I believe, mostly because it's now way more expensive to pay for a copy of something than to just copy it, which encourages frequent casual theft. With micropayment systems based on digital cash, I would be able to ask a nickel for this column, and you might be willing to pay before reading. You aren't likely to pay after reading it.

And third is being paid to receive junk mail. I heard this idea a couple of years ago from computer software pundit Esther Dyson and more recently in some detail from *InfoWorld* reader Greg Henry. With a micropayment system connected to your mail server, you could ask that strangers pay for the privilege of sending you messages.

You tell your server that you wish to be paid a dime to receive a message from a stranger and say a quarter for each additional megabyte. Advertisers could use digital cash to make it worth your while to receive their messages, as they do now with information and entertainment. Automatic mailers, finding your attention too expensive, could invest promotional dollars more productively elsewhere. Spamming might be brought under control this way.

Iway commerce is ramping up. I can tell that by how often I am now asked to type my credit card number into some on-line form. When digital cash starts flowing, and especially when I can't leave my Home page without it, watch for a jump in GNP.

A Penny for My Thoughts on the Next Internet

January 22, 1996

Is it unfair that only people with money can get a decent education, a heart transplant, a sailboat, a sushi dinner, or an Internet address? I say, wait a minute, that's exactly why money was invented.

Far from being the root of all evil, money is a technology for exchanging value. Money has repeatedly proved superior to its predecessors, barter and plunder.

Agreeing on how much things cost is difficult, but money is a separate subject, a neutral and useful technology, right up there with language, fire, the wheel, and those little plastic things that hold your nostrils open when you're asleep.

Money goes back several millennia. Its evolution parallels the growth of trade, industry, prosperity, longevity, literacy, science, art, and democracy. How money evolves over the next few months will determine in large part how quickly the Internet recovers from its catastrophic collapse (or collapses) in 1996.

How the many new kinds of digital money evolve over the next few years will determine whether commerce on the World Wide Web ever amounts to so much as a blip on the gross national product.

Not many of you thought my last column on digital money was worth a whole 2 cents. (See "On-line services in for small change on the Next Generation Internet," Dec. 25, 1995/Jan. 1.) A few of you, buying into this haves vs. have-nots thing, thought that the Internet and everything on it should be free. You said it's unfair that only people with money can get on the Internet.

And anyway, you said, because most of it is free today, it will always be free.

A few of you wisely agreed with me that advertising will increasingly pay for Internet access and content. But then you went overboard, saying the Internet will therefore be free, like television, only somehow better.

Many of you, especially those with heavy Internet appetites, favor paying for your Internet under various all-you-can-eat flat-rate subscription schemes. I suppose you favor flat-rate pricing only as long as it's low.

And a few of you got it exactly right and agreed with me that the Internet needs a kind of digital money that supports subpenny transactions. You saw clearly, as I do, that inexpensive monies will stimulate fantastic growth in online markets for intellectual property, especially newspaper and component software.

How many times while browsing the Web have you clicked on a hyperlink and regretted it? Suddenly, darn, you're stuck downloading a document of several megabytes through a 14.4Kbps modem from a slow server in Amsterdam.

You wait and wait, ending up with another meaningless Web error message.

Or you reach up and impatiently click Stop Loading. Worse yet, the megabytes from Amsterdam finally arrive and you find that, because they're a subsidized labor of love, they're somebody's home movies or yesterday's news.

Why not have the rendering of hyperlinks indicate the commitment you'd be making if you clicked on them? Wouldn't it be economically sensible if clicking on a hyperlink helped finance its content? Well, consider having hyperlinks rendered with the sizes, locations, and prices of the documents they reference. The prices would include whatever their owners might want to charge plus the price of transport based on document size and your location.

So, encountering a description of an *InfoWorld* column or a software component on the Web, you might in the hyperlink see its size, location, or price, or all three. Should you decide to click on it, the document comes back, automatically paid for right out of your electronic wallet. Or, if the price exceeds some threshold, when you click on the hyperlink your electronic wallet warns you and asks for confirmation.

Next week, in addition to making the 1995 *InfoWorld* Iway Commerce Award to a digital moneyman, I'll explain an experimental system for supporting subpenny Internet transactions.

The following week, we'll learn about a credit chip working its way to your PC.

In the meantime, because 2 cents was too much, would you consider paying maybe 2 mils for this column?

Consummate Your Internet Relationship, Spend Lots of Money

June 3, 1996

There's nothing wrong with the Internet that a lot of money can't fix. Money of many different kinds. Including Mondex.

First there's government money. The Internet started 27 years ago with some of the best-spent money in the history of government. A little more government money — not another runaway jobs program — is needed for continuing Internet research at universities.

Then there's monopoly money. When politicians can't raise taxes, they create monopolies to collect money more discreetly by overcharging choiceless customers. Trouble is, monopolies become runaway jobs programs and don't serve customers all that well.

Which is why today, thanks to telephone monopolies, the Internet obeys not only Moore's Law but also Grove's Law: Bandwidth doubles every hundred years.

Telco monopoly money is now oozing into the Internet with the promise of wet cement. Telcos are becoming dominant Internet service providers (ISPs). Let's preserve competition among ISPs by demonopolizing telecommunications, please.

Then there's investor money. Wall Street is gaga over the Internet. Investor money is flowing in. Trouble is, investors expect their money back, with more than interest. Soon? Then there's advertising money. Companies pay to put products in front of customers. Advertising pays for most newspapers, magazines, radio, television, this column, and other professional sports. Advertising is a major source of money for the Internet, but keep in mind that, ultimately, money flows through companies from their customers.

Which brings us to customer money. This is really the only money that counts.

The daily choices made by customers are the very consummation of democracy. The Internet thrives to the extent that it offers attractive choices to customers who then can spend their money in large amounts.

Therefore, we'd better attend to how the Internet is going to collect and distribute customer money — money that will pay for things bought through the Internet, including the Internet itself, money that will surge through Internet markets carrying messages between supply and demand. Well, as I reported in *InfoWorld* late last year and early this year, the race is on to establish money mechanisms for the Internet.

It's clear there will be a wide variety of Internet monies, including the micromonies soon to ignite renewed growth in software and publishing.

New among Internet money contenders is Mondex, a proposed "global electronic cash payment scheme." Mondex money is carried on smart credit card-size cards.

What's next for Mondex money is for it to be carried on the Internet. I recently spoke with Tim Jones, who helped invent Mondex in 1990 at the British bank National Westminster.

Unlike most proponents of electronic money, Tim Jones has panache. He is a former rock star. He dared to become a Martian management consultant in the launch issue of the glossy *Mondex Magazine*. And he is awesome on the phone, well covering electronic money's ground, from financial instruments to semiconductors.

Unlike many of us, Mondex has a life outside the Internet. For example, in one trial, consumers are using Mondex cards to buy newspapers and place calls from public telephones in Swindon, England. Mondex is testing and franchising its scheme around the nonvirtual world.

Unlike most Internet money, Mondex is based on hardware. The Mondex card carries a reverse-engineering-resistant microprocessor with memory, unique identification, secret keys, and encryption algorithms. Digitally signed cash is downloaded into Mondex's "electronic purses" at automated teller machines, by telephone, or card to card, consumer to merchant, or consumer to consumer.

Jones is now promoting standard smart card readers for personal computers so that Mondex money can flow over the Internet.

Join in watching the evolution of Mondex. Mondex cards are not anonymous, but Jones says they might be. Mondex algorithms are not public — for scrutiny only by well-meaning security experts — but Jones says they might be. Mondex cards are not able to transfer values of less than a penny, but Jones says they might be. They will be, when Mondex catches on. I do look forward to the day when I can pay the freight for downloading a large Java program from India by just popping a Mondex card into a public Internet.

Pay-As-We-Go Internet Puts Your Money Where Your Consumption Is

September 21, 1998

Advocating the Pay-As-We-Go Internet™ is a dirty job, but somebody has to do it. And when I do, as I did here last week (see "Get into the mind flip and do the time warp with anticiparallelism," Sept. 14), disagreeable people throw back in my face how angry I am with the telephone monopolies, which meter telephone calls. Telopolies are giving network usage metering a bad name.

Many of life's other essentials are metered. Water and electricity are metered, for example. We even pay for highways as we go, by the mile, paying metered gasoline taxes and tolls at carefully spaced booths.

But why pay as we go? Why pay e-postage? Why pay for downloaded Web pages? Why pay for gigapacket meters? Because flat-rate billing really works only when the flat rates are high.

Some say most telco costs are for billing, not bandwidth. And since bandwidth will soon be free, there's no sense building all the infrastructure that would be needed for Internet metering and usage billing. Flat rates will suffice.

Well, it's probably not true that most telco costs go for billing. And even if it is, bear in mind that for decades telcos have been increasing their costs to increase their regulated profits.

No, the problem with telco metering is not the metering. It's the rates. They've been ripping us off, and we should be angry about that, not about the metering.

Those who say bandwidth will soon be free have some strong arguments. Semiconductor densities are doubling every 18 months, photonic bandwidths are doubling every 12, and wireless bandwidths are doubling every nine.

To these arguments, I say "great!" but Internet traffic is now doubling every four months. The number of Internet users is going up. The time each of them spends on the Internet is going up. The bandwidth consumption of new applications is going up. Do the multiplication.

It's great that bandwidth is getting cheaper, but like memory, it will always be scarce — it's price elastic. We have economics to deal with scarcity. The Internet can no longer be an economics-free zone.

Metering Internet usage and charging for consumption is what we need in the next-generation Internet. Paying as we go will deter waste, and the prices will serve as distributed coordinators between supply and demand.

The first Pay-As-We-Go systems we need are for settlements among Internet service providers. Sure, telcos settle for carrying one another's calls, but that's not their problem. Their problem is a lack of competition, not settlements. We need settlements among our thousands of competing ISPs, or we'll likely lose them and be stuck getting our Internet from the telopolies.

The second Pay-As-We-Go systems we need are for billing Internet users. As users consume various resources, microcharges will be accumulated and bills periodically sent. ISPs could do this, but it might be better to use separate entities — the way credit cards gather charges from many merchants for many holders.

The third Pay-As-We-Go systems we need are for e-postage. Competing e-mail servers will have to pay competing ISPs for the bandwidth consumed to transmit their mail; they will have to settle up with one another for messages forwarded; and they will have to send e-postage microbills to individual users. E-postage will deter spam while paying for Internet capacity and the timely evolution of e-mail services.

The fourth Pay-As-We-Go systems we need are for Web downloads. Like anybody else generating Internet traffic, Web servers will pay traffic costs. They will also incur server costs. And of course they will want to bill for the value of the content delivered. Web server bills will join those ISPs and e-mail carriers in the Internet's competing microbilling systems.

Now, once we have a Pay-As-We-Go Internet and the bills to come with it, who will pay them?

Well, a lot of Internet bills will be paid by Internet users the way they now pay for food, water, clothing, housing, transportation, and other necessities. But a lot of these bills will be paid by advertisers, which now pay for most of television — strong evidence that we don't want them paying all of our bills.

Then there are the proverbial have-nots.

Won't a Pay-As-We-Go Internet leave the have-nots out of the Information Age? Well, we can argue about that and then when we decide, let's not make the same mistake that we did with the telopolies. It's better to give subsidies to the have-nots to pay as they go on the Internet.

Companies Start Offering Infrastructures for the Pay-As-We-Go Internet

November 23, 1998

One of my least popular ideas, ever, is the Pay-As-We-Go Internet™ — a nextgen Internet with infrastructure for usage metering and billing.

Many of our Internet bills will be paid by advertisers and governments, but with the right infrastructure, we'll be paying more of our own bills. We won't want an Internet in which we get only that for which advertisers and governments are willing to pay.

And although flat rates should not be outlawed, metered rates should be offered and will be chosen by many Internet users to pay as we go for access, services, and content. These will be metered by the second, by the kilopacket, by the megameter, by the message, by the call, by the page — whatever works.

Why pay as we go? Light users will rebel at paying high flat rates that subsidize heavy users. Internet service providers will find heavy flat-rate users unprofitable; ISPs are already capping unlimited usage plans. Metered prices will help to coordinate supply and demand. And usage metering will deter waste, for example, spam.

I've had the honor of getting a recent Pay-As-We-Go column picked up by the Cable News Network, which even ran a poll that asked, "Would you be willing to pay as you surf the Net?" That week 93 percent of 3,451 CNN viewers voted no.

Many CNN viewers think that because they need the Internet, it should be free. Many think the Internet is already paid for by the government and should therefore be free. Many think that if the Internet was metered, they would have to stop using it, no matter what the price. So they've been telling me that I'm a heartless, rich, greedy capitalist pig in the pocket of large corporations. Well, I'm not a pig.

One university student wrote that advocating the Pay-As-We-Go Internet makes me "worse than Hitler." I recommended that he read a book, *Explaining Hitler* (Random House), recently out from my childhood chum Ron Rosenbaum.

I also recommended that this student learn some economics. He said he is, but Marx still haunts American universities, so I'm recommending another book, *Eat the Rich, A Treatise on Economics* (Atlantic Monthly Press), by P.J. O'Rourke, chief of the foreign affairs desk at *Rolling Stone*.

Despite all of this rejection of the Pay-As-We-Go Internet, I've heard from many companies preparing to provide metering and billing infrastructure for ISPs. Here's a partial list ranging up the San Francisco peninsula.

GRIC Communications, in Milpitas, provides metered billing and settlement services to 400 ISPs in 100 countries so they can offer global roaming, remote access, fax, and telephone to 16 million dial-up Internet users.

XACCT Technologies, in Santa Clara, provides an IP billing system that enables ISPs to have flexible pricing models for e-mail, telephone, video, virtual private networks, content — and to give their customers meaningful bills.

Portal Software, in Cupertino, provides customer management and billing software to enable ISPs to have varied pricing plans for new services.

Ipass, in Mountain View, provides 500 ISPs in 150 countries with infrastructure to support roaming services, remote access, and, early next year, exchange point settlements.

Narus, in Redwood City, will announce its technologies on Dec. 2 and its products in early 1999: wire-speed probes that will enable ISPs to analyze traffic and bill for unified messaging, video, telephone, fax, host services, and content.

I'll be back with more about companies providing infrastructure for the Pay-As-We-Go Internet. Although they seem focused on selling to ISPs, corporate information systems may need Pay-As-We-Go infrastructure, too, perhaps for intranet charge-backs or auditing ISP service-level agreements.

What problem is metering supposed to solve?

Rebuttal by John Levine

John R. Levine <collapses@johnlevine.com> has been writing, consulting, and opining on and about the Internet for over a decade. His recent books include "The Internet For Dummies, 7th Edition" and "Internet Secrets, 2nd Edition" (See chapters 2 and 31 for more on the topic of this rebuttal) In his spare time he serves as Water and Sewer Commissioner for the Village of Trumansburg, N.Y.

Much though it dismays me to say this about my esteemed colleague and occasional dinner companion, Bob's missing the point. The Internet is already metered where it matters.

Since we're talking about paying for the Internet, and since in a previous life I was an economist before I settled down as a computer geek, let's start with a look at how it's paid for now. The structure of the Internet is basically a pyramid, with the bandwidth flowing from the top of the pyramid to the bottom, and the money flowing from the bottom to the top. At the top are a few dozen backbone providers, running networks at 155 mbits per second or faster with data centers full of $100,000 routers and a full suite of buzzwords including ATM, SONET, and so forth. Below that are ever-larger numbers of ever-slower connections, down to the dialup, cable modem, and DSL connections that individuals and small businesses use. At each level, the bandwidth gets divided up into smaller and smaller chunks. For example, I get my home connection (a T1, but they also do dialup) from a tiny ISP owned by my local independent phone company, who in turn gets its connection from a larger ISP about 100 miles west of here, who in turn gets its connection from Sprint, one of the backbones.

Conversely, the money flows upward into larger and larger chunks to match the size of the bandwidth. I pay a few hundred dollars a month to my ISP for my T1, and dialup users pay about $20 per month. The ISP in turn pays a few thousand dollars a month to its upstream connection, the larger ISP, who in turn pays about $10,000 per month to its upstream, Sprint. There are a few minor complications that sometime obscure this picture, such as reciprocal compensation which allows ISPs to charge the phone company for incoming phone calls; and the irrationally exuberant investors who keep pouring money into ISPs, letting them sell service below cost year after year; but the basic simple model remains.

This all works because there are huge economies of scale in providing Internet connections. A T1 is about 30 times as fast as a 56K dialup connection, but doesn't cost anything like 30 times as much. What's more, Internet traffic is bursty, with a typical connection having a flurry of activity as a user retrieves a web page or picks up mail, followed by a period of quiet. This means that an ISP can serve 100 dialup users from a T1 with good performance. When they ``oversell'' like this, they're not cheating users, they're using a statistical model to provide service at a reasonable price. As long as the customers' behavior matches the model, everything works. We'll get back to this crucial point shortly.

There are two ways to manage the amount of data that flows through a connection, by controlling the size of the pipe, or by counting the data as it goes by. High volume Internet connections are charged in much the same way as industrial electricity users are charged. Providers use a combination of the capacity of the connection, the total amount of data transferred per month, and the peak usage. In the upstream provider's statistical model, the main aspect of customer behavior that matters is the peak usage — that is, how much data flows over the customer's connection during the busiest 15 minutes of the day. As long as the upstream can handle all the customers' peak usage, the network will work, and non-peak usage doesn't matter, because by definition there's plenty of capacity to handle the traffic. So the provider makes the customer's charge depend on the peak, to encourage each customer to limit his peak usage, and thereby limit the overall peak. This approach works pretty well when there are relatively few customers, and each customer uses a lot of bandwidth. What happens when you have vast numbers of dialup or DSL customers?

There are two rather fundamental differences between dialup/DSL and high-speed customers. The first is that there are a lot of dialup customers, and when you have a lot of people, you can predict their overall statistical behavior quite well. (Students of statistics refer to the law of averages or the central limit theorem; fans of sci fi recognize it as the basis of psychohistory in Isaac Asimov's Foundation series.) The other difference between dialup/DSL and high-speed is that the expensive parts of providing retail Internet service are the phone lines and modems and the support personnel, not the upstream connection. So, if you're an ISP and you know how many modems you have and how many DSL customers, you can predict quite accurately the amount of upstream bandwidth you need and the number of modems you need. It's therefore easier and cheaper just to buy them than to hammer on the users to try to get them to be less wasteful.

The one place this model fails is with outliers, people who don't act the way the model says they will. Since the expensive resources are modems and phones, the outliers are the ``campers'' who stay connected all day and all night. Campers are a problem because each one ties up a modem that otherwise could serve six to ten normal users. But rather than punishing everyone by instituting metering, it's much more effective to say ``no camping,'' with a monthly hour cap, per-session time limits, or the like. Although hour caps are the most common way to deter camping, they're not really the right answer — ISPs' modems are only fully busy a few hours in the day, about 6 to 10 p.m, and the ISP wouldn't care if you were on 500 hours a month as long as it wasn't during those busy hours.

Some users consume a lot more bandwidth per hour than others, but that turns out not to be a big issue. The amount of bandwidth a user can demand is strictly limited by his connection speed, making it hard to use enough to throw off the model. Overall, this means that metering the data transferred by individual users would be a waste of effort because the ISP already understands and can handle what those users do, while metering the campers' data would be pointless since the place they break the model is in peak hour connect time, not in data transfer or even non-peak connect.

Well, if it's not worth metering packets, is it worth metering anything else? The answer is the same one we've already seen: it's worth it only when you have users whose behavior breaks the ISP's economic model. Web hosting companies, for example, generally have a

Continued

(continued)

per-site monthly bandwidth cap that is far higher than most sites ever need. Their problem is the Web equivalent of campers; that is, sites that serve vastly more data than normal. In practice, these sites are either full of JPEG images of naked ladies or ZIP files of stolen software, and it's quite effective just to ban warez sites (they're illegal anyway) and to set special higher rates for porn sites.

How about metering e-mail? Sending e-mail uses very few network resources. (Spam exists because the recipient of mail bears most of the cost of handling the message.) That means charging users for outgoing mail won't accomplish much other than driving users away to ISPs that charge less. Bob has proposed inventing a complex system of e-postage, in which senders pay recipients to defer the costs of receiving messages. This ignores the detail that nobody has the faintest idea how you would build such a system (how am I supposed to remit a $0.02 payment to a recipient in Thailand, or vice versa?), and this system would just substitute one set of social problems for another.

Instead of spamming, bad guys would use a variety of tricks to induce victims to send them large amounts of mail so they could collect the e-postage. Even worse, e-postage would kill the vast number of legitimate mailing lists that exist on the Net. The computers on my home network send out about 30,000 messages a day, nearly all from mailing lists I host for friends and associates. I do this for free because it costs me nothing because I already have the network connection and servers. If I had to hassle with per-message payments, I wouldn't bother. One could imagine a system in which people waive payments from lists to which they've subscribed, but that offers yet another opportunity for screw-ups and fraud. Spam is a social problem, not a technical one, and it needs social solutions, not complex technical band-aids.

I could go through a bunch of other analyses of other services, but they'd all come to the same conclusion: metering is a solution in search of a problem. So, Bob, can we argue about something else instead, please?

The Telco Empires Strike Back

It's human nature to root for the skinny, weak underdog against the great big, nasty bully. That's why we all go to movies like *Star Wars* and why we all hate telephone monopolies. If you get your jollies watching battles between ARPA knights and Imperial storm lawyers, with our rights to fast Internet access being held hostage, you'll love this chapter. It's got battles; it's got an evil Empire; it's got Big Lies; and it's even got lobbyists. Read these columns and you'll see how, in a far off galaxy called Washington, huge telco monopolies are pulling the strings that keep you and me limping on and off the Iway at a snails pace.

Telephone Companies Are Slowing Communication Links

April 20, 1992

Comdex is as far into the future as many of us normally get to look. And so, just before heading off to Chicago, I was fortunate to be in London attending quite a different kind of conference, at The Royal Society, founded in 1620 by England's Charles II. I went to hear the latest on my favorite subject, communications — but only as it will be after the year 2000.

After a day and a half of presentations, I found myself smoldering, waiting for someone to mention Ethernet. But no. And then I began to notice that the speakers weren't talking about IBM Token Ring either. Nor about NetWare, TCP/IP, or OSI. And amid almost constant praise for optical fibers, not a word about FDDI.

Speakers seemed to be carefully constructing their sentences so as to avoid any mention of PCs or workstations. Instead, sprinkled among numerous references to something they called the network, I heard speaker after speaker dismissing my PCs as just so much "customer premises equipment."

It wasn't that this conference was in London. And it wasn't that this conference's futuristic agenda transcended PC LANs. No, it was because I, a personal computer advocate, had stumbled into a meeting of big-time telephone people. These were people who took themselves seriously enough to discuss whether it was the penetration of telephones, to more than 20 phones per 100 people, that finally killed communism in the Soviet Union.

I.D.T. Vallance, chairman of British Telecom, kicked off the conference by admitting how dangerous but necessary it is to predict the future. He beat subsequent speakers to the punch by celebrating the "relentless compounding" of advances in microelectronics and photonics.

Dr. J.S. Mayo, president of AT&T Bell Laboratories, followed by adding software to the list of the three key communications technologies. He noted the existence of chips capable of hundreds of millions of instructions per second and of fibers carrying gigabits per second, projectable to a terabit per second. He looked forward to wireless, hi-fi, video, and even virtual reality telephones but lamented that the slow building of ISDN and fiber infrastructure would leave us with plain old telephone service ("POTS") deep into the third millennium.

Dr. G.J. Handler, vice president of network technologies at Bell Communications Research, felt compelled to break the news that software complexity and the inertia of current infrastructure would slow the proliferation of new telecommunications services. He noted that the United States has $100 billion invested in current telephone facilities, and that today's telephone switches require 10 to 20 million lines of software and therefore it takes five years to introduce a new service. And, by the way, the telephone companies want to offer us those services so that their existing businesses won't become commodities.

And then, finally, a PC owner, J. DeFeo, director of information technology and services businesses for Barclays Bank, broke the PC ice. He said his PCs and workstations were already hurting without ISDN and wondered what was taking the telephone companies so long.

So it seems that the evolution of our PC-based enterprise (and later inter-enterprise) networking systems may be throttled in coming years by the telephone companies. Like most businesses, they want to avoid becoming a commodity. But the installation of raw data transmission services is being held up while the telephone companies figure out how to write the 20-million-line programs (which they think they need to offer all the modern data services that they think the PC community wants). Further, the phone companies will be slow to write off their vast infrastructure investments.

The telephone industry needs a mind-set change. Stop thinking of all of our computing equipment out here as being small, dumb, and cheap. Sure there is $100 billion invested in the telephone network, but there is $500 billion invested in computing equipment. Let's have the transmission facilities we need and skip those centralized telephone services that are holding things up.

Let's have growing competition in the telephone industry.

What Iways Need Now Not Deregulation, but Demonopolization

June 26, 1995

Regulating Iway monopolies is so complicated that lugs such as me and you can't possibly understand the Telecommunications Competition and Deregulation Act now moving through Congress. Does this mean we should slouch back, have a beer, and let sophisticated telco lawyers expertly tinker with the bill on our behalf? No, because there ain't nobody qualified to tinker with our 60 years of accumulated telecommunications regulatory apparatus — nobody I'd trust, anyway.

It's dangerous to fool with mean Judge Green, three overlapping subcommittees in Congress, five Federal Communications Commission members, 51 state utilities commissions, a long list of executive branch agencies, bureaus, councils, offices, forces, and the swarm of lobbyists that regularly take them all to lunch. No, our only hope is to bulldoze the rickety old thing and rebuild from scratch.

The Competition and Deregulation Act aims to free everybody in telecommunications from regulation so they can compete with everybody else, thereby lowering prices, increasing choices, and spurring technological advancement. Amen.

Senate Bill 652 has passed, but the Competition and Deregulation Act is still under consideration as House Bill 1555, and the usual suspects are busy amending the hell out of it.

Local telco monopolies say they are for the Act. Consider their ad in my June issue of *The American Spectator.*

"Consumers should be able to choose the companies they use for each and every telecommunications service... That's why Congress should authorize full competition in local phone service, cable and long distance — now," the ads say. Amen.

No matter what the ads say, however, telco lobbyists are meeting daily with members of Congress and their staffs, pressuring for amendments that free them to compete while having their monopolies protected. And long-distance telcos don't want local telcos coming into their markets until there is effective local competition. Cable companies want their price controls lifted even before the telcos are ready to give them a run for their money.

Democrats want universal service mandates. Republicans want decency. And I want competition. The situation is overconstrained. Congress might reach gridlock on the bill.

Here is the problem: The bill is misnamed. Competition and deregulation are not compatible when you're dealing with big old companies with 99 percent market share. We will actually have to regulate such monopolies, at least in the interim, so as to create and then sustain their competition. The International Communications Association (ICA), which lobbies on behalf of telco customers, notes under S.652 as it stands, telco monopolies will suddenly be unregulated and without competition to keep them honest. ICA estimates, therefore, that over four years residential telephone rates will more than double to $40 per month.

Therefore, I propose we bulldoze S.652 by renaming it the Communications Demonopolization Act of 1995, and that we begin rebuilding with three simple new rules.

First, S.652 should cap all telco prices at current levels forever. No big windfalls while competition ramps up. I know that telco costs are declining and so, therefore, should prices, but let them do so under competitive pressure, just for practice.

Second, S.652 should prohibit all mergers and acquisitions among telecommunications companies with more than, say, $1 billion per year in sales.

Having telcos buy cable companies, for example, would not create the competition we need. Such business combinations would not leverage scale or integration to benefit consumers; they would leverage monopoly at the expense of consumers.

And third, S.652 should focus the FCC on standards and practices that foster competition. Antitrust enforcement should, as the Clinton administration is recommending, go to our emergent hero Anne Bingaman in the Department of Justice.

Doing so should result in divestitures.

It's late, but not too late to get involved in enacting the kind of telecommunications law we ought to have. Contact ICA. Get on the Web and read.

Call your representatives in Congress. Don't sit back and watch us lose this chance to open our Iways to competition.

Hey, Congress: Local Telco Monopolies Need Breaking Up

November 20, 1995

Congress is probably still messing around with the optimistically named but fatally flawed Telecommunications Competition and Deregulation Act of 1995. A joint committee is probably still pretending to agonize over minor differences between House Bill 1555 and Senate Bill 652, both of which miss the point entirely. The reconciliation is probably still dominated as usual by lawyers lobbying on behalf of organized special interests, in this case the huge local telephone monopolies. I've been finding out, alas, that more than a few of my Republican buddies are slimy politicians, too.

So now I'm agreeing with AT&T, which is arguing that turning the local telcos loose to provide long-distance telephone service is not our current top priority. And we're both agreeing with Democrats in and around the White House.

This tells you how much of a snit I'm in.

To relieve my snit, I walked across the bridge to a small, quiet conference at MIT. There I ran into Internet pioneer Bob Kahn. We talked about a new book his Corporation for National Research Initiatives (CNRI) just published in its series on the history of infrastructures. CNRI's first book was *Emerging Infrastructure: The Growth of Railroads*. CNRI's new, second history is *Natural Monopoly and Universal Service, Telephones and Telegraphs in the U.S. Communications Infrastructure, 1837-1940*.

What impact might *Natural Monopoly* have on the current shenanigans in Washington over telecommunications reform? Kahn says CNRI is planning to publish 20 books of infrastructure history, and so it's too soon for the series to help much in shaping national information infrastructure. But I'm desperate.

CNRI's telephone history shows how competition was important in the transition from telegraph to telephone. I think the book shows how to accelerate the transition from telephone to interactive home video, World Wide Web appliances, and other cool stuff like that. We won't see any of this anytime soon if it's left to the complacent, bumbling local telephone monopolies.

Although state public utilities commissions and the Federal Communications Commission were chosen in 1934 to be The New Deal's regulatory regime for telecommunications, competitive models have worked before and after. For example, the Bell Co. formed AT&T in 1885 to provide long-distance telephone service.

The book says, "What drove AT&T's research and development in long-distance telephone technology in the late 1880s was the coming expiration of key patents in 1894, when AT&T foresaw intense competition that did, indeed, occur."

Between 1894 and 1907, independent telephone companies proliferated to meet customer demand that AT&T had ignored.

Quite a bit later, in the 1960s, the first major step in telco demonopolization was taken with the decision to allow you to buy non-AT&T customer premises equipment such as, say, Hayes modems. That worked. In the 1970s, the provision of long-distance telephone service was demonopolized. That worked. And now it's time to demonopolize local telephone service.

How else to light a fire under the companies we're expecting to pave the Information Superhighway? Why is it a priority of the pending legislation to let the local monopolies into long distance, which is already competitive? Why is it a priority to encourage even greater concentrations of market power through telecommunications mergers? Congress, stop listening to monopoly lobbyists and start listening to, er, well, me. It's the demonopolization of local telcos, stupid.

The current legislation has been hijacked by the local telco monopolies in a lobbying coalition called The Alliance for Competitive Communication. Thanks to them, about the only competitive thing left in the Telecommunications Act of 1995 or 1996 is that, at last report, it allows cable TV companies to offer voice in competition with telcos. Amen.

Anyway, whether or not there is a 1995 act, I'm preparing for the Telecommunications Demonopolization Act of 1997. By then a few more CNRI infrastructure histories and hopefully the rest of the wheeling and dealing Washington elite will be out.

For your copy of *Natural Monopoly*, contact CNRI.

A Rebel Challenge to the Imperial Telco Empire

March 3, 1997

A long time ago, in a galaxy far, far away, Ben "Obi-Wan Kenobi" Barker was an ARPA knight on the planet BBN Corp. Barker has now reappeared in the Texas desert as chief of the Data Race Inc. And we are relieved to learn that, unlike Cerf Vader, this ARPA knight has not been tragically turned to the telco side of the force.

More than 300 Web generations ago, the ARPA knights launched the Internet rebellion against the Imperial Telco Empire. Today, Barker and his insignificant rebel band in San Antonio are rising up against the Empire once again. The Data Race is penetrating the twisted-pair defenses of the Telco Empire's central office: the Death Star.

OK, perhaps I go too far in portraying our oppressive telecommunications regulatory regime and its pitiful telephone monopolies as the Imperial Empire from Star Wars. Such an overly dramatic portrayal begs the question: Who would be Luke Skywalker? Who would be Yoda? (I'd probably be Jabba the Hut, because only he would think up e-postage.) Anyway, let me introduce you to Data Race's Be There (BT) Personal Multiplexor, a premiere product at InfoWorld's Demo '97 conference last month in Indian Wells, California.

In short, Data Race's BT is a pair of exotic three-processor modems, one in your PC at home and the other in a remote-access server at your place of business.

Software in your PC and its BT modem connect you through the Empire's plain old telephone service (POTS) to software in your company's BT server. The server, in turn, connects you to your company's PBX and LAN.

With BT (not to be confused with British Telecommunications, soon to be confused with MCI), it's just like being there back in your office, receiving voice and fax calls exactly as if your home PC were an extension of your office phone system. And you can simultaneously be connected through your BT modems to your office LAN and the Internet. All for a cost of $500 per PC modem card and $15,200 per eight-port server.

Assuming your home is a local POTS call from your office and assuming not too many of your neighbors get busy signals trying this at home, you can telecommute all day for no extra charge beyond that flat monthly Imperial Telco tariff.

Data Race's 33.6Kbps BT modems drive voice, fax, and data simultaneously over any POTS line. The BT modems digitize and compress voice to about 8Kbps. They interleave voice packets with fax and Internet packets. Imagine, with BT you can speed up Web downloads just by not talking.

Digital data-packet switching on top of analog voice-circuit switching is such an abomination that dial-up modems hiss and squawk every time we force them to do it. And so I advise you not to listen when BT dials up. But the Telco Empire gives Barker and his Data Race no other choice in penetrating the Death Star's defenses.

Of course, Barker knows what he would do if the Death Star were no longer fully armed and operational. Instead of making digital data packets look like analog voice calls so that they can then be redigitized and circuit switched, Barker would jumper past the Empire's voice circuit switch that now separates your home and office in the Death Star.

This would allow your home and office or your home and an Internet service provider, to be connected all the time, without the rigmarole of touch-tone dialing, at much higher speeds, at much less cost, without tying up the 121-year-old Empire's obsolete but undepreciated circuit-switching apparatus.

The Federal Communications Commission, intending to implement the Telecommunications Act of 1996, issued regulations giving rebels throughout the Empire access to local wiring in all Death Stars.

The Empire has for now repelled this attack on its Death Stars by appealing to the Supreme Court. There, Imperial stormlawyers will be light-sabering the Act and the FCC for years to come. In the very long meantime, you can "be there" by uniting with Barker and his Data Race.

If you happen to see the updated *Star Wars* trilogy in coming weeks, notice how perfectly the Emperor Palpatine resembles the CEO of your local Imperial Telco.

Telco Empire Strikes Back with Monopoly Embrace and Subsidies for Schools

April 28, 1997

In our last episode of Internet Wars, Arpa Knights returned to attack the Telco Empire's central-office Death Star. Their allies were an insignificant rebel force of ISPwoks armed only with points of presence and modems. The alliance hoped to penetrate the Death Star and win galaxywide megabit packet access to the Internet.

In this week's episode, the Empire strikes back. Defending the Death Star against competition, the telcos have deployed a fleet of Federal Communications Commission cruisers carrying legions of Imperial stormlawyers.

A Pacific Bell commander was overheard bragging that PacBell's acquisition by SBC will create the fourth-largest telco — which is good news for whom? Since Imperial stormlawyers brought us telecommunications reform in 1996, we've learned that telcos will not be competing, but merging. If there's one thing worse than a few big, regulated monopolies, it's fewer, bigger, unregulated monopolies.

The PacBell commander dismissed cable TV as competition against the Empire. The FCC has conveniently capped prices on cable, making it hard to fund upgrades for Internet service.

The PacBell commander reported that the Empire is investing heavily to meet the growing demands of Internet modems. But carrying digital data packets through the Death Star over analog voice circuits using modems is an anachronistic abomination. We need direct multimegabit packet access.

The PacBell commander then mentioned the Empire's aggressive deployment of Digital Subscriber Lines (DSLs) for high-speed Internet access.

"Aggressive" like ISDN deployment was aggressive? We don't want DSL deployed monopolistically. We want DSL deployed competitively, which means Internet service provider (ISP) interconnection and collocation within the Death Star. Imperial stormlawyers are fighting interconnection in court. And it turns out collocation is permitted only to regulated "common carriers."

The PacBell commander declared war on lesser ISPs, many of which rely on PacBell for circuits. The FCC, Department of Justice, Federal Trade Commission — somebody — should insist that PacBell and other telco monopolies divest their vertically integrated ISPs.

Finally, the PacBell commander demanded that ISPs pay access fees ("modem taxes") into the FCC's Universal Service Fund. FCC Chairman Reed Hundt said reassuringly that he's against taxing ISPs "for now."

So, there it is. This week the Empire is back, bringing ISPs under monopoly regulations we've been trying to dismantle for 30 years.

More proof? Chairman Hundt and the telcos now fervently support Internet subsidies for schools and libraries (S&Ls). This is yet another Empire ploy to bring ISPs under its thumb, this time using our children as a force shield to protect the Death Star.

On May 6, the FCC will vote to allocate a couple billion dollars to pay for S&L Internet subsidies. These billions will burden only people who use telephones, especially urban business data rate payers; probably you.

Socialized education and monopoly telecommunications have been around for more than a century. Still, there are fewer telephones and televisions in classrooms than Apple IIs. If we are to believe the Clinton Administration, the Internet, with ISP discounts to S&Ls, will be in every classroom four years from now.

You can argue against the FCC's S&L Internet subsidies, but I won't. Instead, I'll object to what the FCC is shrewdly calling these subsidies: discounts.

As I wrote Dec. 9, 1996 (see "ISPs should help kids and libraries, but forced discounts repeat mistakes"), the FCC will soon vote that ISPs, each according to its ability, must give discounted Internet service to schools and libraries — to each according to its needs. Then ISPs will have to beg reimbursement of these S&L discounts from universal service funds collected from telcos by the FCC.

We could give tax money to S&Ls to buy their Internet, but the FCC plans to drag ISPs into the Empire by forcing them to seek S&L discount reimbursement from the Empire. Then ISP prices, costs, and "modem taxes" will fall under the jurisdiction of the petty commissars at the FCC and our 51 public utilities commissions.

If you'd like to discourage the FCC from imposing S&L Internet discounts, contact Chairman Hundt. Hurry.

After Steering Clear of Microsoft's Pathway, Ferguson Takes on FCC

May 5, 1997

Charles Ferguson downshifted into a questionable left turn across Market Street in San Francisco. A few blocks ahead was Il Fornaio, where Ferguson and I would wail long into the night about Internet profiteering among telephone monopolies.

I tried not to sound as if I were begging Ferguson to slow down. He laughed and said it only seemed like we were going too fast because his Miata was low to the ground and its top was down.

Just then the proverbial truck started pulling out from a dark side street into our path. Instead of hitting the breaks — as I was trying to do — Ferguson downshifted, swerved, and accelerated past certain death by a hair.

Some weeks before, I had met Ferguson after a talk at Harvard University about Vermeer Technologies. The exciting part of Ferguson's story was what happened when Microsoft's truck pulled out from a dark side street into the path of his accelerating 18-month-old Web-tools company. He downshifted past certain death by selling Vermeer to Microsoft for a reported $135 million.

Today, Ferguson, with a doctorate in political science from MIT, is a visiting scholar at the University of California at Berkeley and MIT. I often walk slowly over to rendezvous with him among the glitterati at Sonsie, a bistro on Newbury Street in Boston. Please don't tell them we're only gossiping about local exchange carriers (LECs).

LECs are the villains of a 184-page essay Ferguson just wrote that I urge you to read. His essay "analyzes policy issues related to future local telecommunications services, particularly the digital infrastructure needed for Internet services, electronic commerce, open-systems HDTV [high-definition TV], videoconferencing, and future voice telephony."

Ferguson's essay concludes that the Federal Communications Commission policy fails to give Internet service providers the right to interconnect or collocate their data networking equipment with the monopoly LECs, creating barriers to entry and retarding technological progress.

Antitrust policy has permitted monopolistic practices, mergers, and cooperation among competitors. As a result, local services could remain dominated by LECs "whose technological performance and strategic conduct are severely inappropriate for a modern information economy."

Ferguson's essay details, for example, the current T1 scandal (my word) and why LECs do not offer us High-bit-rate Digital Subscriber Lines (HDSL) for 1.5Mbps

Internet access. In short, LECs, without fear of competition, charge on average $500 per month for 1.5Mbps T1 service, in addition to $3,000 for installation. These prices explain why T1 is growing only 40 percent per year vs. 200 percent to 300 percent annual growth for the Internet.

Still, by the end of this year, there will be nearly 2 million T1 circuits, accounting for upward of $5 billion to $10 billion, or 4 percent to 8 percent of LEC revenues. Many of these circuits are used for Internet access, contributing to as much as 25 percent of LEC networking profits.

Now although T1 prices have not been dropping, HDSL has been lowering T1 costs. A pair of 1.5Mbps HDSL terminals costs $600 to $1,200 total. With a half million HDSL lines already in service, these costs are rapidly declining.

It is understandable why LECs aren't reducing T1 prices according to volume increases they are getting from Internet buyers nor from technology advances they are getting from HDSL. The LECs make big money from T1, just as IBM once did from mainframes, and they lack competition.

Why are LECs permitted this Internet profiteering after the Telecommunications Act of 1996? Why are four out of the eight major LECs now considering mergers instead of competing with one another? Why was Bell Atlantic just given the green light to merge with Nynex?

The widening investigations in Washington into campaign finance and the behavior of Janet Reno's Department of Justice should look closely at LEC lobbying and Reed Hundt's FCC.

Meanwhile, read Ferguson's essay, *The Internet, U.S. Economic Growth, and Telecommunications Policy*.

Some LEC trucks will likely pull out from a dark side street into Ferguson's path, but expect him to downshift, swerve, and accelerate past certain death by a hair again.

Don't Buy Monopolist Jive: GRIC Provides Global Competitive Access, Billing

June 23, 1997

My predictions batting average is not 1.000. For example, I struck out when the Internet escaped gigalapses during 1996. I'll long remember how mercilessly many of you insisted I pay the price. So, I'm asking, Who will be eating my December 1995 predictions column now that it's clear I hit a homer on the Telecommunications Act of 1996?

As I warned in 1995, the Act is bogus. It was supposed to bring competition to local telecommunications. Not. And our highly competitive and rapidly evolving Internet is gravely threatened.

When the Act passed in early 1996, many celebrated the long-awaited opening of competition with local-exchange carrier telephone monopolies, which I'll call telopolies. Many ignored the bad sign that prominent among the Act's party-goers were telopoly lobbyists.

Well, has competition flourished? No.

Instead, gobble gobble gobble, MFS bought UUNet (done), WorldCom bought MFS (done), SBC bought Pacific Bell (done), British Telecom bought MCI (pending), and Bell Atlantic bought Nynex (pending). And now SBC is brazenly trying to undo two decades of telecommunications demonopolization by buying AT&T (or vice versa).

Of course, telopolists know public sentiment is anti-monopolies and pro-choice. Using what former Clinton strategist Dick Morris called triangulation, telopolists trumpet that they must merge monopolies and integrate Internet service providers (ISPs) to become, yes, more competitive. How stupid do they think we are?

What's worse than a few big regulated monopolies? Fewer, bigger unregulated monopolies. We need more great ideas for keeping the Internet competitive such as Hong Chen's Global Reach Internet Connection (GRIC).

Hong Chen left China to study computer science in the United States and he got his Ph.D. in 1991. Interested in software for "advanced interactive media," Chen and his Taiwanese wife, Lynn Liu, founded AimQuest in 1994. They've raised $9 million in venture capital. They grew as an ISP.

In 1996, AimQuest established GRIC to provide global roaming services for subscribers of member ISPs. AimQuest, having sold its ISP business, now employs 70 people developing GRIC software and services in Milpitas, Calif.

Chen says GRIC's membership — 105 ISPs with 5.5 million subscribers in 40 countries — is growing fast. A series of big deals is pending. Netcom, with 700,000 subscribers, is so far GRIC's largest member in the United States.

But even small ISPs, for a $5,000 software license and annual minimum fees of less than $1,000, can offer their traveling subscribers access to the Internet from around the world.

A GRIC member's traveling subscriber calls a local access number provided by his home ISP. He logs in with his name, password, and home ISP. These are authenticated through the home ISP and the session recorded at GRIC.

Monthly, GRIC collects and redistributes billings to member ISPs so they can charge subscribers for global services rendered, now 30 cents to $1 per log-in and 6 to 10 cents per minute. Settlements are also exchanged so that members can pay one another for services rendered. GRIC's take is 10 percent to 20 percent.

GRIC is developing new services, which its growing membership can offer globally, such as remote access to corporate intranets, fax, telephony, videoconferencing, and paging.

Chen estimates that the 2002 market for these and other global Internet services will be $60 billion. His dream is to be the first mainland Chinese founding CEO to take a Silicon Valley company public.

Irresponsible opportunists offering Internet services, especially telephony, say that long distance on the Internet is free. What they mean is they've so far been able to get away with not paying for the backbone bandwidth their services consume. Chen says that when Internet backbones start demanding payment, GRIC will offer global backbone settlement services.

What recourse do GRIC members have if service is poor or fees high? Chen says his strategy is to make a fair profit. Because we seldom agree on what's fair, and because we've had enough of governments deciding for us, I told Chen that a competitive market for GRIC will likely develop.

Demand Coppertone from Phone Companies for Cheap, Fast 'Net Access

July 7, 1997

Last week I asked nicely for a simple, low-end 1998 repackaging of tried-and-true packet-switching technologies. I asked for "imps" to provide businesses, schools, libraries, and homes with small, interim LANs and more affordable multimegabit packet access to the Internet. (See "Little imps could bring 'Net plumbing to schools, businesses, and libraries," June 30.)

This week I ask, not so nicely, for "coppertone" rather than more modem dial tone. Our imps need more affordable multimegabit packet access to Internet service providers (ISPs) directly through plain-old dry metallic copper wires.

But local telephone companies are not losing any sleep about getting their 121-year-old analog voice circuit-switching monopolies out of the Internet's digital data packet-switching way. Telopolies might slowly be getting around to offering circuit-switch-bypass Internet services, but not soon or cheaply enough. And, in the meantime, they're biting the ears off would-be competitors.

So, I propose small interface message processors — not IMPs, but imps. These imps will route Internet packets among their Ethernet ports and to adjacent multimegabit Internet packet access demarcs (little pads to complement our little imps). These pads will someday contain cable-TV modems, satellite-tracking antennas, and eventually lasing diodes for fiber transmission.

But, in the long interim, we want High-bit-rate Digital Subscriber Line (HDSL) pads that exchange packets with ISPs at more than 1Mbps.

The pad I want in my basement has an RJ-45 Ethernet port for connecting to my imp and an RJ-48C port for connecting via HDSL to my ISP. Getting copper is the hard part of HDSL between RJ-48C pad ports and ISPs. Copper wires are easy; the problem is rapacious telopolies.

The good news is that some of you can already buy inexpensive coppertone from telopolies. My ISP and I got some coppertone just last week. Now, don't ask anyone at your telephone company for coppertone or HDSL; this will get you nowhere. Instead, order a "burglar-alarm circuit," put some HDSL electronics at each end, and bingo, you can have 1.5Mbps for a fraction of what telopolies charge for T1 lines.

The folks at my own ISP, Midcoast Internet Solutions, in Owls Head, Maine, say that if Nynex allowed coppertone, they'd convert four of their five 1.5Mbps lines to HDSL and save $2,000 of the $3,000 they spend each month on T1.

The bad news is that your local telopoly may not be willing to provide you with burglar-alarm circuits. They may be planning to offer their own HDSL. They, of course, don't want any competition while they're deploying ISDN and their daring new colors for Princess telephones. They need the cash from T1 overcharges to pay for mergers with other telopolies and ISPs.

Pacific Bell says it's eager to deploy DSL. Of course, it is not so eager as to let anyone else provide DSL. The alarm companies have lobbied for years with the Public Utilities Commission to keep coppertone, and PacBell is always trying to withdraw or substantially increase the tariffs. PacBell offers DSL service in some locations, but the price is high — some say ridiculous. When it announced DSL, PacBell said $50 per month. Now it is saying $200 to $300 per month. Nice not having competitors.

US West, another telopoly, offers more than $10 billion in "one-stop" communications to 25 million customers in 14 states. One thing US West wants to stop is coppertone. In May, the telopoly said it is taking burglar-alarm circuits off the market.

US West says it's not keeping competitors from providing HDSL, but avoiding cross-talk interference in trunking cables. Telopolies say cross-talk is a big problem when providing DSL competitors with coppertone, but it's manageable when they're providing DSL themselves.

Since AOL's megalapse last August, telopolies have been fear-mongering about long Internet calls collapsing the telephone network. They want ISPs to pay more for dial-up ports. It seems to me that coppertone should get special credits — not high prices — for reusing old depreciated plant and reducing the load on the voice network. But telopolies want more for dial tone — the modem tax — and more for coppertone.

Next week, because the telopolies have sued the Federal Communications Commission over rulings opening competition under the Telecommunications Act of 1996, and because turnabout is fair play, I'll propose a class-action lawsuit against the telopolies, like the one now against tobacco companies. I'll be looking for a Coppertone (which rhymes with Carterphone) Decision.

Illegal Business Practices, Spreading Lies Just Business As Usual for Baby Bells

August 11, 1997

Roy Neel must have trouble facing himself in the morning. Either that or he's a lawyer. On July 23 in *USA Today,* Neel defended incumbent local exchange carriers (ILECs) against complaints that they are resisting efforts to open up local telephone markets to competition.

With a straight face, Neel wrote that ILECs are opening up their markets and were opening them even before the Telecommunications Act of 1996. Alas, that's why ILECs have been forced to fight the Act and Federal Communications Commission rulings in the (not tennis) courts — to defend "real" efforts to bring competition to telecommunications.

Neel actually wrote that ILECs "welcome competition," are making "real progress toward all-out competition," and are offering "real choices."

Among propaganda professionals, this is known as The Big Lie.

Neel and his 70-some staff are paid to tell The Big Lie. Neel is president of the 100-year-old United States Telephone Association (USTA) in Washington.

Without shame, Neel continued his *USA Today* rebuttal, saying the FCC should drop efforts to bring competition to local telephony and, instead, "look into the stall of competition in the long-distance and cable areas — two areas where American consumers are desperate for real choices."

Get real, Neel. Long distance and cable could use some more competition, sure, but they already have lots. In long distance, we now routinely choose from AT&T, MCI, and Sprint, to name three. Cable operators get competition from broadcast TV, satellite TV, radio, and video rentals.

So who is stalling competition in telecommunications? Neel's 1,200 USTA members, who, if the truth be known, account for 160 million telephone lines; $20 billion per year in capital investments, which now total $298 billion; 500,000 employees; and $100 billion in annual revenue. They are all hanging tough against the march of progress.

USA Today does not believe USTA's Big Lie.

"In case after case, Baby Bells resist opening markets. Their customers pay the bill," the editors of *USA Today* recounted.

Since the AT&T breakup in 1984, long-distance service rates have fallen by 22 percent. Local telopoly rates are up 53 percent.

Here, on July 14, I proposed we sue Neel's members. Again, somebody please organize an antitrust class action against the local telopolies. They are guilty of agreeing to not compete in each other's territories. They are guilty of tying their copper monopolies to voice and Internet services. Through this illegal tying, ILECs perpetuate their monopolies in voice and leverage those monopolies unfairly into expanding Internet markets.

The response of *InfoWorld* readers to this idea of suing the telopolies has been gung ho. I'm buried in infuriating reports of telopoly abuse. I hope you're all getting ready to join when we find a way to break the USTA.

Thanks to *USA Today,* we now know that an antitrust suit against telopolies is not unthinkable. Electric Lightwave, in Vancouver, Wash., has been fighting US West's efforts to hamper its competition. Electric Lightwave sued on June 30.

Through a rhetorical sleight of hand, Neel pushes responsibility for competition onto long-distance carriers — unattractive characters who would retire if they could ever stop restructuring. What Neel doesn't want you to notice is that the most qualified competitors to his members are...his members.

But local telephone companies don't compete. USTA says that competition among its members is not prohibited nor unheard of, but only a couple possible examples come to mind from a thousand companies over a hundred years. The acquisition of Nynex by Bell Atlantic is unfortunately going through exactly because our antitrust watchdogs see no possibility of these two adjacent USTA behemoths competing.

I've been warned that breaking telopolies to make way for the Information Age is a fool's errand — that taking on the $100 billion USTA threatens my credibility, similar to predicting Internet collapses. But if we don't, who will? And if not now, when? Keep your ideas flowing and checkbooks at the ready.

FCC Chairman Hundt Shares Our Fears of Telopoly Abuses of the Internet

September 15, 1997

Last week, standing in his office atop the Federal Communications Commission building on M Street in Washington, I thanked Reed Hundt for serving four years as chairman of the FCC. I took the liberty of thanking him on your behalf.

In two weeks, Congress is scheduled to begin confirmation hearings on four out of five new FCC commissioners. Why anyone even remotely qualified would take Hundt's job, I'll never know. Can't be the money. Not even Hundt's photo of Clint Eastwood begging him for a radio-station license seems worth it.

Being no Clint Eastwood, I was surprised they let me in to the FCC after savaging Hundt here in May. I'd gone after Hundt for playing Robin Hood to schools and libraries with our telephone bills and, worse, throwing Internet service providers to the regulatory wolves (see "FCC's Hundt takes a step forward, two backward with subsidies and taxes," May 19). Nameless members of Hundt's staff said my attack on the chairman was nothing compared to the usual, and Hundt agrees with me (or vice versa) on most everything else.

Hundt is not leaving his high office gracefully. He's recently been sticking his thumb in the eyes of the telephone monopolies.

Great stuff.

I worried here last month about the so-called Internet Protection Act of 1997 (IPA97) now before Congress (see "Don't let the name fool you: Beware the Internet Protection Act of 1997," Aug. 25). Hundt is flat out against IPA97, and now instead of being worried, I'm scared.

Hundt's view is that IPA97 is part of a determined effort by telopoly interests to move jurisdiction for the Internet out of the FCC and down to the state level, where telopolies and their public utilities commissions hold sway. But, Hundt asks, is the Internet mainly a network for local or intrastate communication, or is it more at the interstate or even international level?

Hundt is sympathetic to those, including me, who urge the debloating of Washington. But, throwing the Internet in pieces to telopolies and their local authorities is not a place the devolution battle should go. If the Internet is to be regulated at all, we agree, it should be by the FCC, and in large part to prevent burdensome regulation and taxation by local authorities.

Hundt's view on the Telecommunications Act of 1996 is more surprising. He's angry with the legal profession, the courts, and Congress for allowing telopoly lawyers to thwart competition by halting the Act's implementation. (So it's no wonder the leading candidate to take over AT&T is a regulatory lawyer.)

In a recent *Wall Street Journal* article, Harvard Law School's Laurence Tribe attacked Hundt and defended telopoly litigation to halt implementation of the Telecommunications Act of 1996. Tribe wrapped himself up in the Constitution — a sure sign that Hundt is right.

Tribe represents the worst of the telopolies — SBC Communications — and he likes trying his cases in the newspapers. Tribe is arguing that it's unconstitutional to name telopolies in the Act. I'd say the U.S. Department of Justice should return the favor by naming them in an antitrust countersuit.

I asked the chairman how he felt about my urging of a class-action antitrust lawsuit against the United States Telephone Association (USTA). Recall, these are the local telopolies, who in obvious violation of antitrust law, do not compete with one another and who are unfairly leveraging their $200-billion circuit-switching monopolies into today's emerging $1.5-billion packet-switching markets (see "Illegal business practices, spreading lies just business as usual for Baby Bells," Aug. 11).

It's a good sign that the chairman did not pat me on the head and tell me to run along.

Instead, Hundt said such suits would be stronger if launched by governments — how about the United States vs. USTA? He reminded me how state attorneys general broke open tobacco litigation. When I asked whether the FCC would be taking any antitrust action against the telopolies, Hundt smiled and said I was asking the wrong guy.

Who is the right guy? Joel Klein, head of the Antitrust Division of the Department of Justice. If anybody out there knows Klein, please tell him he can always come back to Microsoft later, after breaking the telopolistic USTA.

I invited Hundt to speak with computer executives gathering at Agenda 98, the industry conference I'm co-producing in its 11th year with Stewart Alsop next month in Arizona.

I'll get back to you with what Hundt says to, and gets told by, that audience.

Have the Telcos Actually Bought and Paid for Tamed Antitrust Bulldogs?

November 24, 1997

Much to their surprise, I've taken to thanking people in government service. There should be fewer of them, of course, but we do need some good ones. What I can't figure out is why, except for my thanks, anyone good would put up with the hassles.

Last week, I thanked Daniel Rubinfeld, Deputy Assistant United States Attorney General for Economic Analysis. He didn't say, "You're welcome" because I was hassling him at the time in preparation for the following little expose.

Just remember, I'm out to break the telephone monopolies, including especially the 1,200 local exchange carriers (LECs), which meet regularly in restraint of trade at the United States Telephone Association (USTA). (See "Illegal business practices, spreading lies just business as usual for Baby Bells," Aug. 11.) USTA members' combined revenues top $100 billion, for which they do not compete, period. And like Microsoft, they're hot to leverage their monopolies into emerging Internet markets. Meanwhile, they overcharge for inadequate local-loop communications. LECs are a bandwidth bottleneck between us and the Information Age.

So, why doesn't the Department of Justice have an antitrust suit against the USTA? And, given that the only thing worse than a few big regulated LECs is fewer, bigger unregulated LECs, why did the Department of Justice allow SBC to buy PacBell and Bell Atlantic to buy Nynex? Is the Department of Justice too busy with Microsoft to be working the LEC antitrust case or has the Department of Justice been "captured" by the LECs?

Consider the capture of Daniel Rubinfeld.

In September, the Department of Justice announced Rubinfeld's appointment as Deputy Assistant Attorney General for Economic Analysis. His overall economic analysis responsibilities include competition among LECs. The Department of Justice said Rubinfeld is highly qualified — with, for example, a Ph.D. from MIT and a professorship at the University of California at Berkeley.

What the Department of Justice did not say is that Rubinfeld is a principal of the Law and Economics Consulting Group, in Emeryville, Calif. It's probably a coincidence that LECG's initials are LEC followed by G.

A major portion LECG's business is consulting, expert testimony, and litigation support for companies on antitrust and regulatory matters. LECG's Web pages do not list its clients.

The news is that LECG principals plan soon to cash in through an initial public offering (IPO) of stock. LECG billed $20 million in the first half of 1997, and business is so good that Rubinfeld's 4.9 percent of LECG is worth maybe $6 million. He hopes to sell maybe $1 million of it in the upcoming IPO.

But wait — sources estimate that 25 percent of LECG's revenues are from LECs, including Ameritech, Bell Atlantic, Indiana Bell, Nevada Bell, Nynex, PacBell, SBC Communications, US West, and the USTA.

So Rubinfeld heads the Department of Justice's analysis of competition among LECs and holds millions in stock, the value of which is tied to satisfying LEC clients.

Rubinfeld returned my call immediately. He told me his LECG holdings were long ago disclosed. In accordance with the Department of Justice ethics policies, he recuses himself from matters relating to clients of LECG. The SBC and Bell Atlantic acquisitions were completed before he arrived at the Department of Justice.

Rubinfeld assured me he would not act improperly to benefit LECG clients. He invited me to check up on the reputation that won him his high office. He didn't enter government service for the money, but is a liberal Democrat who's making considerable financial and family sacrifices for the honor of serving his country.

I believe Rubinfeld and invite you to join me in thanking him again for his government service. I believe him, by the way, not because he's a liberal Democrat, but because he's a graduate of MIT, where I'm president of the alum association.

But, I ask you, is recusal a sufficient remedy for appearances of conflict such as Rubinfeld's? Is the point of view of the LECs so pervasive among Rubinfeld's colleagues that recusal is mere window dressing?

Consider that another LECG principal, Richard Gilbert, held Rubinfeld's current Department of Justice job several years ago. And that Laura Tyson, former head of President Clinton's National Economic Council, joined Ameritech's board of directors shortly after leaving the White House to become a partner in...LECG.

Does not bode well for demonopolizing the LECs.

Telecom Analyst Ventures Forth with Documentation of Big Baby Bell Rip-Offs

January 26, 1998

Bruce Kushnick just spent seven years writing his "unauthorized biography" of the Bell telephone monopolies. His unpublished, 475-page manuscript exposes how the Baby Bells have been ripping us off since they were born out of AT&T in 1984.

Kushnick has been living off credit card debt in Brooklyn, N.Y. He wears black, vibrates with nervous energy, and jokes about his Bell paranoia.

After receiving a letter from Nynex indicating a "mysterious third party" is after him, Kushnick also wrote a semiautobiographical novel, now a screenplay in development at Warner Brothers. "Touchtone" is about the Bells conspiring to kill a telecom analyst with an unpublished manuscript.

Reliable sources confirm Kushnick is credible. He's been a telecom analyst for 15 years, associating at times with Link Resources, Probe Research, and Phillips Business Information. His former clients include AT&T, MCI, Sprint, Nortel, British Telecom, PacBell, and BellSouth. And the manuscript is heavily footnoted, so his findings can be checked (not that I have).

Kushnick's main finding is that Ameritech, Bell Atlantic, BellSouth, Nynex (now within Bell Atlantic), Pacific Bell, SBC (now including PacBell), and US West are annually overcharging us $14 billion.

But wait, aren't profits on the Bells' $100 billion in revenues regulated by our Federal Communications Commission and 51 state public utilities commissions (PUCs)? Well, actually, no. Kushnick finds that understaffed regulators rely on information provided by the Bells. Independent audits are rare and, despite often finding gross overcharging, result only in slaps on the Bells' thick wrists.

And worse, since the Telecommunications Act of 1996, the most heavily lobbied bill in legislative history, the Bells have been "deregulated," which just means more gouging of their choiceless customers.

And the Bells' gouging is not evident on phone bills. Kushnick finds that zero percent of telephone customers understand their bills. Bells overcharge for calls — for example, 75 percent more for intrastate than coast-to-coast. They overcharge for unordered services — such as home wiring maintenance.

They overcharge the unwary — such as Kushnick's legally blind, 87-year-old Aunt Ethel, who has paid $1,100 since divestiture for the rental of an old rotary telephone. And then there's "digital spew" — such as the posting of bogus charges on phone bills.

Kushnick finds — get this — it's a myth the Bells lose money on local telephone lines. They've been shoveling expenses into their regulated local services while shifting revenues out into unregulated subsidiaries. With line numbers growing, the Bells are lowering per-line head counts, deinvesting per line, and increasing actual prices.

The FCC and PUCs do already report Bell prices are up — and that's scandal enough — but reported prices are for reduced services, for the rare, least-expensive installation, without deposits and substantial charges for initiating services. Reported prices are gross understatements of total prices actually paid. Kushnick finds that telephone bill charges have increased an average of 275 percent since 1983.

Kushnick finds at the bottom line the Bells financially outperform other regulated utilities, 28 percent returns vs. 11 percent. Bell shareholders have enjoyed guaranteed returns 55 percent greater than those by investors in the S&P 500.

The part of Kushnick's expose that angers me most is how the Bells have used the Information Superhighway to win concessions on how much money they can extract from their monopolies. Kushnick recounts extravagant Iway promises, shows them to be just a Bell ploy, and documents how they've not been kept. He tracks billions intended for Iway deployment to Bell executives, to their shareholders, and, of course, to almost all of your elected representatives in government.

Kushnick sees his book as a manifesto for a coordinated effort against the Bells in the jurisdictions of all 51 PUCs. He's looking for a bold, fast publisher. Interested parties, but not Bell assassins, should contact Kushnick.

Kushnick worries the Bells will sue him into oblivion once they catch wind of his manuscript. I've tried to reassure him. First, *InfoWorld* readers can keep a secret. Second, there's The First Amendment. Third, Kushnick is already in oblivion. And fourth, nothing would advance his cause more than the publicity of defending against the legions of Bell storm lawyers. Many of you, I'm sure, would join in the Kushnick Legal Defense and Publicity Offense Fund.

Time to Flex the Long Arm of the Law Against Incumbent Local Exchange Carriers

April 13, 1998
All 100 million of us Web users are on the verge of suing somebody over the slow, unreliable, and expensive Internet access we get using dial-up telephone modems.

Who we gonna sue?

Recall reading here about Bruce Kushnick's 475-page manuscript attacking the Baby Bells, of which we are now down to only five: Ameritech, Bell Atlantic, Bell South, SBC, and US West. (See "Telecom analyst ventures forth with documentation of Big Baby Bell rip-offs," Jan. 26.)

Kushnick still doesn't have a publisher. Read his plans for class actions against the Bells and the Telecom Riot Act of 1998.

This week I've gathered materials for use in various lawsuits against not just the Baby Bells, but all incumbent local exchange carriers (ILECs). There are 1,200 ILECs meeting regularly in restraint of trade at the United States Telephone Association (USTA).

Let's sue USTA and ILECs on the following points.

> ✦ *Universal Service*. This is an old system, dating back to the ill-fated founding of the Soviet Union. It uses telephone monopolies to transfer billions of dollars per year from urban, business, data, and wealthy users of the public switched telephone network (PSTN) toward rural, residential, voice, and needy users. Rural senators and USTA are conniving to bring the Net under their old Soviet-style Universal Service regulations.

For example, there's the FCC's new $2.25 billion Schools and Libraries Corporation (SLC). ILECs are crowding around SLC for new Universal Service subsidies. USTA is ready to help them fill out the forms.

Even if you think have-nots should get subsidized Internet access, we would all be better off if, instead of propping up telephone monopolies, we just gave subsidies directly to the have-nots so they can participate in competitive markets for Internet services.

> ✦ *Access fees*. ILECs and USTA are working to force ISPs to pay additional access fees to the Universal Service Fund because ISPs connect through the PSTN. Instead, because we're already talking about force here, ILECs should be forced to let ISP data packets bypass the PSTN's old voice circuit switches.

✦ *Political contributions*. ILECs should be prohibited from spending monopoly profits on political contributions. They give ILECs undue influence over various legislatures and ILEC regulators in the FCC and the 51 state public utilities commissions.

✦ *ILEC mergers*. SBC's acquisition of Pacific Bell and Bell Atlantic's acquisition of NYNEX should be reversed. Future mergers among ILECs, especially the Bells, should be prohibited by our antitrust watchdogs. The only thing worse than a few, big, regulated telopolies is fewer, bigger, unregulated telopolies.

✦ *Internet services*. ILECs should not be allowed to offer Internet services. There are thousands of ISPs, so we don't need ILECs distracted from the founding purpose of their monopolies — telephone services — nor should we risk letting them extend their telopolies into Internet services through bundling, dumping, and other unfair competition.

✦ *Long distance*. ILECs should never be allowed to offer long-distance telephone services. Again, there are many competing long-distance providers who are not ILECs, and we need not risk extending ILEC monopolies into long distance. It has only been 14 years since we spun the Bells out of AT&T.

✦ *ILEC-ILEC competition*. So, if not allowed into Internet or long-distance telephone services, what will the poor ILECs do? Well, it's time they started competing with one another for the $125 billion that they now divide among themselves annually with zero competition, which is illegal almost everywhere else that it is tried.

✦ *Transmission and switching*. ILECs need breaking up. New wiring and cable companies, Waccos, should own ILEC copper and central offices, renting them to the former ILECs for their voice switching services.

Waccos should also rent wiring and space to competing LECs and to ISPs. Waccos would have to compete against cable television, wireless, satellite, powerline, and fiber companies in local access services.

Above transmission, there would be a layer of competition in switching. This competition, better than monopolies, would drive deployment of transmission and switching infrastructure, which is important now that the Internet is the major factor of production in the information age.

These recommendations will be discussed at Vortex98 in May. I'll be reporting back on that. See you in court.

Don't Be Fooled: Telopoly Deregulation Is a Bad Thing for the Computer Industry

January 25, 1999

Jeffrey Eisenach of the Progress & Freedom Foundation says the computer industry is now a "mature political force." This was accomplished under his auspices by computer executives taking a "principled stand" on the bandwidth battle now raging in Washington between our Federal Communications Commission and the telephone monopolies.

Eisenach says the computer and telephone industries have rallied to eliminate that one remaining obstacle to rapid deployment of broadband Internet access, which is, he says, regulation of the telephone monopolies by our FCC. He says telopolies would quickly deploy $50-per-month megabit Internet access if only the FCC would stop introducing new and unnecessary regulations.

Recently, computer executives from Cisco, Compaq, IBM, Intel, Gateway, Microsoft, Novell, etc., met with their new buddies from Bell Atlantic, BellSouth, GTE, SBC, US West, etc., and in December 1998, they wrote two letters to FCC Chairman William Kennard and demanded deregulation of the telopolies. In return, the telopolies agreed to 10 principles "upon which the next generation of progress in the digital economy will be built."

I say the computer industry is getting its pockets picked.

The 10 principles say that when incumbent local exchange carriers (ILECs) offer Internet services, they shouldn't use their monopolies to squash competing ISPs. They say ILECs should unbundle local loops for ISPs and let ISPs install equipment in telephone central offices. In return, ILECs should be freed from price and other regulations, which, we're told, are discouraging telopolies from speedily rolling out the megabit Internet access services we're all dying for.

Well, the computer industry is being duped into pressuring the FCC to deregulate, but not demonopolize, telecommunications. The only thing worse than a few big, regulated telephone monopolies is fewer, bigger, unregulated telephone monopolies, which is what we've been getting since the Telecommunications Act of 1996.

FCC regulations are not why, in 1998, the television industry deployed 700,000 cable modems vs. the telephone industry's 25,000 Digital Subscriber Lines (DSLs).

ILECs have not been able to resist leveraging their monopolies against ISP competition. The pro rata costs that ILECs would pass to ISPs, after decades of regulated padding, turn out way high; central offices turn out unaccountably full; and wiring services to ISPs turn out to require years of litigation.

Furthermore, telcos would rather sell 1.5Mbps T1 services for a price of $1,000 per month rather than offer comparable DSLs for a $50 per month price tag. Eisenach says cable modems and DSLs offer Internet access for $50 per month, but actually cable is already down to $40 per month, while DSLs run much higher, for example, in Boston, where I would pay $250 per month and more.

ILECs should be told to spin off their Internet services. ILECs should be told to compete in the local telephone switching business in each other's central offices. And ILECs should be told not to buy one another.

In their recent letters, computer executives seem to forget that ILECs are regulated by 51 public utilities commissions (PUCs), not just the FCC. ILECs would like to be thrown to the PUCs, which, after decades of mature political power, they own.

I plan to have my mind changed about telopolies at a ComNet panel I'm running in Washington this week, and in May, at Vortex99, the Internet-telephone-television convergence conference I'm organizing.

Note: Telco critic Bruce Kushnick says his book, *The Unauthorized Biography of the Baby Bells & Info-Scandal,* will soon be available in a 508-page paperback for a price of $49.95.

Meanwhile, I stand by my prediction that cable modems will again outsell DSLs during 1999 — and then on to 1900!

View from the Death Star

Rebuttal by Robert W. Lucky

Robert W. Lucky is Corporate Vice President of Applied Research at Telcordia Technologies. Bob began his telecommunications career at AT&T Bell Laboratories, where he was involved in studying ways of sending digital information over telephone lines, which research eventually led to the invention of the adaptive equalizer. He has served as President of the Communications Society of the Institute of Electrical and Electronics Engineers, and as consulting editor of several technical journals and books.

Recently I heard Bob Metcalfe speak before an audience of telecommunications executives at an industry forum. He speaks like he writes, and he pulled no punches because of the particular audience on this occasion. "More than 300 Web generations ago, the ARPA knights launched the Internet rebellion against the Imperial Telco Empire," he began. Soon he was describing the "oppressive telecommunications regulatory regime and its pitiful telephone monopolies" as the "Imperial Empire from *Star Wars*."

As Metcalfe went through his condemnation of the industry, I watched the telecom executives. For people who were being likened to Darth Vader, they were remarkably genial. Laughter radiated throughout the room. Even the notion of "imperial storm lawyers" seemed to evoke only grins and nodding of heads in agreement. "Yep, that's us," they seemed to be confirming. After the meeting, Metcalfe got the highest ratings of any speaker at the forum.

So the question is this: If the executives who run the industry recognize their caricature as the evil empire from the death star, how can they possibly continue such antisocial behavior? Are they intrinsically evil, ignorant, delusional, or what?

As a career member of the telecom industry myself, I have often thought about why we do what we do, and how it appears to the outside world. Even had the experience of testifying in the AT&T antitrust trial before Judge Greene, and trying to explain why our company had resisted so-called "foreign attachments", like other manufacturers' modems, to the network. I could see the look of disbelief on the judge's face as I went through my pathetic explanation. He shook his head in disgust, and my faltering confidence crumbled. My argument, however, remains: We were simply well-intentioned people trying to do a job in which we believed.

It would be fruitless for me to try to argue Bob's specific points about the anti-competitive behavior and apparent incompetence of the telecom industry. Sometimes he's right, and sometimes industry trends do look ridiculous in hindsight. Arguing ISDN might be like talking to automobile executives about the big tail fins and boat-like cars from the 1960s. Hey, we all went wrong — there isn't much more to say.

As Bob Metcalfe knows, since he has many friends in the industry, there are many knowledgeable and intelligent people in telecom companies. They usually don't lose all their competence when they become managers, but often they have different priorities than Metcalfe might desire. Generally speaking, they have a service religion and the great burden of maintaining a ubiquitous and almost totally reliable network. The concept of being the carrier of last resort weighs heavily upon them. Moreover, they have to satisfy the analysts and millions of stockholders that they have obtained maximum financial performance from the cards they have been dealt. Sometimes, from their point of view, the cards don't seem fair, as when new entrants are given regulatory relief or are allowed to skim cream in the name of competition.

The vivid picture of telecom people as storm troopers from the death star suggests a military conformance within the industry that doesn't, in fact, exist. Sometimes from the outside these companies appear as monoliths, but inside they have many factions working at different purposes.

For example, when the long Internet holding times clogged local access, the engineers went to work to fix the problem with a technical solution. While the engineers worked on fixing the network, the lawyers went off to demand a political solution. Who should pay for the required upgrades, they asked? Shouldn't it be the Internet users themselves? I have to admit it's a fair question. But I believe that the FCC did the right thing in deciding that just muddling through and seeing what would happen would be the best approach. Meanwhile, the engineers continued quietly redesigning the infrastructure to packetize the network, and the executives focused their attention on the big mergers and entry into other companies' businesses. Everybody was happy doing his own thing.

There are many voices here, and no simple solution as to what is best for the companies, the users, and the nation. Not only am I amused by Bob Metcalfe's observations, but also I think he plays an important role in the whole panorama. Of course, he simplifies issues that are often arguable, but he is an effective voice. I suspect that many telecom people often agree with him, and I think that secret knowledge was behind the laughing faces that I observed at his industry talk. For myself, I sometimes get very hot and sweaty underneath this black plastic helmet that I have to wear. And frankly, this heavy breathing thing is getting to be a real drag.

Predictions for All Occasions

I've decided that Nostradamus must have been the technology pundit of his day. For some reason people look to pundits like yours truly to spin elaborate descriptions of what the world will become. What's even more surprising is that many people (including Marxist death threat mongers) listen to my predictions and even hold me accountable for them.

So, against my better judgment, I regularly sit down at my virtual crystal ball and try to make sense of the Future. What do I come up with? Fascinating visions, such as drugstores serving cappuccino, brilliant strategies for fixing the Internet's bad plumbing, the changing lifestyle of Willy Loman, and something called Metcalfe's Law (bigger networks are better). This chapter offers a grab bag of predictions, many that proved to be right on target and others. . .well, no one's perfect.

Want to Know About 2000? Look at 1985

December 28, 1992

What will computers be like in the year 2000? Each year at this time we visionaries are biologically compelled to project technology trends and bemoan belated paradigm shifts. So forgive me, please, for asking, What will computers be like, not next year, not five years from now, but in the year 2000? Some might ask, "Won't that be long after most of us have retired — so who cares?"

Actually, it wasn't me who brought this up, nor was I the visionary sought after. Priscilla Tate, executive director of the Microcomputer Managers Association asked Stewart Alsop for his millennial visions.

The MMA wanted Stewart to join a small group of micromanagers, vendors, and press to flesh out and agree on every last detail of the year 2000. Instead, I showed up, in time to have a carton of that sulfuric orange juice New Yorkers drink to help digest our Danish fat pills.

Micromanagers unite

The MMA provides a forum for exchanging information among its micromanaging members — including many *InfoWorld* readers — and to give them a more compelling way to speak to vendors. (No, the MMA is not a support group for executives trying to resist the urge to meddle in the details of the work of their subordinates.) In the recent past, the MMA has produced reports on software upgrade policies, standards for high-density floppy disks, network software licensing, and "the real cost of graphical user interfaces." In 1993, the MMA is planning technology forums for its members on network management, remote computing, groupware, and international standards. This is a group that has at least one eye on the future.

To lead discussions on the year 2000, Priscilla invited Fred Pollack from Intel Corp., Mac McLoughlin from Compaq Computer Corp., Charlie Tuller from IBM, and me. You really had to be there, especially because the meeting, in order to promote frank discussion, was under a non-disclosure agreement.

You might guess that Fred talked about Intel's next-generation microprocessor (formerly P5, now Pentium) and maybe even about P6 (which I suppose will be called Sexium). You might guess that Mac talked about Compaq's recent successful turnaround and aggressive new moves on products, pricing, and distribution. And you might guess Charlie talked about the new leaner and meaner IBM. You might guess these things, but you didn't hear them from me.

What I told the meeting would not make a good secret. I noted that the year 2000 is not far off in the future — only seven years. Not only will most *InfoWorld* readers still be around, but at an average age of 48, we won't be retired — unemployed maybe, but not retired.

Seven years ago

To project computer technology trends out seven years, I suggested we go back seven years, to the end of 1985, just to get calibrated on how fast things really happen. It isn't as fast as we are often tempted to think.

Lotus 1-2-3, Novell NetWare, Microsoft Windows, and Apple Macintosh were all already at least 2 years old by the end of 1985. Compaq was more than 3 years old. The DOS/x86 platform had been burgeoning for more than four years. The DEC VAX was more than 8 years old. And Sun was escaping startupdom with workstations based on Unix and Ethernet, both of which had been around for well over 10 years.

That was about the time when, unbeknownst to most visionaries, IBM was reaching its zenith (no pun intended), having just delivered the PC/AT, merged with Rolm, shipped the 3090, and announced the IBM Token Ring LAN.

Seven years from now

Surely within seven years microprocessors will be fast enough and memories large enough to shift us into the right paradigms for mainstream artificial intelligence, objects, and multimedia. I can't tell you what killer apps are going to ignite the object-oriented AI multimedia wildfire, but I bet it involves networking — probably ATM. Cellular and ISDN networking will be mainstream by the millennium, but maybe not FDDI if Ethernet keeps nipping at its heels and ATM nips it in the bud. Client/server computing will be old hat, and the last mainframe will have been unplugged — or turned into a NetWare server. And, by the year 2000, Microsoft should be on its third release of Windows NT, and we know that three is the charm for Microsoft.

Will today's commanding computer companies, Intel and Microsoft, unbeknownst to most visionaries, be approaching their zenith in 1992 as IBM did in 1985? Will you be rooting for an Intel-Microsoft comeback then, the way you're rooting for IBM's today?

Will There Be Any LANs in the Year 2013?

January 18, 1993

Almost 20 years ago, arriving at the Xerox Palo Alto Research Center on May 22, 1973, I turned on my IBM Selectric, pulled out a wad of Ko-Rec-Type, snapped on an Orator ball, and banged out the memo inventing Ethernet. So, if nobody gets all worked up about which was the first "true" local area network, I'll say LANs are about 20 years old.

Beginning with this column, I am collecting ideas on where LANs are going — over the next 20 years. I will share some of these ideas in my ComNet keynote speech on February 4 in Washington. And I hope to be really clear about the future of LANs by the time of Ethernet's 20th anniversary.

I know that network hardware is not your top concern, even though it is my life's work. I know you worry about a myriad of issues, from microprocessors to databases to internetworking protocols to implementing client/server applications.

Even if I do say so myself, LANs are a solved problem — they work, they're cheap and, for the moment, they're empty. But will it always be thus?

Between now and Comdex

So I've begun my research. I'm touching bases with all my old Ethernet cronies and reaching out to all my old enemies on the side of IBM Token Ring. I'm talking to editors and analysts. I'm seeking the visions of young turks in the LAN industry, some of whom are kind enough to offer me networking tutorials. It looks as if we have a lot of great ideas about LAN evolution between now and Comdex.

But, what about the longer term? I asked Lee Doyle, director of LAN research at the International Data Corp. Doyle's current worldwide projections stretch out well beyond Comdex, all the way through 1996, when 42 percent of the 156 million PCs installed in businesses will be on LANs. In 1996, the number of PCs, workstations, and multiuser systems on Ethernets will total 47 million.

Token Ring's installed base will grow to 16 million. FDDI will grow to 1.9 million. And everything else will account for some 7.2 million.

Doyle is quick to add that these projections, due to be updated in March, may be greatly affected by unforeseen events. For example, a few years ago, the relatively sudden arrival of standard (10Base-T) and cheap twisted-pair Ethernet broke the momentum of IBM Token Ring.

The Longer Term

Yet Doyle's data only covers the next five years; I'm interested in 20. The basic question is, Will there be LANs in 2013? The basic answer is, Yes.

The application driving LAN evolution is of course multimedia, whatever that is. Although I don't think we will know what multimedia is in 2013, I know that LAN bandwidth requirements will grow — write this down — by a factor of 1,000 in the next 20 years.

Ethernet and IBM Token Ring are going to dominate at the desktop through 2013.

First, they will be sped up by a factor of 10: Ethernet will climb to 100 megabits per second, and IBM Token Ring will reach 128 megabits per second.

But the big changes — the other factor of 100 — will be in their routing hubs.

FDDI will play a role, but only as a backbone technology, and that role will be taken over in most cases by Asynchronous Transfer Mode (ATM) well before 2013.

Wireless will be the only way to go for mobile computing by 2013, but at speeds too low for LANs. (I note that television has been wireless all these years, and now it's going to cable.) Narrow-band ISDN will not eliminate LANs, as many telephone people continue to believe, but it will become an important way of providing the infrastructure for extending WAN internets to small businesses and homes.

Broadband ISDN ATM will become the dominant technology for WANs, for sure. As ATM inevitably invades buildings to replace FDDI backbones, this will be as close as we get to the elimination of LANs — with one big uniform interconnected ATM cell-switching fabric, perhaps extending itself all the way down into desk-area networks.

So, are LANs a technology transient, like time-sharing was? Will ATM fabrics obsolete LANs the way PCs obsoleted time-sharing mainframes? No, not in the next 20 years anyway. Networks will for a long time, if not forever, appear in an even richer hierarchy of modes, like that of transportation.

Get Ready for Personalized Newspapers

April 5, 1993

You have enough blank paper at the top of this page, so all you need now is a pen and a receptive mind. I'll begin transmitting when you're ready.

Ready?

Pick a number between one and 10. Multiply by nine. If the result has more than one digit, add them together. OK, subtract five. Take the new number and find the letter in the alphabet to which it corresponds: 1 to A, 2 to B, 3 to C, 4 to D, 5 to E, and so on. Pick a country that begins with your letter. Pick an animal that begins with the second letter of the country.

And, because we'll be needing it later, write down the animal's color.

Which brings me to my subject this week: the future of newspapers, or, to be more specific, how will the accelerating onslaught of information technology eliminate *InfoWorld* as we know it? At InfoWorld we use PC and networking technologies out the wazoo, but still each week we print 225,000 100-page copies near Chicago on Saturday and distribute them around the United States by air on Sunday so they can arrive at most of your doors on Monday.

Wondering about all these pounds of paper and their timely transportation in this electronic age, I sought the comments of Nicholas Negroponte.

In 1985 Professor Negroponte founded MIT Media Laboratory, in Cambridge, Massachusetts.

Since then, the Media Lab has grown to be one of the most successful and envied research laboratories in academia, and Negroponte has become the most interviewed media technologist on Earth — a professor with a PR department.

My challenge was to get from him something about personalized electronic newspapers that he has not already said. (For more see especially his "Products and Services for Computer Networks," *Scientific American,* September 1991.) Of course all publications will eventually go fully electronic, he said, but (as if to reassure me) not soon, and newspapers will be the last.

Paper is flexible, flat, reflective, and cheap. Computer displays as good as paper will be a long time coming — flexible is especially hard. There is some work on making erasable electronically writable paper, but don't hold your breath.

And newspapers are already very interactive. Ever wondered why daily newspapers are printed on so-called broadsheet paper, weekly newspapers like *InfoWorld* on smaller tabloid-size paper, monthlies often on 8 1/2-by-11-inch stock, and books typically smaller than that? Negroponte says that the more frequent the publication the larger the paper, so that readers can make better use of their scanning abilities to interact with the publication to find what they want speedily.

It is likely that newspapers will become electronic only as interactivity (personalization) can be introduced. Negroponte sees the broadcast of newspaper information at 20Mb per second at night over TV channels, with filtering done close to the reader. In fact, as newspapers go electronic, the editing function will move toward the reader.

With an eye on meeting payroll, I asked about advertising. Bucking the academic trend, Negroponte sees electronic newspapers full of advertising.

And he sees that advertising, especially as it becomes more targeted, will increasingly be seen by readers as news.

In the electronic world, newspapers will know much more about their readers, most of whom will be happy to share that information. So, instead of advertising to all the readers of a newspaper, companies will pay to speak only to those readers intending right then to buy their products. This will be more economical for publishers and advertisers and more welcome by readers.

In Negroponte's words, a win-win-win.

How will all this information be collected about readers? Before I get to telepathy, Negroponte asks you to imagine buying an airline ticket from Boston to Scotland. Within days you receive advertising on fly fishing and golf equipment. What other actions might be observed and what other complicated deductions made by electronic publishers to bring their readers the right buying information just when it's needed? The big idea is the development of an electronic model of each reader. Using this model, information can be filtered or directed to a reader. This model can be built with the readers' help or by electronically observing behaviors in the relevant markets, or, if I may say so now, via telepathy.

In case you doubt that minds can be read, it's time for me to confirm that the color I asked you to write up top is gray.

Metcalfe's Law: Network More Valuable Reaching More Users

October 2, 1995

If you had the only telephone in the world, who would you call? Networks seem to grow more valuable to a user proportionately with the number of other users he or she can call. In a network with N users, each sees a value proportional to the N-1 others, so the total value of the network grows as N*(N-1), or as N squared for large N. This brilliant 15-year-old observation was recently named Metcalfe's Law.

Like any self-respecting dog on its nightly rounds, I am forever sniffing out naming opportunities. When noted author George Gilder started writing about the philosophy of Ethernet, the transforming qualities of the Internet, and what he calls Metcalfe's Law, I couldn't wipe the smile off my face.

Gilder is writing another book, *Telecosm.* Read Gilder's chapter on Metcalfe's Law, which also appeared as an article in Forbes *ASAP* magazine. After that, my law was mentioned by *The Economist* magazine in its recent story on the Internet. And, as I sat through an IT conference in Paris last week, up popped Metcalfe's Law again.

Now I'm getting questions. The editors of *The Economist,* for example, trying to explain the explosive growth of information highways, asked me if Metcalfe's Law is even approximately true, like Moore's Law, which is about increasing transistor densities on integrated circuits.

It's risky for me to play along with this Metcalfe Law thing. On one hand is Moore's Law and what it did for Gordon Moore, the billionaire chairman of Intel Corp. On the other hand is Grosch's Law, which is about the scale economies of mainframes. Herb Grosch was fired from IBM, became a journalist, and is now poor, embittered, and wishing the United States were a Scandinavian social democracy.

Risky, yes, but I'm going for it. Moore's Law (smaller transistors are better) overthrew Grosch's Law (bigger mainframes are better). So maybe Metcalfe's Law (bigger networks are better) can overthrow Moore's Law. Even if I don't end up a billionaire, I have relatives in Norway.

Of course, another danger in playing along with this Metcalfe Law thing is that, if it goes anywhere, out of the woodwork will crawl all those people from whom I stole it. Jeff Raskin thought of it while designing the Macintosh, I'm sure. Ted Nelson laid it all out back in the 1960s, along with hypertext.

Alan Kay will gently remind me that the idea goes back to the 15th century, when it was overshadowed by the invention of the printing press. And then they'll find it in the Dead Sea Scrolls or painted on a cave wall somewhere. There are no new ideas under the sun, and I didn't make that up either.

Anyway, Gilder got Metcalfe's Law from stories about how I sold the Ethernet standard throughout the 1980s. I had a 35mm slide that attempted to quantify the value of computer communication compatibility — from which, by the way, 3Com Corp. got its name. Well, I dug around and found the actual slide, a bona fide historical artifact that is part of the illustration you see above.

The point of this slide is that networks can achieve a kind of critical mass and go BOOM! For Ethernet, this happened big time in 1983. For the TCP/IP Internet, big-time critical mass was achieved in 1993.

OK, Metcalfe's Law might overestimate the value of a network for very large N. A user equipped to communicate with 50 million other users might not have all that much to talk about with each of them. So maybe the growth of systemic network value rolls off after some N.

Also, Metcalfe's Law might underestimate the accelerating surplus of network value over cost. At any one time, the cost of an Ethernet grows linearly with its N adapter cards and hub ports. However, the production volumes of standard Ethernets and the resulting focus of development dollars have driven Ethernet adapter costs down over the last 15 years from $5,000 to $50 per network user.

No, Metcalfe's Law may not be exactly true, but the name has a nice ring to it, don't you think?

Time to Make Predictions for the Brand New Year

January 6, 1997

You probably haven't heard yet that the Internet collapsed horribly again while we were away for the holidays. Let's plan on coming back to that after the investigation is further along. This week, I have the following ideas to run by you about covering the Internet here during 1997.

If I had to choose just one word, other than "collapse," that says what happened to the Internet in 1996, that word would be "intranets." We can celebrate intranets as the slam-dunk use of TCP/IP and the World Wide Web in building internal information systems for company employees. Or we can decry private intranets as futile flight from the insecurity, unreliability, and poor performance of the inexorably bogging and intermittently collapsing public Internet.

Now, in 1997, what's happening to the Internet is, in a word, "extranets." We can celebrate extranets as the slam-dunk use of TCP/IP and the Web in building external information systems for company customers. Or, as private extranets proliferate, we can worry that the Internet is partitioning. Or we can marvel at how Internet service providers (ISPs) are now dividing into various subspecies.

Internet plumbing that needs fixing in 1997 includes the underlying protocol (TCP/IP), the DNS, and the Web's HTTP. Too many routes is the problem with TCP/IP. Robust directory services are needed to enhance DNS. And HTTP needs to open many fewer short TCP connections.

Neither WANs nor LANs will be nearly as big of an Internet plumbing problem in 1997 as telco access. Because my current telephone modem, like my car, seldom runs at half its top speed, I'm not excited about upgrading again to 56Kbps. So let's hope that cable-modem trials scale up, satellites take off, and terrestrial wireless propagates.

Somebody has to light a fire under the lethargic, inept, and obstructionist local telephone monopolies. I really have no basis for predicting a Telco Demonopolization Act of 1997, but we need one.

The flow of money into the Internet will accelerate in 1997. True, America Online recently moved away from more metered Internet usage billing, but, as Netcom just announced, it's inevitable. Web advertising is also ramping up.

And although micropayments will not amount to much in 1997, their technologies will be demonstrated and standards proposed.

Among eventual uses for micromoney will be paying postage on e-mail. Charging for e-mail by size, distance, urgency, privacy, and authenticity will help reverse current unsustainable ISP losses. If e-postage doesn't strike you as a good idea, consider that it will also deter spamming.

Electronic commerce will grow out of Web publishing on our extranets during 1997. We'll learn that commerce is not mostly about consummating secure financial transactions, but is advertising, merchandising, distribution, and support.

Along with Java, of course, network computers (NCs) will ramp up in 1997, and maybe we'll end up calling them server/client computing? Larry Ellison and Scott McNealy will learn what Lou Gerstner already knows: There are worse things than disagreeing with Bill Gates about PCs vs. NCs.

The real trouble starts when Gates starts agreeing with you, as with NetPCs for obese clients and Windows CE for svelte clients. Ask Lou and he'll tell you that the only worse thing that can happen, Larry and Scott, is to find yourself forming a partnership with Bill. Let's leave Microsoft to form a partnership with our Department of Justice's antitrust watchdogs.

Collaborative-filtering technologies that personalize Web sites will run afoul of privacy paranoia in 1997. But Gerstner is right that the next killer apps will not be software but sites on the Internet, and these will be highly personalized.

The Internet continues to converge with telephone and television systems. This does not mean that Internet audio and video will be big before the millennium.

Suitable plumbing for streaming data — Asynchronous Transfer Mode — is not well integrated with TCP/IP.

So, that's what I suggest writing about the Internet here in 1997, in the short term. Please send me your comments and suggestions.

Electronic Taj Mahals Reduce Travel to Session Breaks

January 27, 1997

Chuck House is a 30-year veteran and former chief engineer at Hewlett-Packard. He just began his two-year term as president of the 85,000-member Association for Computing Machinery (ACM). House recently called an informal meeting in Washington at the National Academy of Engineering (NAE) to present his proposal for an ACM initiative.

The proposal is to build 100 prototype "collaboratories" — multimedia rooms to facilitate advanced audio-, video-, and dataconferencing simultaneously among as many as 10 research and development teams — over the next several years.

House's meeting would be hosted by NAE's interim president, Bill Wulf, a leading proponent of collaboratories. House and Wulf wanted to discuss how the Internet might let universities, corporate laboratories, and government research agencies work together better with much less travel.

And so I set my alarm for 4:30 a.m.; drove for an hour to the airport in Bangor, Maine; flew to Boston, thence to Washington; and taxied to my hotel for check-in and thence to the National Academy, all just in time to join House's meeting for lunch at noon.

House proposed that each ACM collaboratory be a room that could accommodate as many as a dozen people with their computers, microphones, video cameras, and large screens. He proposed that these collaboratories be connected through the Internet with facilities to support productive remote group collaborations.

Wulf observed that such advanced collaboratories would be "time machines." Building prototypes of advanced technologies that are impractically expensive today could demonstrate what advanced systems could do much later when they're affordable.

Bob Kahn, president of the Center for National Research Initiatives, reminded us that building and interconnecting House's time machines would be difficult. They would require extensive infrastructure development, including digital objects, libraries, standards, and advances in intellectual property management.

Charles Lee from MCI next gently observed that House's "Taj Mahals" might end up little used, as often happens with videoconferencing rooms. It might turn out that people really want to collaborate from their individual offices and do not want to have to go to group collaboratories.

And so the meeting moved to the idea of "personal Taj machines."

Would such machines focus on substituting for travel or on enhancing interaction? Would the goal be to make remote interaction the next best thing to being there, or better? Would we focus on enhancing the collaboration of distributed meeting participants or on recording their communications for future use by them and others? Would we focus on applications, such as research or education, or on infrastructures for more horizontal applications, such as the remote meetings we all enjoy attending so much? Two-way or N-way meetings? One-to-many lectures or many-to-many discussions? An early assumption of House's meeting was that some upcoming upgrade of the Internet would interconnect the proposed collaboratories.

For example, there is Internet2, spun out of Educom; the White House's Next Generation Internet; and the National Science Foundation's new NSFNet.

Or might the development of House's ACM collaboratories lead to requirements for an entirely different communications infrastructure than that of the TCP/IP Internet? My suggestion to House was that the ACM should soon announce that its annual meeting in 2001 will be conducted virtually, without travel. Past ACM president Peter Denning jumped on the suggestion by calling it "a conference that nobody goes to but everybody attends."

Of course, what's true of many real meetings is that everybody goes, but nobody attends. A lot of their value is what goes on outside the sessions, the schmoozing. Virtual meetings in collaboratories make it easier to schmooze in small ad hoc groups or even one-on-one.

So after schmoozing for several hours at dinner following House's meeting at NAE, I started back to Maine. Turns out that one 5-hour meeting and dinner cost me $1,000 and two half-days traveling — a sizable down payment on a personal Taj machine.

I'd like to wire up my home and stay there. How about you?

Best Get an Early Start When Preparing for the El Niño of Predictions

October 27, 1997

We pundits are already preparing to make our predictions for the computer industry during 1998. Why so early? El Niño. So, here's an outline I'm using to organize my early-December predictions for the Internet. Please e-mail your comments and perhaps save me from again foolishly predicting something like the collapse of the Internet.

My starting point this year is that personal computers are passé.

Network computers are the yet-to-be-named platforms that will replace PCs in much the same way that PCs replaced minicomputers and minicomputers replaced mainframes. You won't often boot NCs, nor will you dial them into the Internet the way we do now with PC modems. NCs will always be on and connected. You won't have to lug your NC everywhere because one will be at your destination and places in between, similar to cash machines.

With the Wintel monopolies artificially perpetuating their clunky PC platforms, it isn't likely 1998 will see much progress here, but now that we are on Internet time, who knows?

Intel and Hewlett-Packard will soon join Digital Equipment in the promotion of 64-bit computing. But thanks to Moore's Law, processors are already faster than we need, especially given that Internet access is bottlenecked by modems running at less than 64Kbps.

Now there are advancing technologies that currently matter more than PC-processing power. For example, wave-division multiplexing is increasing bandwidths along Internet fiber backbones. Spread-spectrum technology, which is sort of the opposite of wave-division multiplexing, is rapidly improving our exploitation of scarce bandwidth in places we've not yet run fiber. And then there's home LANs — dare I predict they'll be mostly Ethernet during 1998?

Maybe cable-television modems will start working in 1998. Powerline networking may get started. Wireless and satellite maybe. And perhaps we'll see the various forms of Digital Subscriber Lines (xDSL) deployed by the telopolies and their would-be competitors.

I'm thinking that new forms of xDSL will be needed. Tragic flaws might be discovered in high-bit-rate DSL and asymmetrical DSL. What new letter will be slapped in front of xDSL during 1998?

Moving up several levels, there's collaborative filtering technology, which harnesses the evaluation power of online communities to deal with information overload. There's micromoney technology, which promises to lubricate economic growth in cyberspace. And there's Java, which is not just a programming language but a religion for software running on network computers. Predictions?

Say, don't Microsoft's attempts to derail Java in the late 1990s feel like IBM's attempts to derail Ethernet in the early 1980s?

It's pretty clear that Microsoft, between court appearances, will continue leading the computer industry during 1998. Its monopoly profits have piled up so high that Microsoft is being forced to outplace its cash, rather than pay dividends, by buying companies such as WebTV, investing in cable television, and propping up Apple to convince various judges that the company has competition in PC software.

The downside of the Department of Justice going after Microsoft right now is that the Department has bigger fish to fry, namely the telephone monopolies. Again, what's worse than a few big, regulated telopolies? Fewer, bigger, unregulated telopolies. Will the telopolies finally get countersued on antitrust during 1998?

Governments everywhere are grabbing hold of the Internet. What will be the Internet's big legislative mistakes in 1998? Encryption? Taxation? Keeping the Internet safe from spam?

Now, I know this sounds like column-eating material, but I'm wondering whether the entire Internet will be passé in 1998?

The Internet is working on its naming and addressing problems. Will URLs soon be as cool in ads and on business cards as telex numbers?

The Internet is working on carrying telephone calls, with router upgrades to enable bandwidth reservation. The Internet is working on carrying television, with router upgrades to enable multicast. Will TCP/IP reservations and multicast work? In 1998? Ever?

Keep in mind that the Internet's TCP/IP protocols, like Ethernet, will turn 25 years old during 1998. Will 1998 see the first signs of TCP/IP's replacement by ATM cells, digital streams, or what? Will IPv6 finally get installed during 1998, or will it be skipped?

I've offered lots of fodder here for 1998 predictions. What have I left out? May I have your comments? Remember to factor in El Niño.

The Internet in 1999: This Will Prove To Be the Year of the Bills, Bills, and Bills

January 18, 1999
In 1999, it's Bill, Bill, Bill, bills, bills, and more bills.

Of course, the sorry spectacle of how Bill Clinton is clinging to abused power is not something I can get into here.

Bill Gates is also clinging to abused power. I've been urging him to have an Antitrust Epiphany, just like his Internet Epiphany in 1995, but it's too late, which is too bad. (See "Survival lessons: Skunks, Microsoft, and Bill Gates' 1998 Antitrust Epiphany.")

We are moving from personal computing, where Gates has his monopolies, to network computing, where, thanks to our antitrust watchdogs, Gates will have to compete just like everybody else.

Chances are, 50 percent of U.S. households will have computers in 1999, and 33 percent will be online. Getting the other 67 percent online will require most of us to move in the coming years from Gates' PCs to somebody's network computers.

Bill Kennard, chairman of the Federal Communications Commission, is working to get us the bandwidth we need to robustly connect our home computers to the Internet. And by "robustly" I certainly do not mean dial-up telephone modems.

Of the 50 million U.S. households with computers, 15 million already have more than one. So Kennard not only has to get serious bandwidth to homes — despite telopolies — but also around homes using LANs over telephone wires, television wires, power wires, or no wires at all.

Next week I'll return to why Kennard should not accede to demands from telopolies and their dupes in the computer industry to speedily eliminate FCC regulation of the telopolies. (Hint: Without FCC regulation, we would be stuck with fewer, bigger telephone monopolies and their 51 public utilities commissions).

Internet bills are being passed at accelerating rates by various legislatures — on taxation, censorship, privacy, etc. It's not going to work to simply oppose them all. We do need law and order on the Internet.

During 1999, the number of Internet users will surge 28 percent to 147 million. Two-thirds of the people who will be online by 2002 are not online today. Governments cannot ignore these numbers. And for the first time, most Internet users — 51 percent — will live outside the United States.

Because I've not received a Marxist death threat in a few weeks, let me repeat my call for a Pay-As-We-Go Internet (TM). (See "Companies start offering infrastructures for the Pay-As-We-Go Internet.") In 1999, we'll be paying more bills for what we use of Internet resources. I know this because I am an expert in all three major branches of economics: macro, micro, and home.

Bills of Amazonian proportions are being paid for an increasing number of things being bought over the Internet. During 1999, Internet commerce, which is growing 30 times faster than most world economies, will reach $68 billion.

Between now and 2002, $900 billion of purchases will be made via the Internet. Did I mention that the Internet can no longer be ignored by governments? Internet purchases will not long be exempt from taxes.

In 1998, the number of women on the Internet jumped from 43 percent to 48 percent. In 1999, women will become the majority of users on the Internet. This is important because recent studies show what I have suspected for a long time: Women are different from men. Women go to different places on the Web. They spend less time surfing. And they are the primary decision-makers in a majority of household purchases.

Now, if you expect to pay your Internet bills out of the proceeds of Internet stock gains, better sell now.

So in 1999, it's Bill, Bill, Bill, bills, bills, and more bills. I'm so excited — just can't wait until 1900!

A Glutton for Punishment: Back with More Predictions on the Future of the Internet

April 12, 1999

The Eighth International World Wide Web Conference is in Toronto from May 11 to May 14. I urge you to attend WWW8, and not just because they've let bygones be bygones and invited me back to speak.

WWW8 is not your run-of-the-mill Web commerce trade show. It has tutorials, workshops, and a developer's day, of course, but for the conference, more than100 respected referees chose only 48 of what they call "papers" from more than 300 submissions.

The papers are more technical than the ones presented at most conferences. Many of the 1,000 attendees are, if you can stand it, from universities and corporate laboratories. For example, there's keynoter Greg Papadopoulos, chief technology officer at Sun Microsystems.

The conference has a track organized by the World Wide Web Consortium. W3C is directed at MIT by Tim Berners-Lee, father of the Web, who will be celebrating, yes, the Web's 10th anniversary.

WWW8 topics will include the Extensible Markup, Extensible Stylesheet, and Synchronized Multimedia Integration Languages (XML, XSL, and SMIL); Java, virtual documents, hypermedia, user interactions, search engines, security, scripting, servlets, and internationalization; Python, payments, protocols, and performance; Resource Description Framework (RDF), graphics, marketplaces, and distributed authoring and versioning (WebDAV); digital object identifiers (DOI), discovery, querying, mining, adapting, and learning; and, of course, open-source software.

I will attend the entire conference and summarize it with one of my patented "terminal keynotes." And I'll try some predictions.

At WWW5 in Boston, I predicted that the Internet would suffer large outages — collapses — during 1996. A confident wag from the back of the ballroom challenged me to eat my column if my prediction didn't come true.

Also during WWW5, Microsoft announced its licensing of Java from Sun. I congratulated Microsoft on this nonanticompetitive move, assuming the company was sincere, which, it turns out, it wasn't.

At WWW6 in Santa Clara, Calif., I admitted that an Internet gigalapse — a loss of a billion user hours in a single outage — had not occurred in 1996, only a 118 megalapse. And so I literally ate my offending column in front of 1,000 witnesses.

Now I'm better known for that dodged gigalapse than for inventing Ethernet. That's quite a publicity stunt.

Similarly, Microsoft has had to eat its Java contract.

Still, the organizers of WWW8 invited me back. And I've been asked again for a prediction — since that's a technology pundit's job.

At a recent WWW8 promotional event, I floated three trial predictions.

First, borrowing from MIT's Nicholas Negroponte, I predict that Web retailing will drive drugstores to serve cappuccino.

Think about why people go to bookstores — to shop, buy, meet people, and drink cappuccino. Why hasn't Amazon.com yet killed them all? Now think about why people go to drugstores. Surely not to buy drugs on impulse or to schmooze with fellow sufferers.

Web retailing will do to drugstores, Wal-Mart, and malls what those did to Main Street. People might still shop there if they serve cappuccino.

Second, continuing my Pay-As-We-Go Internet™ crusade, I predict that not only will we routinely pay e-postage in 10 years but we'll like it. On this prediction we'll have to wait until WWW18.

And third, closer in, I predict that the deployment of broadband Internet access will ramp up during 1999 into millions of households, and that cable television modems will open up their lead over Digital Subscriber Lines. This is because local telephone companies are much more secure in their monopolies than cable television companies.

None of these predictions is quite as good as The 1996 Gigalapse. So I'm open to suggestions.

The Internet Is 30 Now, Maybe, but What About Its Long-Term Possibilities?

September 6, 1999

Last Thursday was the Internet's 30th birthday. Well, maybe it was. That depends on the meaning of the words "birthday" and "Internet."

Professor Leonard Kleinrock is one of several contending "fathers" of the Internet. Back when I was a mere graduate student, starting in the 1960s, Kleinrock was a lead architect of the Advanced Research Projects Agency Network — the ARPAnet.

Kleinrock says the Internet was born with the installation of the ARPAnet's first Interface Message Processor (Imp) in his lab at the University of California at Los Angeles on September 2, 1969.

ARPAnet Imps were packet-switching minicomputers, pre-Cisco routers developed at Bolt Beranek and Newman (BBN), in Cambridge, Massachusetts. BBN, since merged into GTE, which will unfortunately soon likely be merged into Bell Atlantic, thinks the Internet was born earlier and elsewhere.

There are also post-ARPAnet people who say the Internet was not born until the ARPAnet's protocols were replaced by TCP/IP in 1983. Others think the Internet is the World Wide Web, which was born (forgetting Tim Berners-Lee) with Netscape circa 1995. I think the Internet was born in 1973 with the invention of the Ethernet (CSMA/CD) LAN and the Internet (TCP/IP) WAN. And so on.

But hey, there's enough credit to go around. Professor Kleinrock, thank you, congratulations, and happy 30th!

On this occasion, and because we're more interested in the future than the past, let's explore some possibilities for the Internet's next 30 years:

+ *Plumbing.* Cable television modems and Digital Subscriber Lines are interim. Optical fibers and switches will be deployed in the Internet's backbones, in local access, and in homes. The always-on high-speed all-optical Internet, and an auxiliary mobile wireless overlay, will also be deployed into any office or school buildings that might be left.

+ *Space.* During the next 30 years, we'll be going to Mars and beyond. The Internet will be going with us. Vint Cerf, another Internet father, is already working on the Interplanetary Internet. I'm organizing a conference about space computing, ACM1, which is to be in San Jose, California, USA, Earth, in 2001. Cerf will be speaking there.

+ *Travel.* We've barely started substituting communication for transportation. Commuting and business travel will decline in favor of Internet telepresence. Fewer Willy Lomans. Let's wire up our homes and stay there.

✦ *Shopping.* New technologies have to wait for preceding generations to die. I probably won't be around to see the Internet change what the front doors of our homes look like. But, Internet shopping will grow so important that homes will be built with large drop boxes out front so that packages of atoms can be delivered without disturbing us. Packages of bits will in increasing numbers bypass the drop boxes and come into our homes directly over the Internet. Good-bye malls. Good-bye Wal-Mart. Welcome back Main Street, as a place to socialize.

✦ *Learning.* Our government-run schools are already in decline, and they've been losing learning share to television for decades now. The Internet will finish the job. We'll come to realize that schools are not buildings, but communities of learners. Instead of fighting unionized teachers to put the Internet *inside* schools, we'll be using the Internet *instead* of schools.

✦ *Language.* Now, if you're French, it's probably best you stop reading here. Reading further may even be illegal in some jurisdictions where they're bitter about French being passé, no longer the world's lingua franca. The Internet will continue, and perhaps even complete, the long-term trend toward fewer languages. If you think you're in fat city with English, watch out for Chinese, or Martian, or something entirely mongrel.

What do you see coming during the Internet's next 30 years?

Hyperbolically improbable futures

Rebuttal by Jeffrey Rayport

Jeffrey Rayport is Associate Professor of Business Administration at Harvard Business School. His research focuses on the impact of new information technologies on service management and marketing strategies of business, with a focus on digital commerce. As a consultant, Dr. Rayport has worked with corporations and professional practices around the world. He earned an A.B. from Harvard College, a Masters of Philosophy in International Relations from the University of Cambridge (UK), and a Ph.D. from Harvard in Business History.

There's a law that's even older than Moore's and Metcalfe's Laws. You might say it received its ultimate veneration when Bob chose to paraphrase it in the headline of his latest Predictions column. It goes something like this: Prediction is hard, especially when it comes to the future. Call it Berra's Law, after a famous non-technologist and practitioner of the malapropism, Yogi Berra.

Berra's Law packs a lot of truth into a few simple, if slightly inane, words. And something tells me that we should be listening a lot more to the Berras of our world, which is to say a lot of non-technologists, if we are truly serious about predicting the future of technology and business.

Heretical, you say? Not for me, at least, not after having reviewed the last decade of pronouncements from our friendly father of the Ethernet. Most of Bob Metcalfe's predictions, with the exception of Bill Gates' now celebrated retirement from active duty, were literally and directionally wrong.

Bob would be the first to say that the art of punditry depends on making outrageous claims that have the character of wild cards. (You may recall that the term wild card is a term of art that belongs to the technology world. The word refers to potential outcomes that are high-impact, low-probability events.) By proclaiming futures that are both outrageously momentous and hyperbolically improbable — like the Internet's supposed gigalapse breakdown — a pundit can grab headlines for making pronouncements and then grab them again for being wrong. Since all ink is good ink in the punditry business, this sounds like a pretty good strategy. And the more specific the prognostication, the lower the probability goes; hence, Bob's penchant for making extremely specific predictions.

Which only goes to prove that there is plenty of truth embedded in Berra's Law. Prediction is hard. But not even Berra's Law explains the low batting average Bob has achieved in his columns, especially given that Bob's a very smart guy. Can it be this hard, even for him? My answer is that it does not need to be hard, but to make it easier our good Doctor must practice his art in a new way.

Technologists love to talk about the unevenly distributed future. They say the future is already here; it's just unevenly distributed. As a result, technology pundits tend to look for the future by searching through the present, attempting to discover the few fortunate humans on earth who happen to be living with the unevenly distributed technology. For example, in the mid-1960s, technology pundits (though I'm pretty sure we didn't have such creatures among us then) might have sought out users of the Bell System's picture phones to predict the future of face-to-face telephony communications. In the early 1970s they might have sought out scientists making use of the Internet to predict a future of e-mail interchange and groupware. Alas, their predictions about a future of such things would have been both right and wrong. Right because products and services with videoconferencing, e-mail, and groupware have indeed come to pass in our world, but they happened decades after these first sightings — and not in any way consistent with any one business' supposed plans. Moreover, innovations like e-mail have become killer apps of the New Economy, while videoconferencing has taken 15 years to fail to take off.

So what's the flaw here? The problem with looking for the unevenly distributed future in terms of unevenly distributed technology is that it''s tantamount to keeping your eye on the wrong ball. To paraphrase the stock slogan of the gun control lobby, machines don't use technology, people do. In other words, our friend Bob, like so many technologists, is extraordinarily well versed in the arcana of machines, networks, and even software that runs on these platforms, but he seldom, if ever, dwells at any length on that curious species of the commercial world usually known as the customer.

It is true that there was a time when the customer was not someone that any self-respecting tech expert needed to spend much energy thinking about. In a world of too much consumer demand and not enough gee-whiz products to go around technologists rule the roost. Think of the post-World War II era for everything from cars to white goods, from consumer electronics to computing power. After all, in times like that technologists are the high priests of new features and functions. Products rich with features and functions used to enjoy long and prosperous product lifecycles. And technologists who designed them and companies that sold them lived good, profitable, go-go, conglomerate, Nifty-Fifty lifestyles. These were lifestyles made the 1960s, at least until the recent rise of the Internet economy, look like a golden era for business.

The problem is that these dynamics no longer characterize the world. These days, we live under the tyranny of too many products, too many brands, and — in the technology sector, — an accelerated version of Moore's Law. According to this law, the barriers to entry for new products and brands in practically any sector you can think of have fallen dramatically, thanks to the Internet and the effect of Metcalfe's Law.

Add to that the fact that this proliferation of options on the supply side of advanced economies has come part-and-parcel with a slowing of growth on the demand side (to wit, customers are increasingly the scarce resource in the business world today), and you have the problem with prediction.

Prediction can no longer be about what technologies might make possible; it's about what consumers might do with technologies. In this sense, technology punditry should no longer

Continued

(continued)

be about technology. It should be about customers. They make the difference between what gizmos become killer apps, such as e-mail, and what becomes an also-ran of the modern era, such as videoconferencing. They determine the difference between versions of an idea that work on a grand scale (Intranet applications on the Web) and those that don't (groupware such as Lotus Notes).

Without question, therefore, technology remains the fundamental backdrop for technology punditry. How could it not? But it is customers, those notably absent players from the high drama chronicled in Bob's columns, who will carry the day. Perhaps if he spent more time talking to, interacting with, and, perhaps most importantly, observing those humble creatures at work and play, he might achieve a higher success ratio in his crystal ball gazing.

Of course, there's only one problem. Because bad news makes good headlines and good news seldom makes the inside pages, there is the question of notoriety.

Could Bob have become the giant of technology punditry that he is today riding on the back of accurate predictions? I suspect not. And therein, as they say, lies the rub. More often than not, making a study of customers and finding out what they want is a lackluster business. As every market researcher knows, it's excruciating, it's messy, and it's often devoid of clear answers (let alone cool features and functions). At the same time, it's what the dreams of great businesses and great industries are made of. If the technology sector wants to keep on realizing the rewards and blandishments of its golden age, that's where it — and its technology pundits — will surely need to go.

I Think ICANN

The whole business of domain names is tricky. Trying to figure it out you run up against issues like trademark law, gouging companies for their own branding, and demonopolizing control of naming to the point of utter chaos. ICANN (Internet Corporation for Assigned Names and Numbers) took over the thankless job of patrolling this demilitarized zone from Jon Postel, one of the tireless builders of the Internet, but things aren't getting much better. You still can't get the .com designation you want, domain name assignment is still a thorn in e-commerce's side, and somebody still has my Metcalfe.com name . . . and I want it back. If you've ever tried to figure out this confused landscape, or even if you haven't, read on to understand some of the reasons we ended up where we are today.

As the Internet Faces an Identity Crisis, Namestake Tells You Where You Stand

January 11, 1999

The Internet is going through an identity crisis.

Well, actually, two identity crises: one about the identities of those Internet users who want privacy and another about those who want fame.

Those who want privacy are fighting over Internet user identities, cookies, e-mail addresses, databases, and spam. They ask, "Who actually owns information about your buying habits or whether you are likely a deadbeat?"

Those who want fame are fighting over Internet domain names, such as infoworld.com, out of which e-mail and Web addresses are made. They ask, "Who will administer domain names? Are they trademarks? Why can't my e-mail address be bob@metcalfe.com?"

The domain name identity crisis is worrisome right now because of the recent untimely death of Jon Postel, the guru of Internet names and numbers. Not nearly filling Postel's shoes, we have the new Internet Corporation for Assigned Names and Numbers, or ICANN.

There is much controversy about ICANN. We know who died, but who made Esther Dyson chairman? Is this some plot of U.S. military intelligence? Are large corporations taking over the Internet?

Let's be thankful that Dyson has agreed to help sort out the ICANN mess, which I think will develop along the following three scenarios.

First, there's the scenario of those who had a hand in building the Internet. They'd like names and numbers assigned much like they are now, without regard for the real world, because everything about the Internet is, man, like, totally without precedent. They think, for example, that domain names should be given out first come, first served, so those who slyly speculate in other people's trademarks can continue to disrupt Internet commerce.

Second, there's the trademark lawyer scenario. They'd assign Internet names and numbers as they have assigned trademarks in the past: for the usual fee. They think, for example, that a "challenge period" should precede domain name assignment, so trademarks can be protected.

And third, there's the scenario of domain names as nothing more than a level of indirection in Internet numbering, allowing sites to move without notifying every last database and spreading loads among sites with the same service. Perhaps all of that money you just spent buying your domain name from some identity speculator will come to naught because soon maybe nobody will care what your domain name is.

Well, Tom Barrett of Thomson & Thomson still cares. Barrett just opened Namestake, which brings onto the Web the services of Thomson & Thomson, a 75-year-old company that gets paid to search for names in trademark registries around the world.

If you are interested in trademarks, visit www.namestake.com. There I learned that metcalfe.com, metcalfe.net, and metcalfe.org are all in the hands of total strangers.

Namestake is also watching trademarks used as keywords in Web searches. Your competitors may be paying so that people searching for you get banner ads from them. Namestake showed me people buying the keyword "metcalfe" so that my fans get their ads — and I don't even get a cut. Were I to complain, the portals would kindly offer to sell me the use of my own name as a keyword.

My favorite abuse of the current domain name system is the famous new top-level domain: not .com but .tv. If your business is about television, find out how to buy www.yourbrand.tv at www.internet.tv.

It turns out that .tv is the two-letter country designation of the southwest Pacific island Tuvalu, which is willing to let you use .tv for $1,000 the first year and $500 each year after that, unless of course there's a conflict, in which case your trademark goes to the highest bidder.

While ICANN tries to untangle various domain name scenarios, go to www.namestake.com to see what's happening to "your" name on the Internet.

Jonathan B. Postel Wins '98 Internet Plumber of the Year Award Posthumously

February 15, 1999

Jonathan B. Postel is my pick for *InfoWorld's* Internet Plumber of 1998 award.

For three decades, Jon was a steadfast steward of the Internet. On Oct. 16, 1998, while passing his baton to the new Internet Corporation for Assigned Names and Numbers (ICANN), Jon died following heart surgery.

I hadn't found time recently to thank Jon for the Internet. Please join me in thanking him now.

Jon and I met in 1970 while we were graduate students working on the ARPAnet, the Advanced Research Projects Agency (ARPA) Network. Jon was at the University of California-Los Angeles working under Professor Leonard Kleinrock with fellow fathers of the Internet Vint Cerf and Steve Crocker.

In 1972, Crocker, then at ARPA, asked Jon and me to become ARPAnet "facilitators." Sporting huge beards, jeans, and sandals, we started visiting military bases to teach various clean-cut colonels about packet switching.

Our ARPAnet missions were undertaken toward the bitter end of the Vietnam War. To the besieged military, Jon and I (twice Jon's size) probably looked like Thunderdome's Master-Blaster. We were escorted out of the officers club at Tinker Air Force Base because of our appearance.

Shortly thereafter, our paths diverged. Jon went to the Information Sciences Institute of the University of Southern California, where, after 21 years, he was director of the Computer Networks Division.

Over the years, Jon's role at the technical core of the burgeoning Internet grew. In 1969, he'd started editing the ARPAnet's Request for Comments series, through which the Internet Engineering Task Force still makes standards today. Jon was still editing when he died. In 1981, Jon became what was later called the Internet Assigned Numbers Authority (IANA), responsible for the Internet's DNS, Internet addresses, and protocol conventions — Internet plumbing. Jon was the first member and a trustee of the Internet Society. And much more.

Jon was the kind of person who makes people like me feel opinionated, greedy, and loud. He was quiet, patient, and, well, stubborn, too. But the only difference between being stubborn and being a visionary is whether you are right — and he was, much more often than not.

One of my hobbies is tweaking the fogies who built the Internet. They too often forget that their baby has grown up and left home. I've often wanted to throw a party, thank the fogies for building the Internet, and send them off into well-deserved retirement. I never meant to include Jon among those retirees, and I'm sorry I never told him that.

On Oct. 7, 1998, Jon gave written testimony before the U.S. House of Representatives. He defended the new Internet Corporation for Assigned Names and Numbers. ICANN is to be the new nonprofit, nongovernmental, international organization that will take over the responsibilities from Jon's U.S.-funded IANA.

Jon had been working to build consensus about ICANN among the Internet's diverse and often shrill stakeholders. The controversy turned ugly. Jon, of all people, was accused of various conspiracies. I would have stormed out in disgust, but Jon persisted, as usual, in working to ensure the Internet was taken care of. Nine days later, Jon was dead. Some lay Jon's death at the feet of those who attacked ICANN.

This *InfoWorld* Internet Plumber of the Year award is intended as a gentle message of support in Jon's name to ICANN's initial board: Esther Dyson (interim chair), Michael Roberts (interim CEO), Geraldine Capdeboscq, George Conrades, Greg Crew, Frank Fitzsimmons, Hans Kraaijenbrink, Jun Murai, Eugenio Triana, and Linda Wilson.

ICANN, do as Jon would have done. Keep open, act wisely, and get the job done. Thank you for taking on the difficult task of passing Jon Postel's Internet baton one more time.

I Think ICANN, I Think ICANN . . . the Time is Now for DNS to Get an Overhaul

May 3, 1999. The Internet Protocol (IP) Domain Name System (DNS) began as mnemonic plumbing — an indirection to save typing IP numbers like 123.45.67.89 all day long.

But with electronic-commerce booming, domain names have become valuable intellectual property. And it's often expensive and sometimes impossible to get www.yourtrademark.com.

Which is why I think we should abolish the .com designation.

This came up last week near Los Angeles at the Internet Corporation for Assigned Names and Numbers (ICANN). I flew there to deliver *InfoWorld's* 1998 Internet Plumber of the Year award in memory of Internet pioneer Jon Postel. ICANN is moving into new offices in the Information Sciences Institute at the University of Southern California. ICANN's future CEO will enjoy an oblique view of Marina del Rey, one of the few compensations for facing a lot of contentious but soon moot issues.

ICANN is a private international organization authorized by the U.S. Department of Commerce to take over the work of Postel and his team, and until recently it was called the Internet Assigned Numbers Authority, or IANA (www.iana.org). IANA has been a U.S.-sponsored DNS registry since even before Al Gore invented the Internet.

ICANN allocates blocks of IP numbers. This will get interesting as the Internet upgrades to IP numbers such as 123.45.67.89.0.123.45.67.89.0.123.45.67.89.0.123.

ICANN also tracks protocol port numbers. If Sun puts the dot in .com, then you might say that ICANN puts the http:// in .com — it's port 80.

But what's keeping ICANN in the news is DNS. The day I was in Marina del Rey, Mike Roberts, ICANN's interim CEO, was in Washington announcing the next step toward demonopolizing DNS registrations.

Now, instead of Network Solutions Inc. not giving you www.therightname.com, your ISP will soon not be getting you the domain name you want from the six competitive DNS registrars, including NSI and America Online. There will be 35 registrars by July. Whoop-dee-doo.

All of these registrars will be reselling registration services provided to them by NSI for $9 per name, and you will mostly still be unable to get the .com domain you deserve.

ICANN administers the Internet's top-level domains (TLDs) including .com, .net, .org, .edu, .gov, .mil, and .int, as well as some 240 country-code TLDs, such as .us, .ca (Canada), and .tv (Tuvalu).

ICANN's really big problem is not demonopolizing DNS registrars, but getting DNS and trademark law aligned. The .com designation is worldwide and not aligned with any trademark jurisdiction.

Maybe ICANN can ignore trademarks because the Internet is exempt from the established rules of real-world commerce. Maybe the World Intellectual Property Organization will invent the .com jurisdiction in the real world.

Or maybe we can adopt my quick fix. I urge that ICANN abolish all but the geographical top-level domains, letting each country administer its own DNS servers under its own trademark laws.

Or let's do what Postel recommended. He foresaw Web browsers, search engines, and directories dealing with Internet names. He saw DNS plumbing fading back into the woodwork from which it has inappropriately burst.

ICANN has another problem for which I have a quick fix. Who will pay for its offices and staff salaries? The plan might be that fees be paid ICANN by registrars, who will in turn charge you for www.therightname.com.us.

But Postel years ago reserved most of the single-letter and single-digit domain names. I urge ICANN to auction off these domains to endow itself. How much might my former company pay to get 3.com? Or, if we abolish .com, how much for 3.com.us, 3.com.jp, and the rest?

ICANN at midstage

Commentary by Esther Dyson

Esther Dyson is the Chairman of EDventure Holdings and of ICANN.

Why ICANN? ICANN is a result of the Internet's scaling-up and its increasing maturity. When the Net was small and few people cared about it, it was okay to have the technical infrastructure managed by a single person — especially one whom everyone trusted, the late Jon Postel.

But the management of the Net is no longer a one-man job. What began as a convenient directory service for a small technical community is now a vital public resource for the millions of people who use the Net. It requires an organization, and the organization needs to be accountable.

Accordingly, there is a need for technical policies that meet with general community approval, and standards that meet community needs. Those policies and standards are what ICANN is all about.

ICANN sets policy for the single-source parts of the Net — the coordination of standards that must apply everywhere, the allocation of addresses that can't be duplicated, and, for now, the Domain Name System that people use to name and find servers (e-mail hubs and web sites). ICANN has already affected the DNS, by introducing competition into the service of registering domain names in the .net, .org and .com spaces. There are now multiple registrars competing with NSI in the business of selling domain names to individuals and organizations. But Network Solutions Inc. still maintains the only global registry where all the registrars store names in a single database — a "monopoly," if you define the relevant market as the .net, .org and .com namespace.

There are two issues: One is the ability of a single registry to charge unreasonably high prices; and the other is control by a single, unaccountable entity over who gets which names and how names can be found and identified.

The United States Government handles the price issue by setting a price cap on the fees that Network Solutions can charge for access to the registry. This issue is also addressed by ICANN's opening of the retail registration market to any qualified company (which should foster both price competition and better service).

ICANN will deal with the second issue by managing the process — assuming Internet consensus wants it so — of introducing new domains and competitive registries. In the long run, a free market, that is a market where people are free to choose, is clearly the best solution.

Some argue that ICANN should simply throw everything open; others feel that it should introduce competition gradually, with a few, carefully controlled, Top-Level Domains each year. Others think the Domain Name System itself will become obsolete shortly, as new forms of catalogues, directories and naming systems replace the current obsession with .com names.

Eventually it will become clear that a .com name does not guarantee commercial success, and perhaps the current obsession with dot-com will die down.

Whether it's trademarks or domain names or listings in some supersuccessful search engine, the challenge remains the same: How do you ensure a way to avoid letting a single entity control that space, while at the same time not imposing utter confusion on consumers? The current approach is to try to allow the community to regulate itself, using ICANN as the vehicle for developing consensus policies.

Over time, as likely new TLDs, current ccTLDs (country-code TLDs such as .fr, .jp, .uk, .cn), and potential new TLDs become part of the mix, market forces will guide development. But what happens if a service such as RealNames or an advertising-supported directory from Microsoft or Yahoo! gains a de facto monopoly in the future? Will ICANN be the vehicle for dealing with that, or will we fall back on national and multinational antitrust and diplomatic bodies? The answer to this question may well lie in how well ICANN does the job it has now.

The Open-Sores Movement

Not believing that the development of operating systems should be like some giant quilting party run by people with a tendency towards antisocial behavior, I am not a fan of Linux. Even my dislike for much of Microsoft's shady shenanigans hasn't sent me rushing to join the Open-Sores fan club, though the dues are about as reasonable as they can get.

In my effort to help you all see the light about Linux, I have likened this movement to communism, but let's be fair: Linux lovers have labeled me as disagreeable, lazy and clueless. So we're even. Bottom line: Windows won't be Linux roadkill, and Bill Gates won't have to mortgage the ranch.

Linux's '60s Technology, Open-Sores Ideology Won't Beat W2K, but What Will?

June 21, 1999

Closing the eighth International World Wide Web Conference, I predicted the Internet's stock bubble would burst on Nov. 8, 1999. A thousand people hooted at my specificity.

Next, I predicted that the Internet would gigalapse before the end of Y2K. I said I wouldn't eat my column, again, if the Internet doesn't gigalapse, so the audience booed.

Then, having just sat through a ceremony honoring open-source software guru Richard Stallman, I predicted that Linux would fizzle against Windows like all previous Unixes have. The audience, which I'd expected to run me out of town on a rail, fell suddenly silent.

Taken aback, I stopped, looked around, and asked, "What?"

A few long seconds passed before a single, sad voice answered, "We are in mourning."

That sad voice was not Nicholas Petreley's, whose column hangs above mine. Petreley disagrees about the fate of Linux and his beloved Open-Source Movement. He is editorial director of *LinuxWorld*. He's written that Windows will be Linux roadkill. He won't quietly mourn this column.

Why do I think Linux won't kill Windows? Two reasons. The Open-Source Movement's ideology is utopian balderdash. And Linux is 30-year-old technology.

The Open-Source Movement reminds me of communism. Richard Stallman's Marx rants about the evils of the profit motive and multinational corporations. Linus Torvalds' Lenin laughs about world domination.

Disagreeing even on how to pronounce Linux — "leenucks," says Torvalds — they flip the collective finger at Bill Gates, the software Romanoff whom they'd like to trap in a basement somewhere. Eric Raymond breaks with Stallman, like Trotsky waiting for The People's ice pick. A Soviet Linux lies ahead, with successive five-year plans every three.

OK, communism is too harsh on Linux. Lenin too harsh on Torvalds.

How about the Back-to-the-Earth Movement? How about Linux as organic software grown in utopia by spiritualists?

If North America actually went back to the earth, close to 250 million people would die of starvation before you could say agribusiness. When they bring organic fruit to market, you pay extra for small apples with open sores — the Open-Sores Movement.

Stallman and Torvalds would have us return to the time when software was so new that one person working alone could change the world over the weekend. But modern software, like feeding 6 billion people, is more complicated than that.

Stallman's EMACS was brilliant in the 1970s, but today we demand more, specifically Microsoft Word, which can't be written over a weekend, no matter how much Coke you drink. Multinational corporations are themselves technology invented to get big things done, things that sustain us in the complicated modern world.

Unix and the Internet turn 30 this summer. Both are senile, according to journalist Peter Salus, who like me is old enough, but not too old, to remember. The Open-Sores Movement asks us to ignore three decades of innovation. It's just a notch above Luddism. At least they're not bombing Redmond. Not yet anyway.

The hard part of being down on Linux and the Open-Sores Movement is worrying about that menace hanging over us at year's end. No, not Y2K, but Linux's nemesis, W2K, Windows 2000, the operating system formerly known as Windows NT 5.0.

W2K is software also from the distant past — VAX/VMS for Windows. But it will overpower Linux. NT, now approaching 23x6 availability, is already overpowering Linux. NT and NetWare constitute 60 percent of server software shipments. All Unixes make up 17 percent, and Linux is a small fraction of that. When W2K gets here, goodbye Linux.

Let's hope there's something coming soon that's better than both Linux and W2K. What would that be? Java or what? Let's be looking.

Linux Redux: Enough of the OSnic Slurs, Let's Count Linux Versus W2K Users

July 5, 1999

Flaming Linux is too easy. I am ashamed of myself for not resisting the temptation to take cheap shots in my column two weeks ago. (See "Linux's '60s technology, open-sores ideology won't beat W2K, but what will?" June 21.)

Flaming an OS is a lot like slurring a people's ethnicity. All too predictably, I got back hundreds of e-mails from angry people who sounded as if they were defending their OSnicity.

The first third of these responses generally agreed that if it's to overtake Windows, Linux must calmly temper its free-software ideology and rapidly advance its Unix-like technology. They said it will; I say it won't.

The second third generously overlooked my OSnic slurs, carefully rationalized the vitality of Linux, and apologized for the third third. They also said Linux will better Windows because Linux is reliable, free, and you can recompile it yourself whenever you need to fix bugs or add features. Thanks.

The third third of responding e-mails were flames. They said I'm disagreeable (which I deny) and lazy, clueless, old, senile, an irrelevant has-been, a lapdog of the Microsoft monopoly, and not really the inventor of Ethernet, which was a bad idea anyway. Devastating.

Now I have a third reason that Linux will not beat W2K, which is the obsessively anti-Windows, toxically anti-Microsoft, sometimes anti-capitalism, often anti-American, and always antisocial flaming that passes for discourse around the Open-Source Initiative. I should not have fanned the flames by joking about the Open-Sores Initiative.

But calling it OSI does recall Open Systems Interconnection, which, despite my backing, wasn't such a great idea either. It would be fun to watch Linux users take kernel-compilation time to organize the process for renaming OSI.

Linus Torvalds was recently asked how many Linux users there are. He answered that he had no idea because nobody really counts Linux users. Then he added, "About more than 10 million." See how easy it is to slip from programming to promotion?

Dan Kusnetzky is director of operating systems at International Data Corp. IDC is a 35-year-old, $100 million market-research company, which along with *InfoWorld* is part of International Data Group, on whose board I serve.

Kusnetzky has been selling OS counts since 1996 at www.idc.com. He gave me these for free.

During 1998, 4.4 million new units of server OSes were shipped for revenue. Of these, Windows NT Server was 38.3 percent, 1.7 million units, up 38 percent over 1997 and projected up 20 percent per year for the next five. NetWare was 22.8 percent, up 8 percent over 1997. Unix was 18.8 percent and is projected up 13 percent per year from here. And Linux was 15.8 percent, 700,000 units, up 190 percent over 1997 and projected up 20 percent per year for the next five.

Also during 1998, 89 million units of new client OSes were shipped for revenue. Of these, Windows 95 was 57.4 percent. Windows 98 was 17.2 percent, up 39 percent over 1997. Windows NT Workstation was 11.1 percent, up 34 percent. Mac OS was 5 percent, up 9.9 percent. DOS was 3.8 percent, 21.5 percent below 1997. Linux was 2.1 percent, 1.9 million units, up 28.8 percent over 1997. Unix, which has a higher revenue share than Linux, was 0.8 percent of units shipped.

A problem with these numbers is that they count only OS units shipped for revenue. Kusnetzky agrees with Torvalds: Nobody has figured out how to count units of free Linux.

Nicholas Petreley routinely defends underdog OSes. He responded to my Linux/OSI attack last week. (See Down to the wire, June 28.) Petreley trusts me to change my mind about Linux if facts warrant. He knows that deep down, I'm rooting for Linux, or any OSnic group that gives Microsoft a run for its money, especially after next year's antitrust breakup.

Unix Certification Undercut Open-Sourcers

July 26, 1999

It feels as though millions of readers have responded to my two recent Linux columns at www.infoworld.com/print links. So how can I stop now?

It also feels as though the open-source software movement has launched a new marketing campaign. In response to Microsoft's "Where do you want to go today?" the movement has been saying, "Linux — because Microsoft is an oppressive monopoly." But now, responding evermore persuasively to the concerns of corporate America, the open-source movement's marketing message has become, "If you don't use Linux, you suck."

And then, contrary to doctrine, Linux recently ran slower than Windows NT in benchmarks conducted by MindCraft. When it came out that the tests were sponsored by Microsoft, *PC Week* oversaw a rematch. Alas, the outcome reconfirmed that NT is actually faster than Linux (at least between crashes). See poor MindCraft vindicate itself at .

Speaking of craftiness, there's NetCraft, which counts server types on the Internet. Open-source believers love NetCraft because most of the 6 million servers it probes run the open-source Apache Web server on the open-source Linux. See, which is cool.

NetCraft, not MindCraft, is quoted widely in open-source circles as to the truth about the dominance of Linux. Why isn't anybody weighting servers by how important they are or craftily counting servers behind firewalls?

Speaking of benchmarks, Linux and the open-source movement got another boost last week from Bill Gurley, who is now a venture capitalist writing columns for Fortune.

Gurley wrote, "Open-source works. . .The leading open-source operating system, Linux, is also gaining steam. According to Red Hat Software, there were 12 million Linux users at the end of 1998. . .[It] turns out that you can make money off freely available software code. Perhaps the best example of this is Red Hat Software, a company that packages, distributes, supports, and, more importantly, brands a version of the Linux OS."

In the fine print, Gurley disclosed that his firm, Benchmark Capital, is an investor in Red Hat. See.

Turns out Benchmark owns nearly 10 percent of Red Hat, which filed to go public in June and raised nearly $100 million. So we're left to wonder whether Gurley has put his money where his mouth is, or vice versa.

Anyway, this makes Linux an inflator of the current Internet stock bubble, which I've predicted will burst on Monday, Nov. 8, 1999.

Eric Raymond is one of open-source's most effective champions. He complained that I'd confused the Free Software Foundation (FSF) with his Open-Source Initiative (OSI).

OK, sorry, I should more carefully distinguish the freeloaders at FSF from the free marketers at OSI. Trouble is, I'm not alone.

Then I asked Raymond two haunting questions. First, why is Linux not certified Unix? He answered, "Because so far, nobody in the Linux community has ponied up the money for The Open Group's certification process. . . Equally, The Open Group's process has a lot of built-in assumptions that are a bad fit to the way our community is organized. . .There were some negotiations last year; they seem to have bogged down after the proprietary Unix vendors got wind of the idea. I'd personally like to see it happen, but the Linux community as a whole doesn't care much about [Unix] certification." See.

Next, I asked if any next-generation OS could emerge from OSI. Raymond answered, "Something will eventually replace Linux. . .probably a persistent-object system like Jonathan Shapiro's EROS. And yes, it will come from the open-source community because, by the time Linux nears the end of its life cycle, trying to build critical infrastructure software in closed-source will (correctly) be regarded as the height of lunacy."

If Open-Source Software Is so Much Cooler, Why Isn't Transmeta Getting It?

February 10, 2000. Linus Torvalds gave the keynote speech at LinuxWorld Expo last month, right after announcing Transmeta Corp. Am I the only one to see that Torvalds and other open-source software revolutionaries are acting out the finale of George Orwell's *Animal Farm*?

Orwell's farmhouse is full of open-source pigs, which are now almost indistinguishable from the proprietary humans they recently overthrew.

It's true that I have been unkind to the "Open-Sores" Movement. But to be clear, anyone is welcome to beat Microsoft with better software, even a utopian community of volunteer programmers.

May the best software win

And don't get me wrong, even if he disappoints Richard Stallman by not always referring to GNU/Linux, Torvalds is a genuine hero of the open-source revolution.

But with Torvalds saying some animals are more equal than others, why is the sanctimonious open-source press still cheering him on? Are the likes of Slashdot.org, just gobbled by VA Linux, also porking out in Orwell's farmhouse?

Torvalds wrote and now controls Linux, the open-source operating system, due this summer in Version 2.4. By day, he is a programmer at Transmeta. Transmeta just announced Crusoe, its low-power microprocessors for mobile computers.

The architecture of Crusoe chips is based on VLIW (very long instruction words). It has "code morphing" to convert and cache software in speedy VLIW codes. And it comes with Mobile Linux, with Linux extensions for power management. According to Transmeta, Crusoe is two-thirds software and one-third hardware.

So what I want to know is, if open-source software is so cool, and if Torvalds "gets it," why isn't Crusoe open source? For a start, why aren't the Crusoe chip's mask sources published for modification and manufacture by anyone?

And yes, Mobile Linux is open-source, but not the "code morphing" software Torvalds helped write. Transmeta has taken the phrase Code Morphing as its proprietary trademark. And what the code does, according to Transmeta, has been ... patented.

Worse, Crusoe is touted for running Intel X86 software, and in particular, Microsoft Windows. Doesn't the open-source community say Windows is beneath contempt?

Torvalds showed up at LinuxWorld Expo touting open source, of course, but then went on to revise two of its bedrock principles.

Torvalds talked at LinuxWorld about fragmentation – the emergence of too many Linux versions. Being old enough to have watched Unix fragment during the 1980s, I worry.

But instead of holding to the party line that Linux will not fragment, Torvalds now says there is bad fragmentation and good. One can assume, because he's in charge of both, Transmeta's Mobile Linux will fragment Linux 2.4, but in a good way.

Then Torvalds talked about commercial companies, which aren't so bad after all: Take for example Transmeta. His audience, packed with employees, friends, and family of newly public Linux companies, did not boo him back out into the barnyard.

Where is the outrage?

So just to keep Torvalds honest, I'm thinking that Crusoe chips, which are mostly software, should be open-source and basically free. Chips have to be manufactured — with white coats, ovens, and stuff — so maybe it should be OK to sell open-source Crusoe for the cost of its silicon, trace metals, media, and manuals.

And how about this? To keep pigs out of the farmhouse, how about bundling Crusoe chips with Transmeta shares? This would cement commitment to Transmeta products and its inevitable IPO.

Until the Internet stock bubble bursts, this would provide Transmeta with funds to pay to make the chips and to pay for Super Bowl ads. This would be breaking new ground in The New Economy.

Bob, we run the Internet

Rebuttal by Eric Raymond

Eric Raymond is an Open-Source Evangelist and author of The Cathedral *and* The Bazaar. *Eric has been heavily involved with the Linux File System Standards Group, the GNU Emacs 19 development and was one of the principal developers of the ncurses library. He co-maintains the Sunsite archive, the largest and most popular software repository in the Linux world.*

Rebuttal: Linux's '60s Technology, Open-Sores Ideology Won't Beat W2K, but What Will?

Far more than a thousand people are hooting now, Bob, after your Internet stock bubble conspicuously failed to collapse on schedule on November 8th. But it's hard to believe that you ever took that prediction, or any of the other flamage in this column, seriously; unless, that is, you're already suffering from either senile dementia or a masochistic fondness for making yourself look like a buffoon.

Actually, buffoon may be too mild a word for anybody who says the Open-Source Movement reminds him of communism. You're equating a peaceful movement of volunteers with a brutal, murderous ideology that has caused the slaughter of hundreds of millions. Even at this late date communism will doubtless cause the murder of at least a few hundred thousand more before it's finally consigned to the dustbin of history. You might just as well say the local Boy Scout troop's bake sale reminds you of Nazism.

OK, so you admit that's not really fair. It isn't much brighter of you to suggest that we're a bunch of granola-munching ecotopians off in Cloud-Cuckoo Land. In case you haven't noticed, Bob, we run the Internet. The nervous system of the New Economy is *ours*. Sixty-six percent of all the web sites in the world use an open-source web server, and 85% of the live content on the Web consists of Perl scripts. You can't send mail or even resolve a single Internet address without using the open-source code and infrastructure *we* build and *we* maintain.

Finally you get your figures wrong — even in July when you wrote this IDC was already saying that Linux had pulled even in market share with all other Unixes combined. NT will reach 23 x 6 availability the day water flows uphill. And those of us who have been paying attention aren't worrying about Windows 2000 — we're laughing. We're laughing at Windows 2000, and at you and everyone else who is betting their reputations that it won't be the biggest flop since the Edsel.

Rebuttal: Linux Redux: Enough of the OSnic Slurs, Let's Count Linux Versus W2K Users

Once again, your writing suggests that there's little you love more than tickling your tonsils with your toenails. Open-source rhetoric doesn't look so "toxically anti-Microsoft" now that it's been exceeded in scope, volume and devastating pointedness by a federal judge's findings of fact, does it now?

But that's not the biggest howler in this column. How you could mistake the rhetoric around the Open-Source Initiative as being anti-capitalist, anti-American, or anti-social is beyond me — though the phrase "willful idiocy" does suggest itself. OSI exists specifically to make nice at capitalists, which we've been doing pretty successfully, if the frequency with which outfits like IBM, Apple, and Novell actively seek our endorsement is any indication.

And you wonder why you get flamed...

Rebuttal: Unix Certification Undercut Open-Sourcerers

The half-life of your predictions is shrinking, Bob. Mindcraft was not just "sponsored" by Microsoft, it was performed in a Microsoft lab with Microsoft techs helpfully looking over Mindcraft's shoulders. And barely a month after this column came out, the truth about the "Mindcraft II" rematch came out — it was just as slanted. This time, however, it looks like the failure to apply the same level of optimization and updates to the Linux kernel as they did to NT's was due to incompetence, rather than actual conspiracy.

Then, of course, there's that telling phrase "between crashes." We both know those weren't Linux crashes, don't we, Bob?

He that would make his own liberty secure must guard even his enemy from oppression: for if he violates this duty, he establishes a precedent that will reach unto himself.

— Thomas Paine

The Day the Internet Stock Bubble Burst

If you've ever had to buy a tee shirt at Disneyland, a meal from some hotel's room service menu or a bottle of wine in any restaurant, you're used to inflated prices. But your little purchase didn't precipitate a stock market crash. In these columns I contend that overpriced Internet stocks will do just that. I even had the total gall to name the day the sky would fall — but because the universe is perverse, it didn't.

Well, no matter what anyone says, timing isn't everything, and it may be that, although I had the date wrong, I had the trend nailed. To those readers who own outrageously priced Internet stocks, (and to the three of you who don't) these columns offer a seer-like perception about a topic I admit to knowing nothing about: the stock market.

Internet Stocks: Don't Get Greedy — Take Half Off the Table Before It's Too Late

March 15, 1999

You have questions, I have answers. Here are two: Sell half of your Internet stock now. And $R(A,S)=(A+S)!/(A!*S!)$.

Autonomy CEO Mike Lynch and I just had dinner again. Lynch is the brilliant Cambridge mathematician who taught me the Monty Hall Paradox. (See "Autonomy's sorting tools can help you find some of the best deals on the Net.")

Lynch now has another paradox, which he shares with many Internet companies. He took Autonomy public in July. On the one hand, thanks to 80 percent growth in recent months, Lynch enjoys a market capitalization well into the triple-digit millions.

On the other hand, Autonomy's market cap is much larger than its annual revenues, which are barely into the double-digit millions. Just to keep his stock steady, Lynch must keep delivering phenomenal growth and eventually, profits.

So, it's safe to say, Autonomy's stock is going up, or down, or will stay the same.

I keep telling young Internet companies: Don't go public. But if presidents can't resist interns, how can we meanies expect young companies to resist the public stock market?

True, going public gives young companies stock with which to buy one another, so they can achieve critical mass or offer one-stop shopping. And they get what's called liquidity, with which shareholders convert stock into beer.

But then, young Internet company CEOs wake up to find that attracting employees is difficult. High-priced stock options are not worth much.

And if the stock falls, shareholders and employees, who were enthusiastic on the way up, go berserk on the way down.

Worse, going public turns programmers into Rule 144 securities experts who all of a sudden can't program.

So why are Internet stock prices so high?

The economy is strong, thanks entirely to Bill Clinton, and the Internet has a limitless upside, but the main reason Internet stock prices are up is that many dowager corporations are looking for Web gigolos to take them to the Internet Riviera.

Say you're an elderly telco, or even Microsoft. Without good growth ideas, your monopoly profits pile up. What better way to feel young again than to be seen around town splurging on young Internet companies?

And while attending Wall Street parties, where dowagers hang out, gold-digging Internet companies are encouraged to flirt with one another. Surrounded by lawyers on the boards of their newly public companies, young CEOs are rudely informed by merger and acquisition pimps that it's their fiduciary responsibility to merge and acquire.

But trees don't grow to the sky. And so I urge, if you are holding any highly appreciated Internet stocks, sell half.

If prices fall, feel good about shares you sold. If prices rise, feel good about shares you kept. In the meantime, have fun by walking a different route to work every day.

More routes to work

Back to the puzzle some of us have been escaping with these past three weeks. If work is A avenues west and S streets north of home, how many different shortest routes are there? The shortest routes, of which there are R(A,S), are all of length A+S blocks.

Last week, I claimed recursively that R(A,S)=R(A-1,S)+R(A,S-1), with R(A,0)= R(0,S)=1 terminating the recursion.

This week, after counting permutations and eliminating duplicates, I claim that R(A,S)=(A+S)!/(A!*S!), where N! is N factorial, or N*(N-1)*(N-2)*...*2*1.

In Excel's Visual Basic, my recursive and factorial functions agree.

I've noted that along the six blocks between my townhouse and IDG headquarters in Boston, there are interesting alleys, and that the opposite sides of avenues and streets are quite different. So my routes to work increase from R(2,4) to R(6,13), all of length 6 blocks. This is 27,132 — 50 years of walking variety.

Last Week's Stock Market Slide Was Just a Temblor Compared to the Big One

April 26, 1999
When, exactly, will the Internet stock bubble burst? And I mean burst, not like last week, which was just a minor blip by comparison.

Well, I don't know. My assets are in a blind trust that routinely underperforms market averages.

And even if I did know, why would I tell anybody?

But the National Venture Capital Association (NVCA) recently invited me to address its annual meeting. And there weren't enough seats for all the venture capitalists (VCs) who could afford Boston's Ritz-Carlton.

According to the 1999 NVCA Yearbook, 1998 was the seventh straight record-breaking year for VC fundraising and investment. Exactly 547 companies raised $25.3 billion, bringing their capital under management to $84.2 billion. They invested exactly $16.7 billion in 2,859 growth companies, 60 percent in information technology, with $3.5 billion going into Internet-related ventures alone. Exactly.

Chatting up NVCA attendees, I learned that nobody knows anything exactly about the future of Internet stocks.

VCs know trees don't grow to the sky, all stocks eventually sell for 10 times earnings, there is too much money chasing too many deals, and Internet stocks have run off the end of a cliff.

But VCs aren't looking down. They are scrambling to take their ripe (and not so ripe) portfolio companies public before the bubble bursts. The trick is to get in on the ground floor and get out early.

When it was my turn to talk, I took it upon myself to predict the exact day the Internet stock bubble will burst.

With Y2K looming, I used the following date-day algorithm, thanks to reader Peter Sprague, for calculating on which day of the week a future date falls.

Take the future date's year and set A to 2 if 1999 or 3 if 2000. Set B to the result of using the date's month as an index into the vector [2,5,5,1,3,6,1,4,0,2,5,0].

If the year is 2000 and the month follows February, add 1 to B, because 2000 is a leap year. Finally, add A, B, and the day of the date's month, divide by 7, and use the remainder ("modulo 7") to select the day: 0 for Sunday, 1 for Monday ... and 6 for Saturday.

So, for example, Jan. 1, 2000, is 3 (for 2000), plus 2 (for January), plus 1, modulo 7, which yields Saturday. What a relief to know we'll have a whole weekend to work out any Y2K problems that might arise.

Among those Y2K problems will not be the bursting of the Internet stock bubble. Internet stock values are grossly inflated by "dowager corporations looking for Web gigolos to take them to the Internet Riviera," so investors are sure to bail out way before any Y2K problems arise.

Some say Internet stocks are not worth their multiples, but the eventual winners will be, so place your bets. Others say investing in all Internet stocks will prove profitable even though nine out of 10 will fail. This kind of thinking will inflate the bubble, at least through the summer, if I know anything about stocks, which, again, I don't.

The bubble will burst sometime after October reports of disappointing third-quarter earnings and warnings about fourth-quarter shortfalls are announced. The pressure to get out ahead of year-end tax-loss taking will build.

Therefore, the Internet stock bubble will burst on — don't quote me — Nov. 8, 1999. Sorry they jumped the gun last week.

Just to be sure, let's run a quick check with our date-day algorithm. Taking Nov. 8, 1999, we get 2 (for 1999) plus 5 (for November) plus 8, modulo 7, Monday, which, after a weekend of hand-wringing, is a likely day for a stock market bubble to burst.

Hearing this, an NVCA member asked me how deep the stock crash will be and how long it will last. I said that I don't know — thousands of points, and it will last a year.

Won't be long before Yahoo! is again a race of exclamation point-less men from *Gulliver's Travels*.

Advertising Dependency Will Help Burst the Internet Stock Bubble on Nov. 8

August 30, 1999. Only 10 weeks until Nov. 8, 1999, the day the Internet stock bubble will burst. And hurting the most will be companies that rely too much on selling Internet ads.

Don't know much about the stock market, but I've been predicting this burst since April 26.

Why risk such an exact prediction? Because Freeman Dyson is right: It is better to be wrong than to be vague. And this time I've not agreed to eat anything if I'm wrong.

Why Nov. 8? Well, first of all, it's a Monday. And as if that weren't enough, third-quarter earnings (if any) and fourth-quarter estimates will be out, and disappointing.

Further, year-end tax-minimization plans will be exaggerating fears about year-2000 software bugs.

And then there are the "lock-ups," which prevent early employees and investors from selling stock in newly public Internet companies. Many more lock-ups will expire before Nov. 8, creating excess supply to fuel the big sell-off.

TheStreet.com has an Internet stock index. It peaked at 824 during my April warnings. Last week, it was already down 33 percent. Many recent initial public offerings (IPOs) are "below water." Their lock-ups have expired.

They're trading below IPO prices. So, we're told, the Internet stock bubble has already burst.

Don't be fooled. Many Internet IPO prices were surreal. There is a lot more bubble bursting to do than 33 percent. And leading the way down will be companies too reliant on selling of Internet ads.

AdForce is a hot young company that does not sell Internet ads. It serves companies that do. AdForce tools and services help Web publishers and their agencies to target, schedule, submit, select, deliver, account, audit, and analyze advertising campaigns.

AdForce went public in May and reported an unprofitable second quarter with revenues of $4.2 million, up 433 percent from last year, after delivering 18 billion ad impressions, up 38 percent from last quarter. A new data center gives AdForce 450Mbps of access to 10 terabytes of storage, increasing its ad selection and delivery capacity to 450 million impressions per day.

Working at IDG, a company with hundreds of millions of dollars in ad revenue, I think highly of my theory that Internet ads will turn out not nearly as profitable as those in print and broadcast.

AdForce doesn't exactly agree with me. The company believes that tighter targeting of demographics and psychographics will eventually result in higher advertising prices, measured quaintly in costs per thousand impressions (CPMs).

However, AdForce concedes that Internet CPMs are currently in decline. With no paper handling and bandwidth aplenty, competition for the attention of Internet users is fierce. Internet CPMs are now generally below $1.

Growth is masking price declines. AdForce alone is adding a billion new ad impressions per month. But by November it will be clear that you cannot give everything away for free to attract eyeballs for sale profitably to advertisers.

Business models will have to show increasing revenues from sources such as access, transport, services, subscriptions, pay per view, and transactions.

Adding to the November woes of companies running rich on Internet ads is that we are growing tired of banners. AdForce reports clickthrough rates at 1 percent.

The ad community is hustling to boost clickthroughs with animations, vertical banners, audio, and other rich media advertising. So one new application of always-on Internet access will be the overnight downloading of exciting ads onto our disks.

While steaming up about that, mark my words. These advertising trends and uncertainties will come to a head in the stock market on Nov. 8. And I won't be able to resist saying I told you so.

The Final Days: Last Net IPOs Before Wall Street Bubble Bursts on Nov. 8

October 4, 1999

The Internet stock bubble will burst on Monday, Nov. 8, 1999. Or so I've been predicting since April.

Judging from my mail, many of you resent my making such an unhappy and excessively precise prediction about your Internet holdings.

True, Wall Street is off my beat. And true, picking an exact day is foolhardy. It's just that I can't resist sharing this hunch.

Recently, I've received a stream of offers to buy "friends and family" stock in upcoming initial public offerings (IPOs). Aha!

Wall Street is rushing to get another batch of companies public before the bubble bursts. About 25 of the 50 companies in the IPO hopper are Internet companies.

Being designated as a company friend means that you can buy a limited amount of stock at the IPO price before the stock is traded to the public. It also means you can sell immediately, unlike the company's early employees and investors whose stock is generally locked up for six months — investment bankers don't want those insiders selling into a new market.

So, with Internet issues now routinely popping well above IPO prices in their first few hours of trading, being a friend is an easy way to make a few thousand dollars in a few hours.

Because I write this column, give speeches, and organize conferences mostly about the Internet, I do not allow myself to make investments in stocks except through a blind trust. So, I decline to be an IPO friend. More journalists should do the same. (Editor's note: InfoWorld's editorial code of conduct prohibits its employees from directly owning any stock in computer technology companies.)

John Shoch is an old-fashioned venture capitalist and a friend of mine. He believes it's the job of a company's investment banker to price its stock to move up 15 percent in the days following an IPO. When a stock runs up much higher than that, it means that the banker has failed the company. The money that goes to friends from selling stock soon after an IPO should actually have gone into the treasury of the company and would have if the banker had set a higher IPO price.

Friends are not the only beneficiaries of underpriced IPOs. Favorite customers of banks also benefit.

Despite what they say at road-show dinners, these customers often "flip" new issues — buy them and then sell them, all in the same day.

And then there are the bankers themselves. They get a commission for selling IPO shares — 7 percent as I recall from 3Com's IPO — so you'd think they'd want the IPO price as high as the market will bear.

But banks want their buy-side customers to make killings on IPOs and, oh, by the way, to make killings themselves. They buy shares in their own IPOs and sell into the run-up.

It's too much in a banker's interest to underprice an IPO. The dirty deed is typically done on the eve of an offering. The young company, which goes public only once, finds itself surrounded by Wall Street, which goes public all the time.

Shoch has a proposal. Companies should make IPO agreements with bankers so that when stocks run up, say double, lockups expire.

This would better match supply and demand for new stocks, dampening the roller-coaster ride and shifting gains from speculators toward investors.

What's wrong is that Internet stocks have become a Ponzi scheme. Eventually, Ponzi schemes run out of suckers. When they do, Wall Street heads for the Hamptons.

The least sophisticated investors, the public, the greater fools, and heavily armed day traders are left holding the bag. Don't be one of those.

Now, as much as I worry about you, I worry even more about the Internet.

After the stock market bubble bursts on Nov. 8, and Wall Street wakes up with a long-term hangover, how are Internet companies going to get properly financed?

Day of Reckoning Arrives. The Internet Stock Bubble Burst Today, Didn't It?

November 8, 1999

Today, Nov. 8, 1999, the Internet stock bubble burst, or so I've been predicting since April.

I'd been warning about Internet stocks since March 15. But it was on April 15, during a National Venture Capital Association panel at Boston's Ritz-Carlton, and in this column on April 26, that I first announced today's stock burst.

Now, follow my verb tenses carefully. I'm writing this column a week ago, on Oct. 31, just before attending Weird Al Yankovic's Halloween Concert in Portland, Maine. So I can't say how exactly right I am today. All I have are stock data from the market close on Oct. 29.

Oct. 29? Yes, we just passed the 70th anniversary of The Great Stock Market Crash of Oct. 29, 1929. That Black Thursday ended The Roaring Twenties and began The Great Depression. On that one day, the Dow Jones industrial average dropped by 13 percent.

Funny, but *The Wall Street Journal* just last week updated the Dow Industrials by replacing Chevron and Sears with Intel and Microsoft. Intel and Microsoft are not Internet stocks, but they've arrived among the Industrials just in time to drag the Dow down.

But forget the Dow; let's use the Internet Index at www.thestreet.com. Its 30 Internet leaders rocketed during early 1999, from December's low of 302 to a high of 824 in, yes, April. After I predicted today's burst, the index turned south and, by August, was back down into the 400s.

Many said then that the Internet bubble had burst. But not me. On Aug. 30, I reiterated my Nov. 8 prediction.

In the September issue of *Red Herring* magazine, Editor Anthony B. Perkins looked at the 133 initial public offerings (IPOs) of Internet stocks since Netscape in 1995. Their combined market capitalization (share price times number of shares outstanding) was then $410 billion, which is impressive. Annual revenues were not so impressive at $15.2 billion. Even less impressive were the profits of these companies, at a loss of $3 billion.

Perkins calculated that, to be worth their August prices, assuming profits of 5 percent to 15 percent and price-to-earnings ratios at 40, the Internet IPOs would have to grow their revenues by 80 percent per year for the next five years.

Consider that Microsoft grew 53 percent its first five public years, and Dell grew 66 percent. Even assuming Dell's growth, the size of the Internet bubble came out as an excess market cap of $130 billion, or 33 percent.

So, in September, Perkins said sell, whereupon TheStreet.com's index turned up, from August's 400s to 750 on Oct. 29.

Akamai was yet another sign. This fine Internet company was founded 14 months ago by people whom I know from around the MIT Laboratory for Computer Science. Akamai generated $1.3 million in revenue for the nine months ending on Sept. 30.

Morgan Stanley priced Akamai's IPO at $26 per share. On the big day, Oct. 29, the 250-employee company's new stock closed at $145 per share, giving it a market cap of around $13 billion, less than Chevron but more than Sears.

The Weird Als who buy Internet IPOs saw interest rates not going up much and must have thought, hey, Akamai is worth five times more than what Morgan Stanley just estimated. This makes me think that investing in Internet stocks is beyond gambling; it's more like rooting for sports teams. So we should ask, "How do you like them Akamais?"

Now, hot off the presses, sight unseen, I recommend *The Internet Bubble: Inside the Overvalued World of High-Tech Stocks — and What You Need to Know to Avoid the Coming Shakeout,* by Anthony B. Perkins and Michael C. Perkins. They warn investors to get out while the getting is good, which, according to my prediction, was before today, Nov. 8, 1999.

Life on the Exponential Curve

A Rebuttal by Steve Jurvetson

Steve Jurvetsin is Managing Director of Draper Fisher Jervetson, a venture capital firm located in Redwood City, California. He was the founding VC investor in Kana Communications, Hotmail, Interwoven and Lightwave Microsystems. Mr. Jurvetson also serves on the Merrill Lynch Technical Advisory Board and the Microsoft Advisory Board for the Silicon Valley Developer Center. Upside Magazine recently chose him as one of the 100 "most influential people in the digital world."

The easy response to Bob Metcalfe's prophecy of doom is that it is wrong. There was no great market crash in 1999, and especially not on November 8.

A more interesting question is whether he was just off in his timing. Are Internet stocks wildly overvalued and due for a crash? And why do so many people argue that the Internet is overvalued, even as the stocks keep climbing?

I think there is a natural human tendency to presume convergence to linearity. Life on an exponential growth curve is perpetually unsettling. In retrospect, everything might make rational sense. Look at the run-up in Yahoo!'s stock price in 1997, which can be attributed to a shift by the investment community to a per-subscriber valuation model, like the one used in the cable industry. But, during 1997 itself, the rise of Yahoo! was bewildering. People shook their heads and said the stock couldn't go any higher, month after month. At the 1998 ETRE conference, Bill Gates shared an interesting disclosure: "I think Microsoft's stock is overvalued. I can't see how it could ever double again from where it is today. But, I have had this same thought every single year since we first went public!"

In retrospect, we say that, of course, Microsoft was a great stock to buy. When it comes to the information technology industry, we should not presume linearity. We should recognize network effects, increasing returns to scale, and Metcalfe's Law — that the value of a network grows with the square of the number of nodes. A good idea can spread more quickly over the Internet than was possible before in the physical world, where manufacturing and distribution fundamentally limit the rate of product adoption. The Internet is a wonderful substrate for the realization of intellectual property value, and should grow faster than Dell or Microsoft.

What's more, the Internet *is* the economy. Most modern businesses are information businesses at their core. Looking at GNP forecasts, the projected growth for the U.S. economy can be attributed to the Internet. We are in the first inning of its growth. Internet access from companies like NetZero is now free, and web appliances from companies like iTV cost $19. As Nintendo and the VCR companies can tell you, there is enormous consumer price elasticity when products drop under the $149 and $99 barriers. The $1,000 PC and $20-a-month fee for access have been huge adoption barriers. So, we should expect a second wave of consumer Internet adoption driven by price and appliance-like ease of use.

The business-to-business use of the Internet is just beginning and is forecast to be well over ten times the size of the consumer Internet. By improving real-time communications, computerization improves most business processes, including sales and support, which are fundamentally communication exercises. Trade is a form of structured communication. Excess inventory is a byproduct of poor information flow. The Internet provides a lingua franca that works throughout all businesses. My Macintosh can talk to your PC; we can start building business applications without worrying about the plumbing. And that is a remarkably liberating substrate for business-to-business e-commerce. Small businesses, in particular, are a huge growth area, given how poorly they are served today.

Then there's international growth. IDC estimates that by 2005, 70% of the online population will be non-English-speaking. This is a huge upside change for the largely English-only Web of today. Imagine when China comes online, probably via cell phones and Web appliances. Forrester estimates that European e-commerce will exceed that of the U.S. in just three years. Yahoo already has over 100 million subscribers outside the U.S.

So, against a backdrop of the most profound business and investment opportunity in the history of the world, there are certainly a number of individual stock excesses. The quarterly pace of financial reporting is glacial compared to the market shifts that occur in a three-month period. People trade stocks in a vacuum of market information. Any dynamic system with long feedback paths is prone to oscillation — this is true in Internet stocks, VC funds flow, and DRAM capacity planning. We should expect a lot of volatility, and some of the swings may feel like crashes. For many consumer Internet stocks, there is also a Beardstown-lady effect that occurs when consumers use an online offering, form an opinion, and buy the stock from the convenience of their homes. Many of these volatile stocks trade more like a futures contract on the commodities exchange than a traditional equity. As a result you see some speculative bubbles that last for short periods of time — not years.

So let's look at the entire Internet basket of stocks. I pose a question: Which do you think will be more valuable in five years, the PC industry or the Internet industry? If you could own one basket of stocks, which would it be? Regardless of where prices are today, which will be more valuable in five years?

Most people I know choose the Internet, without question. The PC is becoming a commodity. Metcalfe points to Perkins and Perkins' recently published book, *The Internet Bubble,* to argue that the Internet is overvalued. Using the same data from that book, we can compare the market cap today of the Internet basket to the PC basket. Guess what? The valuation of the PC basket is more than twice as high as the entire Internet basket. If you take AOL out of the Internet basket on grounds that it is a pre-Internet anachronism that will be made obsolete by the free ISPs, then the ratio is PC over the Internet, by more than three to one.

Continued

(continued)

Metcalfe seems uncomfortable with the notion that several of these Internet companies will fail. The public and private markets are blurring, and many of these Internet companies are at what WitCapital calls the "venture stage." As venture capitalists, we are quite comfortable with the notion that some of our investments will fail, but the winners can more than compensate. The wisdom of betting on a portfolio, despite enormous risk on an individual stock level, has been borne out time and time again. This is the land of revolutionary change and disruptive technologies. It's not for the bond or dividend investor mindset.

Metcalfe also insists that all stocks will eventually trade at a P/E of 10; however, if you wait for a stock to mature to a P/E of 10, you miss the hyper-growth phase of every technology industry.

Metcalfe's argument also misses the notion of asset valuation. Imagine a stock that owns all of the non-income-producing land in Texas. While some may lament it's total lack of earnings, others would try to figure out if there are oil reserves or developmental potential in the future. Subscribers are an asset in the land-grab of the Internet. Human attention has proven to be "monetizable" in every media in the history of the world — print, TV, and radio. The Internet has greater opportunities for personalization than any of its predecessors.

It took many years for TV advertisers to discover the soaps, and then the popular 30-second spot. The Internet has grown much more quickly than any preceding media grew, but it has not yet matured. The Internet should command a per-subscriber valuation in excess of the $2,000 per sub that a cable company commands today.

Bob also repeats the oft-heard refrain that there's too much VC money chasing too few deals. But there are also more entrepreneurs than ever before. We have funded more Internet companies than any other VC firm, yet we are backing 20 of the 20,000 business plans we get each year! I wonder if the thousands of unfunded entrepreneurs think there is too much money? I would argue the contrary — the Internet is underfunded, and has been for every year of its existence.

It's always easier to accept this fact in retrospect. Every VC wishes he or she had made more Internet investments in '94, '95, '96, '97 and '98. It's the same message every year: "There's too much money sloshing around." But let some time pass, and the venture capitalists will look back to 1999 and lament once again that they didn't fund more Internet entrepreneurs.

It's life on the exponential curve again. In the business flux of the information age, and with the shift from corporate behemoths to a freelance economy, a larger number of people will find fulfillment in the artistic expression of their ideas and in the dramatic impact that small groups can have at the product and project level. A good idea no longer needs a corporate crustacean to change the world. This is no longer an opportunity for a very small number of lucky people. Individuals and ideas are empowered as never before. This is a very exciting time. Bring on the new wave of entrepreneurial democracy!

Epilogue: Punditry

Punditry is what I do, for a decade now, since retiring from 3Com in1990. And here's what I've learned.

Yes, I know; pundit is a word often used in the pejorative along with other p-words, such as pedantic, puffery, and pontification. But, if it's good enough for William Safire, it's good enough for me. And anyway, a little self-deprecation goes a long way.

I started out in 1990 calling myself a journalist. But too many people complained. Daily newspaper reporters looked down on me because I'm well paid to cover business. Business journalists said I was only in the computer trades, which reminded me of what Harvard people say about MIT people. Trade journalists said I was biased and wrote opinions, as if they aren't and don't.

What I'm not is your typical journalist. I find that my colleagues are mostly struggling young English majors. As a result, they show strong tendencies toward Luddism and Marxism.

In contrast, I am a successful old engineer-entrepreneur. I am enthusiastic about Silicon Valley technologies and ideologies.

I find myself in pressrooms explaining the difference between silicon and silicone, and the differences among revenue, profit, and cash. In return, they explain to me when you're supposed to use "between" as opposed to "among."

It is a conceit of journalists that they stick to the facts. Too often they vent their opinions subliminally through story, source, language, and fact selection. They also vent not so subliminally out in the open on page one, as is now the sad standard at even my hometown newspaper, *The New York Times.*

But it's my job to opinionate. As a technology pundit, I write columns, give speeches, and organize conferences, all of them overflowing with opinions. My conceit is that a lot of people should be interested in my opinions. I'm even hoping someday to win a Pulitzer Prize.

The large and growing audience for my punditry is made up of those who buy information technologies for their companies — many my former customers at 3Com. My secondary audience consists of those who sell information technologies. My columns are syndicated internationally, but are written for Americans.

Here's what I don't try to do for my readers. I don't try to evaluate products for purchase — *InfoWorld* has a huge test center for that. I don't try to get scoops on industry happenings — *InfoWorld* has a huge news department for that. And I don't try to suck up to my readers to get them to feel good and to like me — everybody else is doing that.

Here's what I do try to do for my readers. I do try to find technologies that are likely to be important to them over the next five years. I do try for conceptual scoops — noticing a technology trend before anyone else does and explaining its heretofore unappreciated significance.

I do try to entertain my readers. I do tell them jokes, present puzzles, make excessively precise predictions, and attack people who they think are cool. I do try to attack high fliers, with the goal being soft landings. I do try to find clever ways of explaining complicated things, preferring the risks of oversimplifying. I do try to write well and fight constantly with the young things on *InfoWorld*'s copy desk who are used to editing news and not literature.

For example, I often ignore my editors and write sarcasm. This sometimes backfires, flooding me with mail that agrees with me against myself — people don't read as carefully as writers would like them to. But mostly my sarcasm works, and my readers and I have more than the usual amount of fun.

I do all this with the intent of attracting reader attention, waking them up, and making them think. I really do want people to read my columns, listen to my speeches, and attend my conferences.

There is a temptation here, to wander from the truth in order to get laughs, but I resist. And I really do want that Pulitzer — hear that Columbia?

(For any of you wishing to nominate me for one Pulitzer Prize or another, forms are available at http://www.pulitzer.org.)

But what I mainly do for my readers is tell them about stuff that interests me. I figure that if it interests me, then it will be good for them to know about it.

One of the ways to get people thinking is to make predictions. And I follow advice attributed to Freeman Dyson, Ester's dad, that it is better to be wrong than vague.

It's interesting that I am now better known for having predicted the collapse of the Internet in 1996 than I am for having invented Ethernet in 1973. Go figure.

Now, it's relatively easy to predict the future. It's harder to make precise predictions. And it's hardest of all to get the timing right.

My peculiar point of view on predictions was formed between 1970 and 1990. IBM monopolized the computer industry then, much as Microsoft does today. IBM was in the habit of making industry standards just by announcing them. I used to call such standards not de facto, not de jure, but de ibmo standards.

I was a proponent of the Internet against IBM Systems Network Architecture (SNA). In particular, I was out promoting my baby, Ethernet, and growing my company, 3Com.

All around me was IBM and their hangers on. They were promoting SNA and doing quite well. Whenever IBM's earnings went up, IBM was "the best managed company in America;" but when earnings went down, it was macroeconomics.

When Digital Equipment Corporation (now Compaq), Intel, Xerox, and I proposed Ethernet as a local networking standard in 1980, IBM was caught with its pants down. Angered, IBM turned all of its monopoly power against Ethernet and, I felt, against poor little me, personally.

For years and years and years, I was surrounded by senior corporate executives, Wall Street analysts, reporters, pundits, venture capitalists, competitors, customers, employees, friends, and family members, all of whom told me regularly that Ethernet was about to be killed by IBM's famous Token-Ring LAN. It was hard to argue otherwise.

Fortunately, I was stubborn.

Well, it turned out, after a really long time, that they were all wrong. Ethernet was the straw that broke IBM's back. Starting in 1985, when IBM and 3Com both announced Token Ring products on the same day, Ethernet, with a five-year head start, took hold. After that, Big Blue lost its ability to make industry standards by fiat.

And now, perhaps you've noticed, I can live with people disagreeing with me. Water off a duck's back. In fact, if I find myself in the mainstream, I know something is wrong.

Actually, I find out that something is wrong via e-mail. My e-mail address is published weekly — metcalfe@infoworld.net. And for a decade I've been receiving, reading, and responding to 50 e-mails per day. Sure, after some particularly obnoxious column — attacking the open sores movement, for example — I'll get a thousand, but 50 is my usual number.

Now, I do get a lot of ugly e-mail. But, see, I'm an expert in statistics. Since I have many more than 500,000 readers, and since on any given day I only hear from a self-selected sample of 50 (one hundredth of one percent), what I get from e-mail cannot be projected reliably over my whole readership. And so I'm confident there's this silent majority out there that's behind me all the way.

On the other hand, when my e-mail runs positive, I am sure it's because I'm right.

So I know a lot about disagreement. When my readers disagree, they say I have sold out; that I have conflicting investments; that I am a right-wing kook; that I am stupid, lazy, and uninformed. Some repeatedly threaten to stop reading my column (I wish they would), and some to cancel their *InfoWorld* subscriptions.

Because InfoWorld accepts advertisements, some readers say that my incorrect opinions are what our advertisers want — I have been bought. This point of view is encouraged by the fact that I am from the dark side, having been a large vendor myself at 3Com, and worse, I was *InfoWorld*'s Publisher/CEO for two and a half years and sold tens of millions of dollars of advertising.

It's true that I was *InfoWorld*'s Publisher and at the same time wrote an *InfoWorld* column. And it's true I found that too hard to do. The separation of church (editorial) and state (advertising) is hard enough without having to do it inside one's head. So, I chose being a full time pundit. I no longer hang out much with my friends on the advertising side.

Readers are prone to think that advertising influences editorial because journalists confirm it all the time. You will never hear a journalist who has been fired say that it was because he failed to show for work, missed deadlines, wrote poorly, failed to check facts, or sexually harassed fellow employees. It's always because the journalist, says he, boldly stood up to advertising pressure and was fired at the specific request of an advertising executive intending to quash an unfavorable story. Rubbish.

This tendency to attribute disagreement to advertising pressure is quite strong. I have been attacking Microsoft in print since 1991, and still, for example, when I attacked Linux, I got tons of e-mail saying I am Microsoft's lapdog.

Another frequent accusation from disagreeable people is that I must own stock in the companies I promote and in the competition of companies I attack. I have to say that too many journalists, and especially pundits, are flying too close to the sun here — they have complicated rules about not writing about companies they own (or disclosing that they do in fine print). To avoid the aggravation, I keep my small fortune in a blind trust, like politicians do, which ought to set minds to rest.

Now, as for the accusation that I'm a right-wing kook, guilty as charged. Again, Luddites and Marxists can go jump in the lake. Most journalists are lefties, so I don't think I'm doing much damage by being right. Let them squeal.

Once in a while my writing escapes *InfoWorld,* which it has to before I win the Pulitzer, but then the trouble begins. CNN.com picked up one column I wrote on why people should be paying more than a flat fee for using the Internet.

Turns out that people who watch CNN are not the same as those who read *InfoWorld*. I got my first two death threats from CNN.com readers — Luddites and Marxists typically resort to violence against those who disagree with them. The FBI looked at the threats and said not to worry. What, me worry?

Please don't doubt I'm going to win a Pulitzer Prize. If I don't win one for technology punditry, I have a foolproof back-up plan. I always carry a loaded camera for the next time I run into a scorched fireman carrying a crying baby out of a burning building.

Now, about YOU becoming a technology pundit. As technology becomes ever more important, the market for technology pundits is expanding. I can use some help. I can stand the competition. And too many of the wrong people are interested. To get started, why not gather your opinions about this book, write them down, and send them as a book review to some newspaper, magazine, web site, the Pulitzer nominating committee, or directly to me at metcalfe@infoworld.net.

Index

Notes

Notes

Notes

Notes

Notes

Notes

Notes

Notes

Notes

Notes

Notes

Notes